THE
JAMIE
OLIVER
EFFECT

This second edition published in 2008 by
André Deutsch
an imprint of the
Carlton Publishing Group
20 Mortimer Street
London W1T 3JW

First published in 2006

A CIP catalogue record for this book is available from the British Library

ISBN 978 0 233 00256 9

The publishers would like to thank the following sources for their kind
permission to reproduce the pictures in this book.

Page 1: Geoff Wilkinson/Rex Features
Page 2: (top) Flo Smith/Alamy Images; (bottom) Terry O'Neill/Getty Images
Page 3: (top) John Angerson/Alamy Images; (bottom) Craig Barritt/Retna
Page 4: (top) PressNet/Topfoto.co.uk; (bottom) William Conran/
Empics/PA Photos
Page 5: (top) Rex Features; (bottom) Myung Jung Kim/Empics/PA Photos
Page 6: (top) Peter Dench/Corbis; (bottom) Russell Boyce/AFP/Getty Images
Page 7: (top) Colin Shepherd/Rex Features; (bottom) Fred Duval/
Film Magic/Getty Images
Page 8: (top) © CBS/Everett Collection/Rex Features; (bottom) Gregorio
Binuya/Retna

Every effort has been made to acknowledge correctly and contact the source
and/or copyright holder of each picture and Carlton Books Limited apologises
for any unintentional errors or omissions, which will be corrected in future
editions of this book.

Typeset in Liverpool by E-Type
Printed and bound in the UK by CPI Mackays, Chatham, ME5 8TD

THE
JAMIE
OLIVER
EFFECT

THE MAN · THE FOOD · THE REVOLUTION

Gilly Smith

André Deutsch

In memory of Eleanor Stephens

CONTENTS

ACKNOWLEDGEMENTS

Thanks to Jed Novick, husband, editor and cook extraordinaire, who propped up our world while I sat at a computer night and day. To Mark Sutton for fixing it every time I spilt red wine on it, to Gill Hudson, as always, for getting me into this writing game in the first place, to my editor, Jane Donovan, and to my publisher, Miranda West.

Thanks also to all the chefs and foodies who fed me with their stories, insights, and in some cases, even food. To Alice Waters at Chez Panisse, Alistair Little at Tavola, Antony Worrall Thompson, Craig Sams, chair of the Soil Association, David Lewis of Green Core Foods, Diane McRae, food consultant, Eric Treuille of Books for Cooks, Franco and Ann Taruschio, Gary Hunter, Gennaro Contaldo, Gill Hudson, Gillian Carter, Heston Blumenthal, Jean-Christophe Novelli, Jo Bates, Kevin McKay, Lizzie Vann, Michael Kuhn, Monica Brown, Pat Llewellyn, Pete Hansard, Ruth Rogers, Rose Gray, Rupert Ivey, Ruth Kelly, Sally Clarke, Simon Woodroffe, Susan Spungen, Stephen Alexander, Tim Lang and Tom Aikens. I did invite Jamie Oliver to contribute to this book, but his organisation declined on his behalf.

Thanks to the Soil Association, who opened the door to a world of food, food people and food issues, which will fill my books for years to come.

And to my children, Elly and LouLou, for inspiring just about everything I do, for watching endless Jamie DVDs with me, cooking with me, and forgiving me for not taking them swimming as much as I promise. This is for you.

Gilly Smith
2006

CHAPTER 1

THE ADVENTURES OF A HUCKLEBERRY FINN

Where does the energy of a man like Jamie Oliver come from? How does he manage to keep his wife Jools from walking out the door? How does he stop a three year old's tantrum with the words, 'Want to cook?' If Jamie Oliver can teach his mates to cook, his wife to wait, and ensure that by the time they get there, his kids will be eating good school food, what do the next ten years hold? If he can make Capitalism cool, train kids the world has given up on to bake bread *and* change government policy, maybe the *Daily Mail*'s April Fool joke could become a reality. Can he really run for office, or is his plan more of a global revolution?

'He knows what he's got,' said a friend. 'He has killer instinct, a warrior instinct. He sees what he wants, and gets it. He'll never give up – he's that type of guy – and that's quite inspirational.' Jamie himself would probably say that it's all down to being in the right place at the right time, and a lot of luck besides. He might also say that his childhood shaped his entire career. Psychotherapists would probably agree. His parents, Trevor and Sally Oliver, are successful in love and business, the kind of role models that Jamie would describe as 'superb'. Even his older sister, Anna-Marie Hunt, allowed him to shine without cramping his style. He has returned the favour by giving them all supporting roles in his on-screen life, and acknowledging them as part of his safety net as he walks the tightrope of fame.

Trevor and Sally are famously happily married and for them working together was a natural partnership. Jamie's vision of a future is to recreate that dream team with Jools as front of house in their countryside restaurant. 'It's all I've ever wanted,' Jamie told Michael Parkinson. 'My plans have never really changed.' 'Trevor and Sally are the perfect parents,' said Gennaro Contaldo, who would become Jamie's 'London dad' when he gave him his first job. 'They're very warm and humble. They say, "This is what we are... This is a bit of bread, let's share it." Jamie is just like them – he will share what he has with anyone. He loves people, he loves children and he loves a challenge. He is an unbelievable family man.'

An ex-bank worker, Sally was as good with her figures as Trevor was with his staff and together they had a clear vision. Trevor had always wanted a pub or restaurant of his own and by his early twenties he was already behind the bar at The Cricketers, then a rather shabby old pub in the quiet village of Clavering in Essex, with dreams of what it would become. Jamie has often said that it's his dad who inspired his astonishing self-confidence: 'Dad taught me to believe that anything is possible.'

According to the tests which American corporations use to assess potential employees – rating how grounded and emotionally articulate, how powerful, how given they are to performing and how able they are to think outside the box – Jamie is deeply rooted. To use a food analogy, he has 'great potatoes', and it's all thanks to his family. His Nan, his uncle, his sister and his friends followed him in and out of the *Naked Chef* series, the Sainsbury's ads and through the *Happy Days* tour. The opening titles to the *Happy Days* DVD, made by Jamie's own production company Fresh One, feature Trevor and Sally talking about baby Jamie and how proud they are of him. They even show pictures of baby Jamie, the original naked chef. Jamie doesn't care; he's seen it all before.

This is a man who has the unusual combination of being big in all the personality hotspots: he's the lad's lad who can talk about his feelings, who has stayed with the same girl for 17 years and claims never to have strayed – not even once. He's the happy dad – even if he does find it hard to juggle the needs of a man on a mission with those of his wife and children. He loves his mum and dad, his Nan and his sister, and he cried openly at the death of both his grandfathers. His energy for change is revolutionary and it looks like we've only just seen the beginning of his missionary zeal. He's the cook who found more than one use for his drumsticks, who can sing on stage in front of his foodie fans when most chefs wouldn't even make an appearance in the first place. His ability to think laterally has changed our TV and food culture in the space of a stunningly short period of time and he's inspired us to do the same.

Jamie often seems hyperactive, something that he shares with fellow chefs Marco Pierre White and Jean-Christophe Novelli. Pat Llewellyn, producer of *The Naked Chef, The F Word* and *Return of the Chef,* says it's not an uncommon trait among chefs. 'I can see it in them all,' she said. 'There's a slightly manic thing about John Burton-Race and Gordon Ramsay, too. Maybe it's because it's a nocturnal profession. Gordon lives three or four people's lives – it's extraordinary.' Food campaigner Lizzie Vann said she saw herself in Jamie. 'I was hyperactive as a child,' she has admitted. 'I've never grown out of it – I've just learnt to deal with it. A hyperactive always has to be doing something. You rarely just sit down and read a book. I remember talking to Jamie once and noticing that he can't actually sit back and do nothing. He seems to be someone who also can't sit still for long. Needing to be active all the time can be distracting and even self-destructive so I've tried to capture the energy and channel it into activities that are constructive. From what we see of him publicly, it looks like Jamie is doing the same.'

Jamie's 'potatoes' planted their roots in rural Essex although his earliest memory of leaving his mother shows that they needed some help at first. 'On my first day at school I was clinging on to my mum's hand, screaming, "Mummy, Mummy,"' he said. He compares himself to his more grounded younger sister Anna-

Marie, who started play school at the same time. 'She was like, "Right, you kids over here and you lot over there" – she's the delegator.'

Jamie was the original country boy with acres of countryside to explore. His limitless sense of adventure, of never seeing any barriers in the way to getting where he wanted to go, may well come from that experience. 'When I was younger I used to dream that I could fly,' he has said. 'I can recall quite clearly that when I was about five, I dreamt of hovering above the sofa. In my vivid imagination I felt I could float wherever I want to go.' Anna-Marie has said that they both believed they could take on the world. 'He had his life mapped out from the beginning, and he's achieved it.' She explained where she thinks that kind of confidence comes from. 'Growing up in a pub made us both very confident,' she told the Biography Channel. 'You get exposed to a lot of teasing and criticism that most kids just don't come across.'

As he dammed streams and built dens, Jamie used to hang out with a gang of village boys, including Jimmy Doherty, who in years to come would join Jamie as a TV foodie in the Channel 4 documentary of his journey into becoming a pig farmer, *Jimmy's Farm* (June 2004). Jamie first met Jimmy at nursery in Clavering: 'We were two of the Three Wise Men in our first nativity play,' he told journalist Anna Pukas. They remained close friends, getting their first bikes together and nurturing each other's fascination for aquariums. By the time they were 13, Jimmy, always the outdoor type, would have his own wildlife park with chickens, ferrets, tortoises and snakes, and an aviary full of cockatiels while Jamie already dreamed of having his own restaurant.

Jamie was the leader of the gang, but even then he understood the boundaries, although he confessed to journalist Simon Hattenstone 20 years on that he 'went a bit further' than everyone else to have a laugh. 'I quite enjoyed crashing things, breaking things,' he admitted, 'even if I knew it would catch fire, I'd do it till it did catch fire. When you live in the country there's not that much to do. There's only a bus that comes through once or twice a week and you have to do the old schoolboy things, Huckleberry Finn, build tree-houses, camps... I'm obsessed with traditions and things we used to do, good old things. Somebody was talking to me about it the other day. He said, "D'you remember when the corn had been cut and we had the clods, and they made excellent projectiles, whack you on the head proper?" We also used to nick our mums' brooms, tie our jumpers round the end and we'd have three on bikes and five running, and just beat the shit out of each other.'

'He was always a tearaway,' his dad would tell us on Channel 4's *The Naked Chef*, 'so that's why I got him working at the age of eight.' But it was all done in good humour. The scrumping of apples was always with the knowledge that local farmers were happy to turn a blind eye and Jamie's penchant for practical jokes was almost always limited to those who would laugh. Except for once. A friend told how the gang hid around a corner with buckets of water intended for their mates. The village postman who received the drenching reserved for their mate Dave was an old man about to end his rounds for the day. Jamie was not amused. He hated to see anyone hurt. For him, 'Knock-Knock, Ginger', the childhood game of knocking on doors and running off, was always an awkward experience despite his leading his gang of good-natured hooligans. When an old lady was the unexpected recipient of one of their 'Ginger' runs, the horrified Jamie made up for it by doing odd jobs for her. Apparently, she forgave him.

Jamie and Jimmy's gang included a couple of young gypsy boys, whose parents were potato picking in the area, and he is still friendly with them today. When journalist Miranda Sawyer asked him why he called them 'gypsies', he laughed and said, ''Cos they lived in caravans and picked potatoes for a living, you Wally!' Providing a glimpse of the kind of mentality which would later drive his 'Fifteen' charity, the young Jamie noticed the effect that good food stolen from his dad's pub had on these lads. They would hang around the back of the Cricketers' kitchen in the afternoons while Jamie made baps of turkey and pickle, ham and mustard, salami, and smoked salmon and lemon juice to take off into the woods. 'When I opened up the sarnie and squeezed the lemon on the smoked salmon, they just went "WOW!"' he said. 'That look on their faces was my first feeling of "this is really good" about food that I can remember. It was like showing a kid from the Victorian era what a VW Gold Convertible looks like!'

Jamie's sister Anna-Marie knows they were unusual among their peers. 'Children weren't eating things like avocados in the Seventies,' she said, while his friend Leigh Haggerwood said he even used food to catch his fish: 'We'd go fishing and we would use worms as bait – Jamie used marinated chicken from his lunch box!'

'He's genuinely excited about feeding people tasty delicious healthy food that makes them happy,' said his future mentor chef Alice Waters (Chez Panisse). 'I am, too. It thrills me to give a child a beautiful ripe peach and watch them fall in love with it. I'm a missionary and my aim is to get good food into people's mouths. He thinks the same way: he knows how to make things tasty, and he loves children – that's what drives him. It's very simple.'

Jamie was known in the village for being 'a good lad', one who would help out whenever he could, who would run errands and spend time chatting with anyone who seemed up for it. One villager remembers that when his wife was ill, Jamie knocked on his door to ask if she needed anything. He did the shopping and then spent the rest of the day talking to her about recipes that she'd had passed down from her mother. 'My wife came from a big farming family in Norfolk,' the villager said. 'He loved hearing her talk about having to pluck 20 pheasants at dawn so she could get everything ready for all the guns and the bush-beaters at night. He used to come quite a lot after that and he was always full of life and laughter.'

For the young Jamie Oliver, school was a rite of passage rather than a place of academic achievement although his Art and Geology GCSE's show an early ability to think big while being extremely grounded. Not that he saw it that way: 'Having not been the brightest banana in the bunch myself,' he proclaims loud and proud on his own website, 'I realised that my biggest weapon in life was the determination, enthusiasm, hands-on and "actions speak louder than words" approach my father taught me and I wanted to get this across to others especially those interested in food.' If his energies were not channelled into his schoolwork and were more likely to be put into budding entrepreneurial activities and high jinks, his teachers at Newport Free Grammar school still remember him fondly. One of them recalled, 'As a boy he had a face that betrayed just about every one of his impish emotions so you always knew if he was up to something. Board rubbers had an unnerving habit of dropping off the top of doors as you started a lesson when young Jamie was around.'

But if Jamie was likely to be behind any classroom distractions, his intentions were never malevolent – far from it. His gang took on the plight of a young boy who was being bullied and, without resorting to anything other than peer pressure and a few putdowns, were able to diffuse the situation. 'I always thought that Jamie was much brighter than his tests and exam results revealed,' said the victim (now a teacher himself). 'He had a gift for talking to people with the sort of honest, wide-eyed enthusiasm that's hard to resist. There is no side to him at all.'

David Stephens was another boy at Newport Free who witnessed the early hero in Jamie Oliver. He watched as Jamie interrupted a gang of senior boys giving one of the juniors a kicking in the toilets. 'He just walked in front of my friend and looked the biggest guy in the face and said, "That's enough of that!" And they stopped. There was something in the way he spoke, kind of quiet but confident, that gave the impression that underneath the smiley exterior he might be quite hard.' Jamie knew the gang leader well and smiled back when he mumbled something about it all being just a bit of a laugh. But he didn't move until the junior was safely away. 'He didn't have to do or say anything,' said Stephens, 'but I reckon most people would not have got involved.'

Jamie's lack of academic ability at school was very probably to do with his dyslexia. He admits now that he's never read a book from beginning to end. Jamie is a diagnosed dyslexic and lends his name to campaigns and websites to promote greater awareness of the disorder. According to experts, dyslexics share certain traits and are generally highly creative individuals. They use the brain's ability to alter and create perceptions, and are usually curious about how things work. His future employers at The River Café, chefs Ruth Rogers and Rose Gray, agreed that for them this was the first sign that he would make a great chef. 'He was always asking questions, *always*,' said Gray.

Dyslexics also tend to be highly intuitive, tapping into people who might otherwise have been ignored, and they have vivid dreams – often about how to get the best out of people. Interestingly, considering Jamie's commitment to food production, dyslexics are often highly aware of their environment and think mainly in pictures instead of words – which could account for Jamie's astonishing ability to communicate his passion for food on TV. Dyslexics are known to be able to perceive issues multi-dimensionally, something that would later serve Jamie well in his career with his cross media campaigns. 'Academically I am like my dad,' he said. 'I am a big thinker; I can be bright but only within the context of my own job. I am a doer, and if you tell me that I have to do X, then you can rest assured. I am very trustworthy.'

For a boy who spent his Tuesdays in Special Needs, writing was always going to be a struggle. 'I couldn't spell and I couldn't read very well, and Mrs Murphy would come into class and go [in silly voice] "Special needs?"' said Jamie. 'And we'd all start singing [to the tune of 'Let It Be'] "Special needs, special needs, special needs, special needs…" And me and Jimmy used to go to the Special Needs attic room, and she'd sit there saying, "Con-clusion". There were nine village idiots including me, and the only benefit was when she'd go to the toilet and we could roll up paper and bomb the people in the library below.'

But Mrs Murphy must have been one hell of a teacher for Jimmy Dogherty went on to become the youngest entomologist in his field. Before writing his book *On the Farm* (2004) he earned a degree in Zoology and a doctorate in Entomology, the science of insects. Jimmy was among the mates whom Jamie would try to drag along on the few dates he managed to get. They would all refuse to go with him to cafés like the Mocha café in Saffron Walden. These dates were not a success. 'I was so nervous,' said Jamie, recalling one such date. 'I wrote down 15 things to ask her. By number 10 it was getting desperate – I don't think I enthralled any girl with my conversation!'

While Jamie was busy playing heroes and villains at school, in true Vaseline lens slow motion his world was turned upside down. Sixteen-year-old Juliette (Jools) Norton, the daughter of a model, with the longest legs and the 'best pair of Bristol Cities' he had ever seen, walked into the playground. 'He was totally dumb-struck when he first saw her,' recalled a friend. 'He has his mouth open at the best of times but that day you could have driven a bus in – a double-decker at that!' Jamie was about to leave school to go on to catering college while Jools was to join the Sixth Form at Newport Free. Sexy yet with a coyness that made Jamie and his mates melt, she was unlike any of the Essex girls he'd ever met. What really made his heart race was that she seemed unaware of her allure.

Jools must have noticed that he would blush furiously every time she came into his orbit, but as they slowly became friends, the fire calmed – at least in his cheeks. She loved his sense of humour and he loved her legs. Well, he *was* 16. 'She thought I was an idiot at first,' he said later. 'The first time she really liked me was when we did a big gig with the band.' Jamie and his school-mate Leigh Haggerwood had formed the band when they were 12-year-olds at Newport Free Grammar. He had known Leigh since the age of eight but it was only when Leigh's family returned from an abortive move to Devon that Scarlet Division was born.

Practising in the garden shed was little more than a hobby until Louise Brannan, a young Derbyshire cook, answered the boys' ad for a singer and suddenly the band began to see a future. 'I'd say that Jamie came from the Muppet School of Drumming,' Leigh told the Biography Channel. 'He was just like Animal!'

For Jamie it was job done when his drumming made Jools' pulse skip a beat and transformed their relationship from mates in the playground to mates for life. 'There were loads of people there and she liked the way I was drumming,' he said simply. 'After two years of just being friends, that was what finally did it.' Trevor and Sally Oliver had also been young lovers (Jamie was born on his father's 21st birthday) and they agreed with Jools' parents that the two could go on holiday to Crete that first summer when Jamie was just 17. 'We saved up our money and rented an apartment overlooking the sea in a little village called Stalis,' said Jamie. 'I was already working in restaurants then so I was knackered. The best part of that holiday was just falling asleep on the beach next to Jools in the beautiful late afternoon sunshine.'

Although it is Jools who is meticulous about detail, a self-proclaimed Monica from *Friends*, in those days it was Jamie who worried about everything being just right. We witnessed that same concern when Jools surprised Jamie in *Jamie's Great Italian Escape* (Channel 4). As she flew in from London, Jamie was worse for wear from the previous night's hell-raising with Giovanni, the epicurean fisherman whose spontaneity had stirred his soul. Although Jamie had spent all his reflective moments wishing for Jools to be there to enjoy the scenery and the bustle, and the madness of Italy with him, when she crept in to disturb his siesta, he wanted it to be different. That night he was in charge of Giovanni's kitchen and, with still no delivery from the fruit and veg man, he was worried. It wasn't the romantic moment he'd dreamt of, and he was rattled. This was a sign of the drive to do things properly that he had learnt early on from his father. It was also something he already knew was part of raising the game in the kitchen.

CHAPTER 2

IN THE NAME OF THE FATHER

The Cricketers was one of the original gastro-pubs in Clavering – although the chicken in the basket and scampi and chips served in most 'gastro-pubs' at the time were more likely to leave their punters with indigestion than a revelation of the glories of food. From the earliest Jamie learnt that his home was one which opened its doors to the outside world, where anyone was welcome, a place where they would be wined and dined with warmth and charm.

It takes a special kind of person steeped in social skills to love the pub life but Trevor Oliver's apparent altruism was born of his business mind. 'My dad drilled into me that people came to The Cricketers to be entertained,' said Jamie. Trevor Oliver's attitude to money and making it was old school: see the customer right and they'll come back for more. 'Often they were celebrating a birthday or a promotion or an anniversary, and if you make that celebration a bit more enjoyable, they are all the more likely to come back again and tell their friends.'

Hospitality was not something Jamie could ever be taught in catering college; it was in his mother's milk. 'It was quite an amazing experience growing up in a country pub with all these different characters coming in every day,' he said. 'We were always taught to smile and be polite to people, and make them welcome. So many of my dad's ways were right that I find myself following them even now. "Sometimes it only takes a smile to brighten up a customer's day," my dad used to say, and many's the time nowadays that I think how right he was.'

Jamie's respect for his father is genuine but this didn't stop him playing typical childhood pranks on him. But when he and his mates let off a stink bomb in the pub – which drove his parents' punters out of the dining room so quickly they didn't have time to pay the bill – Jamie learnt his lesson the hard way. Thirty people left without paying, and he received the hiding of his life from his father. Jamie got the message.

Jamie would put his Huckleberry Finn hat away when he was with the pub customers, and villagers remember him as chatty and sociable. By the age of 11 or 12, he was serving food to the punters. Again his training came from Trevor. 'My dad got sent all the quiet kids in the village to work at the weekend,' Jamie told journalist Simon Hattenstone. '"Trev, look after our daughter, will you? She's just a little bit quiet, just a little bit shy." Dad would put her on the buffet for a month over summer and by the end she'd be the most outgoing bird. You can't be shy in the pub trade – it's almost impossible.'

Jamie was very young when he started taking an interest in the kitchen. 'I started cooking regularly when I was about eight as a weekend thing,' Hildred and Ewband report him saying in their early biography. 'But when I was really young, my mum taught me how to make an omelette and I found I was good at it. That was a lovely feeling of satisfaction, of actually creating something out of something else'. By 11 he was taking chicken breasts off the bone and stuffing mushrooms inside the breast: 'But I never thought nothing of it,' he says. 'Mate, it was pocket money.' According to his family, however, the impressionable young Jamie was drawn to the kitchens for a different reason. 'The kitchens were where the cool dudes were in our pub,' said his sister Anna-Marie. While his mother, Sally, recalls: 'They were always telling dirty stories and using language we wouldn't use.'

Jamie's interest in local produce started well before he had any political interest in changing the way we buy our food. It was the yearly family holiday to the Norfolk Broads, where Trevor and Sally would hire a motor cruiser and mess about on the river. For Jamie, the boats were cool, with 'pull-out beds, pull-out telly, pull-out oven, pull-out seats, pull-out everything'. But it was the shopping that he remembers so well, the collection from beaten-up old sheds on the riverbank, with a pot for the money. 'The farm would be a mile up the track and they would trust you to put your money in the little pot, and everyone always did,' he said.

Anna-Marie and Jamie would take the dinghy out, fishing for perch, eels, roach and anything else they could find to throw on the barbecue at the end of the day. But it was Trevor whose lead Jamie was to follow when it came to sourcing the best local ingredients for his own recipes. Essex was surprisingly full of Italian-run greenhouses and market gardens, and it was Trevor's commitment and enthusiasm that allowed him to get in there quickly before everything was dispatched around the country.

By the time Jamie was 14 and on a school trip in France, he found that his culinary skills were making him new friends. For a hungry lad, the stale bread and confitures on offer could never make up for Sally's hearty start to the day. The following year he packed a Calor Gas stove and non-stick frying pan in his bag, and held court on his Alpine balcony as he churned out fried bread and eggs for his grateful mates.

Jamie's childhood cashflow was fluid enough, and he always had enough in his pocket to get by. 'I'm sure everyone thought I was a spoiled brat,' he told Simon Hattenstone. 'I always had whatever trainers I wanted, and I can honestly say I earned every single penny. My old man never gave me handouts. Ever! In fact he was repulsed by the idea.' Trevor believed everyone had to work for their money – and that included the young Jamie. As soon as his son wanted more than the usual comics and toys, he offered him some washing up in the kitchens of The Cricketers. But washing up was not macho enough for a cool and sophisticated eight-year-old, and it was the hardcore action of the kitchen with the real men where he wanted to be.

Peeling potatoes, chopping the vegetables, clearing out the bins – Jamie was anyone's for a bit of spare cash in those days. But while he was dreaming of the £3.75 he would be able to pocket after an afternoon's shift, he was discovering that working for his comics wasn't such a raw deal after all. The chefs who would dole out the chores also realised that they didn't just have to keep the boss sweet and that Jamie was proving to be pretty useful, too. By the time he was 11, Jamie was serving in the pub and at the age of 14, he had moved on from podding peas to helping them cook between 100 and 120 meals on a Sunday night.

While Jamie fine-tuned his entrepreneurial skills at school leasing lockers from his mates (from which he would sell sweets bought on his dad's cash-and-carry account, earning him a cool £30 a week), his father was organising a job for him. It was on the cold starter section at The Starr in nearby Great Dunmow (Essex). Trevor wanted to encourage Jamie to improve his culinary skills, but he was also keen for him to take his understanding of good food up a notch from the humbler kitchen at The Cricketers. Jamie was only 13 years old, but his dad was quickly vindicated in spotting Jamie's potential and within weeks he had replaced a chef of 26. Driving him home that first night, Trevor told him he was proud of him. Jamie said that he 'felt all tingly and funny'.

It must have been something in the genes. Jamie says it is his late beloved grandfather Ken Oliver, who ran The Plough and Sow, in Paglesham, near Southend, whom he acknowledges as his inspiration in becoming a chef. He was thrilled that he saw him become a success before he died of a stroke in 2001 aged 74. It was his father's influence though that would be the driving force in his career and it started young. Toss up the opportunity to go travelling with some mates or get stuck into a career by the age of 17 and most school leavers by the early Nineties would have no hesitation in waxing down a surfboard and heading off on the by now well-worn hippie trail. Looking at the friends he chose to feed during the three Channel 4 *Naked Chef* series, you know that Jamie Oliver would have had a ball on the kind of overseas experience that is part of growing up among his Aussie chums.

But Trevor had drummed it into Jamie that if he hadn't become a head chef by the age of 45, or was still waiting to make enough to have his own restaurant, then he would have failed. 'He told me chefing was a young man's game and that I would want to own my own restaurant as young as possible,' said Jamie – who still gets up at 6.30 every morning in memory of the early-morning water hosing his dad would give him through his bedroom window as a lad. 'He told me people die in bed.'

CHAPTER 3

THE WINTERS OF DISCONTENT

While Jamie was scampering around the Essex fields, food in Britain had reached an all-time low. In 1975 when Jamie was born, most of us still bought our food from local butchers and greengrocers. Although TV dinners were still a decade away from transforming family life, Vesta had begun to produce the first ready meals and products like Angel Delight offered a new generation of working women an opportunity to whisk up a pudding that the kids loved and took no time to make. No one complained at the time; Vesta tended to offer exotic new dishes such as Chow Mein and curries we weren't quite sure how to make anyway, and convenience foods meant more time for the new buzz word: 'leisure'.

Baby boomer chef and culinary alchemist Heston Blumenthal would recreate these dishes in his 'memory food' 30 years later at The Fat Duck and take our senses on a nostalgic ride back in time while giving our bodies the nutrition that it would take 30 years to rediscover. The journey from Angel Delight to The Fat Duck (winner of *Restaurant Magazine*'s Best Restaurant in the World award in 2005) takes us on a trip through British food culture. It spans the course of Jamie Oliver's rise from his mother's knee to becoming arguably the most famous chef on the planet.

The Seventies were already a grim time in British history with the Winter of Discontent bringing a decade of economic weakness, unemployment and strikes under Labour rule to an end in 1979. Even if the effervescent New Zealander Graham Kerr, 'The Galloping Gourmet', was leaping across our TV screens inspiring us to cook and helping himself to another tipple as he stirred lashings of cream into his latest creation, this was no time for feasting. The fact that Kerr was soon to be transformed from hedonistic epicurean to low-fat diet guru by the Eighties was a sign of the times. London had lost its swing only a decade after it led the world in a sexual and style revolution. Just 20 years old, fellow chef and mentor Gennaro Contaldo came to London from the Amalfi coastal village where Jamie would find his spiritual home in his Channel 4 series, *Jamie's Great Italian Escape*, 35 years later. 'London wasn't like it is now,' he told me. 'I found London so behind in fashion and food. My first job was in a fish and chip shop even though I was already a chef. The smell was terrible; they used whale fat. I love fish and chips, but it wasn't my culture. The way that they were cooked was terrible. And then they served them in newspapers,' he said, grimacing at the memory.

The London of the 1970s was not the café society that it would later become and Gennaro reeled at the culture shock of living in a city where food was perceived as fuel. 'I remember when I was first taken into a coffee shop and I expected brioche with my coffee, but I got egg with bacon and a fried slice [of bread] with a mug of coffee. I thought, "My God, that would give you indigestion. Why are they killing themselves?"' Only the bread filled his senses enough to stop him from beating a hasty retreat back to Italy. 'There was a wonderful bread shop with lots of different types of bread and cakes,' he said. 'They were not my type of cakes because they filled them with cream, but the smell of the bread was fantastic.'

Contaldo moved on from fish and chips as quickly as he could to one of the new Italian trattorias populating the city – this time as a waiter: 'I remember thinking, "What is this Bolognese with mushrooms and carrots? They made Carbonara with Béchamel sauce. There were sauces everywhere on the tables. And they made up names of dishes; if someone came from Rome, it would be Spaghetti à la Romana. Of course there's no such thing in Italy. We used to cook meat and call it Meat à l'Amalfitana after the people like me who came from Amalfi." Ruth Rogers of The River Café arrived from upstate New York in 1969 with the heavy meatballs of Italian-American food still fresh in her memory. She remembers the kind of Italian food Gennaro was serving. 'I wouldn't say that food was dire,' she said. 'People were exploring with different ideas and eating cheap and cheerful food. But it was mostly cooked by Italian waiters, I think, so the food was not very adventurous or real.'

Although the scent of espresso coffee had become an essential part of mod culture in the Sixties via Italian cafés in London, it was only in the tiny area of Soho in the midst of the capital's West End where you could find the genuine article. Italian coffee smelt of a lifestyle that people like Rose Gray, now of The River Café, could aspire to. She was a young art graduate, a mother of three children (and pregnant with her fourth) when Jamie Oliver was born in 1975. She lived in London's Maida Vale and shopped in Soho. 'I used to go to Soho every week to buy some Parmesan and salted anchovies, some pasta to stock up on our Italian store cupboard,' she said. 'I've been in love with Italian food since I was an art student in the 50s.'

In the Sixties, cheaper travel pushed open the borders on our rather parochial food culture and families began to try out new flavours. 'When I came here,' said Ruth Rogers, 'there was definitely a sense of foreignness – it wasn't that you were American or Australian, or French: you were just foreign. And I think that's the way it was with food. Now you get people saying that they've heard the new olive oil has arrived. Once you opened up Europe and people were experimenting with the food, they wanted to continue eating it when they got home.'

Sally Clarke, the renowned chef and baker whom Jamie counts as an early source of inspiration, travelled to France every year with her family as a child. 'We travelled further south each year until we got to Italy,' she said. This was an inspiration to the young foodie whose diet at home 'wasn't bland but was fairly limited', and would encourage her to play with new ideas. 'My mother, knowing my love of cooking, was just as happy to give me an Elizabeth David book to play with and head back into the garden, which was her love.'

By the late Fifties and early Sixties, stories about a more Bohemian life in Europe were swapped at universities and art colleges as more young people ventured into France, Spain and Italy. Elizabeth David's seminal books *Mediterranean Food, French Country Cooking, Italian Food* and *French Provincial Cooking* wafted the scent of provincial European food from over the Channel. After the austerity of food rationing and penny pinching of the Fifties, a new breed of arty hippies was beginning to sniff outside of its comfort zone. Rose Gray was finding a wealth of ideas about art, culture and food in Paris and Florence. 'I was brought up during the war in England,' she said, 'and the moment I could travel myself, I went to Italy and France to look at the art.' Art, she says, leads you to food. 'If you're looking at the paintings in Florence, you're also going to be thinking about lunch.'

Gray trained as a designer, but as a single mother she had to think of ideas for making money. When Jamie Oliver, whom she would be mothering herself 20 years later at The River Café, was still a babe in arms, she had her own children asleep at her feet as she made crèpes for the rock crowds at The Rainbow Theatre in north London. 'I saw people making crèpes on the streets in Paris and thought, "What a great idea,"' she said. 'I bought six crèpe machines and, with various girlfriends helping me, I used to make crèpes at pop concerts like Pink Floyd and Rod Stewart. I remember the Alice Cooper gig particularly because everyone was so stoned that they came rushing to my crèpe stand. I used to do bitter chocolate with crème fraîche on my crèpes, and marrons glacés with sour cream and honey and nuts. People adored it. That's why I had to have six crèpe machines – because they'd come out for the 20-minute interval, grab one and rush back in again. There wasn't a lot of time to feed everyone.'

Gray was to become famous for sourcing the best ingredients for the Italian food that she and her partner Ruth Rogers would cook at The River Café by the late Eighties, and her crèpes were no different. Even the flour she used would be from France. It was on one of her shopping trips that she spotted her next money-making opportunity. She began to import wood burning stoves. 'They were beautiful little boxes which you could fit into the fire-places of big old Victorian houses like mine,' she remembered. 'We all had minimal central heating and not much money but you could buy these little wood stoves for £20. All you needed to do was put wood in, and they would act as radiators.' She used her own house as a shop front. 'I used to cook the kids' breakfasts on it,' she said. But as word spread about her pretty French finds, her client list became sexier. 'André Previn and Paul McCartney would walk through the house and choose the wood stoves. It was great fun,' she said. It was an example of the kind of entrepre-neurial passion that was infused into The River Café, and which Jamie Oliver would find himself adding to his pot by the time he was just 20 years old.

Rose's partner, Ruth Rogers, was one of the increasing number of Brits who travelled for business and pleasure, bringing back news of what was happening in French food. It wasn't all good, however. 'I hit Paris just at the point where Cuisine Nouvelle arrived around 1971 when Richard [Ruth's husband, architect Richard Rogers] had won the contract for The Pompidou Centre. Everyone was amazed that you could put a poached carrot on a plate with a Vegetable Terrine. Everyone was minimising and reacting against the classical traditions.'

In the Seventies and Eighties eating out for most people in London was reserved for family events. 'In those days it was just the grand restaurants or the hotels that you would go to for special occasions,' said Gray. Gourmet experiences were not only hard to find – they were not always a great night out either. 'The old fashioned chef was scary and made you feel humiliated,' recalled Rogers. 'The sommelier made you feel stupid, so going out for a special occasion made you feel intimidated.' 'There were also those Indian restaurants that we used to go to,' added Rose. 'I guess that was the colonial thing,' said Ruth. 'Coming from upstate New York, I'd never seen a curry in my life.' Another of Jamie's future mentors, Alice Waters (of Chez Panisse), lived briefly in England in 1968 and although she is credited with inventing Californian cuisine and introducing locally sourced seasonal produce to a US state of health-seeking food fans, it was Indian food she also loved to eat in Britain.

Although most people stayed in and sat around the family dinner table almost every night of the week, in London the celebrity scene was just beginning to bring a touch of glamour to the Seventies. Langan's was where Michael Caine and his exotic wife Shakira could be spotted most nights and where George Best would bring his entourage of beautiful blondes, but it was Neal Street, where Jamie Oliver would get his first job, that was the first to break the mould. 'Neal Street was very, very expensive but very glamorous,' Rose Gray remembered. 'When the Oz trials were on, I remember going to a party and there were pictures of all of them in the loos.'

While food was not the consumption of choice for the celebrities seen in the early London restaurants, Alice Waters loved English produce. 'I used to go down to Harrods every day to the food hall where they were hanging all the wild game. I would go into the countryside and eat garden produce. I have great admiration for British garden produce,' she said. 'You have a great history of sophisticated horticulture. I love reading British writers like Elizabeth Luard on kitchen gardens.'

Gennaro Contaldo had also discovered the market gardens of middle England as well as a passion for British food by moving out of London and away from the 'awful' Italian restaurants to the Midlands. 'I learnt to cook beautiful English food like Lancashire Hot Pot and puddings like bread and butter pudding,' he said.

Sally Clarke remembered what English food was like as she was growing up in the country: 'We had ox and lamb hearts and kidneys. Like most people in the middle-upper classes, we didn't have vast amounts to spend on food and my parents, both being war children, had that mentality.' During the Second World War British food had been bland cold-comfort food with big sauces that kept your fires stoked but did little to stir your imagination. Sally Clarke says it goes back even further: 'You only have to look through a Mrs Beeton's book and you thought, "Blimey, did they really eat that?"'

It wasn't until cheaper travel opened eyes and nostrils that British cooking would change forever, although a trip into a little Welsh market town in the Black Mountains would have done the trick. By the mid-Seventies The Walnut Tree in Abergavenny would have a waiting list of six months with visitors booking from as far away as Japan. It was a culinary phenomenon in a country not particularly renowned for its food culture despite the richness of Welsh ingredients that would rise to prominence by the time Jamie Oliver was promoting locally sourced food. These days Franco Taruschio has moved on, leaving Gordon Ramsay to try to restore his landmark restaurant's flagging reputation in one of his Channel 4 *Kitchen Nightmares* makeovers. But after 40 years Franco is still known as the Godfather of Italian cooking, for bringing the first pasta to Britain in 1963 and growing the first rocket ever seen there. As Franco worked his magic, food-loving journalists began to spread the word about just how good Italian food could be. Even Nigella Lawson, who famously barely ventured out of London to review restaurants for her column in *The Spectator*, headed down the M4 to taste Franco's pasta.

A couple of hours up the A40 into west Wales, a young Pat Llewellyn (producer of *The Naked Chef*) quietly watched her parents create waves in the little town of Newcastle Emlyn, where they ran a small hotel and restaurant. 'They're very into feeding people generously and sending people away happy,' said the woman who would spot 21-year-old Jamie Oliver 20 years later in the kitchens of The River Café. She was brought up with pheasants hanging in the shed and the kind of posh nosh not normally associated with Wales. 'My dad's side were all farmers or grew their own food,' she said, 'but my mother had an understanding of what was going on in the Seventies and brought a tiny bit of sophistication to the place. She read everything – Elizabeth David and all those Robert Carrier partworks. I think my mum and dad probably brought the first Duck à l'Orange to Newcastle Emlyn.' Surrounded by food rather than food shops, Pat's contact with the land would fast-track her understanding of Jamie's passion for locally sourced ingredients and making great food simply. 'My father still does his own tongue and faggots,' she said, 'and there are still rows in the family over my great grandmother's pickled onion recipe; one of my uncles even sent the recipe in to the *Western Mail* and won £5. My family is full of food stories and yarns.'

Trevor Oliver's family came from kitchens rather than farms but the Essex countryside was ripe with local produce and he loved looking around for the best ingredients he could use in his own kitchens at The Cricketers. He may not claim to covet the kind of reputation that Franco Taruschio had already won, and which his own son would gain in years to come, but he was interested in putting the best that he could get on the tables of his customers. He loved the banter with the local market gardeners and used the Oliver charm and loyalty to make sure that the freshest and best produce was kept back for him, often getting the best of the crop before it was transported up to Covent Garden's enormous London market.

The fragrance of fresh herbs and fish, and the banter of market traders ringing in his ears as they drove home, may well have given the young Jamie Oliver an association with fresh produce that would have him shouting its virtues from the rooftops the moment he had an audience. The gypsy boys were his first. 'He really didn't want to eat it,' said Jamie of his mate's first taste of salmon, 'and then when he did, he wouldn't eat anything else all summer. That's when I understood how powerful food can be.'

CHAPTER 4

WHITE HEAT

By 1990, word about the new breed of chef cooking in Britain had made it to Essex. Books such as *White Heat* by gastro-punk Marco Pierre White and *Recipes from Le Manoir aux Quat' Saisons* by Raymond Blanc were influencing a new generation of young chefs with their perfectionism and drive. 'Marco did something that was different,' said Alistair Little, now of Tavola. 'He reworked food in a really intelligent manner. He had a good look at it and broke it down, and modernised it into Nouvelle Cuisine. He kind of dumbed it down but in a really good way.' This was before food sections in the weekend papers, and it was the chat in the kitchens of The Cricketers that drove 15-year-old Jamie to find out more. 'I grew up reading about Marco and Raymond Blanc, and Gary Rhodes and Rick Stein,' Jamie said in a newspaper interview. 'There were quite a lot of the chefs I grew up adoring but a lot of them turned out to be fucking arrogant little shits.'

White Heat's sexy black-and-white photographs of Marco's fiery kitchen by Bob Carlos-Clarke, Marco's mentors (such as Albert Roux and Keith Floyd) and young celebrities like Jason Donovan who ate at his restaurant Harvey's told Jamie – indeed any young chef – all he needed to know: Marco was the perfectionist with attitude. 'A lot of people say I look like a rock star or a designer punk,' he wrote in *White Heat*, 'but I swear it's the job that has carved my face. It's the hours, the stress and the pressure.' *White Heat* was filled with ideas that would make a young lad whose head was already filled with tastes and textures look twice at his meat cleaver. Marco broke the rules. He was the school bully who seduced with his gentleness; a Yorkshire giant with a sensitive Italian core, the tearaway son who sought out the fathers of British haute cuisine like Pierre Koffman, Nico Ladenis and Albert Roux, and charmed his way into their kitchens. He watched and listened until he had learnt his craft. By the age of 33 he had inspired a tribe of young chefs to covet a restaurant of their own and became the youngest chef ever to be awarded three Michelin stars.

'Marco Pierre White turned up at Le Gavroche at the age of 19 directly from Yorkshire,' wrote Albert Roux, whom Marco described as the Godfather of modern British food alongside Pierre Koffman and Nico Ladenis. 'He had no appointment and only £5 in his pocket. I looked up at the shining eyes as he talked about cooking... and I agreed that he should become an apprentice if he would cut his hair!'

'Marco was the transition between the past and the future,' said fellow chef and friend Jean-Christophe Novelli. 'He brought informality to cooking. He was British but he was immaculate in the kitchen. What France had brought to the market was a traditional style, but it meant that you just do the same thing all the time. Marco went to the edges of that. He thought, "Fuck that recipe, let's do a dauphinoise with shellfish reduction!" He pushed the boundaries of cooking and had an attitude that wasn't traditional. He was very rock and roll – he gave these young chefs freedom of expression.'

Marco's attitude to his customers was revolutionary and he was said to throw them out if they complained or arrived late. 'If I came to your house for dinner an hour late, then criticised all your furniture and your wife's haircut, and said all your opinions were stupid, how would you feel?' he wrote in *White Heat*. 'People still come here and expect a three-course meal in an hour. What do they think I do – pull rabbits out of a fucking hat? I'm not a magician.' For a teenager like Jamie Oliver, who had never heard swearing so eloquently and so passionately delivered, what could be more inspiring? Marco was just as much of an inspiration for grown men like Gary Hunter, who would head up the Culinary Arts course at Westminster Catering College in Victoria (where Jamie would study). 'He has had a massive influence. People don't realise just how influential he really is. The amount of lecturers who are influenced by him is astonishing. I had a starter of his at Harvey's and that was the biggest influence of my life. The man is a giant in culinary circles.'

The gossip about this new wave of British cooking was spreading fast and young chefs were staying in all weekend just to be able to take their savings to Books for Cooks in London's Notting Hill on Monday morning. Top chef Tom Aikens was one of them. 'I lived in Balham at the time and I would walk past Harvey's on the way to work,' he said. 'I knew that I wanted to work at that top end of gastronomy for Nico, Roux, Marco or Koffman but it was impossible to get to work for them. This was the Nineties and there were hardly any restaurants of any calibre. There was Le Caprice and The Ivy, but it was nothing like what we see now.'

Tom was in his early twenties when he got his first break working for Pierre Koffman after learning his trade and earning nothing for five months. 'Chefs would work their nuts off,' he said. 'It was so bloody hard to get into these places,' he recalled, referring to the restaurants which Marco had preached as being part of the new wave. 'There was an 18-month waiting list to get work in La Tante Claire,' he said of Pierre Koffman's legendary restaurant in Chelsea's Royal Hospital Road where Gordon Ramsay's now sits. 'Nico [Ladenis] and Marco were churning young chefs out as quickly as they could because there was an endless line of young lads willing to take the shit that they gave. They wanted us to graft and really work.' One of them was a young Gordon Ramsay, who worked there from 1989 to 1991.

Tom doesn't bear a grudge: 'There were so few really good restaurants then but those guys there were amazing. All of them are retired pretty much now. But for me it was the greatest time to be working. You felt so privileged to be working with them because you knew that there were so many people who wanted to be where you were. You were the chosen one.'

Jamie Oliver knew that he wanted to be one of the chosen few too. He had honed his knife skills early in the kitchens of The Cricketers and learnt to make terrines at The Starr in Great Dunmow. It was 1991 and the British had begun to realise that there was more to food than chicken in the basket. London was becoming a serious foodie capital and it was time for Jamie to leave his childhood mates and learn to play with the big boys. The London he would find was reeling from a food revolution that was making it one of the most interesting cities in the world. It was still a place where its residents would buy their food from supermarkets and sit in front of a TV dinner that was heated in a microwave. But London had been simmering nicely for the past 20 years, and was now ready to turn up the heat.

CHAPTER 5

SOWING THE SEEDS OF CHANGE

Things had been changing since the Thatcher Government set its sights on sending the nation out onto the world market to show what New Britain was made of. Margaret Thatcher's vision was a showcase of British progress and innovation. In order to achieve it, she decided to create a national curriculum that put maths and literacy, science and technology on a podium for the rest of the world to admire. What she failed to realise was that by taking Physical Education and Home Economics out of the school day, children would grow up into fat adults who had no idea what a good square meal looked like, let alone how to cook one for themselves and their children. How she imagined they would find the energy to become world-class innovators, she failed to tell us. The concurrent campaign for emancipation gave women a way out of the kitchen while convenience foods allowed them to seem to provide for their families. With cooking skills put on the back burner, it was not long before they boiled dry.

London was influenced by young executives who were travelling to California and New York and bringing home a new enthusiasm for the food they had tasted over business dinners. While France was still setting the standard for haute cuisine and Italy still making the same food it had been feeding its locals for centuries, America was undergoing a massive change in its food culture. It was only a matter of time before Britain caught on.

Much of this was to do with Alice Waters, whom *Cuisine et Vins de France* magazine had spotted as one of the ten best chefs in the world in 1986. She was making waves at her restaurant Chez Panisse in Berkeley, just across the bay from San Francisco, with her single fixed-price menu that she changed daily. Back in 1971, Waters and her idealistic friends at Berkeley had an idea. They would open a restaurant as an experiment in providing a dinner party environment in a bistro, using local organically grown produce that had been harvested ecologically and in season. Building a network of farmers who could supply her, she would help to support the local community of farmers' markets and the wider community. She encouraged Americans to think beyond what they put in their mouths and the effect their purchasing power had on the environment and society. It was a radical idea but Californians lapped it up.

Craig Sams is chair of the Soil Association and the man behind Green & Black's organic chocolate as well as the owner of Judges organic bakery in Hastings, East Sussex. He explained how Alice Waters' idea impacts on the local economy and why every local business leader should be championing it. 'When you go to the supermarket on a Saturday, you're trying to plan ahead for the next week. You end up with food that is past its sell-by date and with food that you feel you have to eat on that day when maybe you don't want to. If you spend £10 in a supermarket, the benefit to the local economy is £12. If you spend it in a local shop, it's £25,' said Sams, quoting independent think tank The New Economics Foundation. 'It's because the owner's profit stays in the neighbourhood. They're more likely to use the local plumber rather than a corporate one and pay rent to a local landlord; the staff is likely to spend its money locally so the money circulates locally. If you buy something in a local shop that came from local producers – like we do in our shop, where the meat comes from four miles away, the vegetables come from three miles away and the eggs and chickens come from seven – then you're talking about £40-worth of benefit to the local economy for every £10 spent.'

By the Nineties, Waters' influence had spread not just across the States but her work with school dinners, growing food in prisons and supporting a network of farmers' markets in America would win her *Bon Appetit* magazine's Lifetime Achievement Award and the James Beard Humanitarian Award. Food was no longer just something rich people ate, or something to do while being seen at the right places. Community wasn't just for the muesli knitters; Alice Waters had combined her talents as the best chef in America to effect social change. Health was about more than a tiny waistline but raised consciousness about the relationship between good food and behaviour. Eating organic, local, seasonal produce was not just tastier but supported the growth and sustainability of real farmers.

Waters says that her interest in food started while she was travelling in Paris in 1963 as she wandered through the enormous fruit and vegetable market in the heart of the city. It was the colours, the bustle of the market traders and customers, and the life that made her feel 'directly connected to the land', she told journalist Susannah Abbey. 'I had an epiphany,' she said. But London in the late Sixties was where the hippie movement met a minor foodie revolution. 'I was greatly influenced by Elizabeth David,' said Waters. 'But I was such a fanatic at the time. We all had such enthusiasm and energy. There was a big free speech movement in Berkeley at the time,' she said, referring to the late Seventies and early Eighties, 'and everyone was setting up businesses in what they believed in and running them the way they wanted to. There was an entrepreneurial culture as well as this beautiful climate that allowed us to grow great produce. It was just at the beginning of the search for organic food and cooking with seasonal produce. It wasn't a new philosophy – it had been around since the beginning of time – but we had moved so far away from it by that time.'

Waters thinks that it was the empty palate of American cooking that was begging to be painted upon that allowed them more freedom than the dense neighbourhood cultures in New York. In contrast to the jealous guarding of French, Spanish, Italian and Jewish cooking in New York, the Californians had more room to play. Rose Gray, who had gone to New York to try out her Italian cuisine on a more sophisticated customer in the mid-Eighties, agrees with her: 'They had no shame about pulling from the Europeans, partly because a lot of Italians and Spanish lived there.' Gray had gone to New York to earn some much-needed cash after four years of cooking in Italy. 'Some friends of mine were opening a night club in New York and they wanted to have a little Italian restaurant inside, so I said OK.' Nell's became hugely successful. 'Everyone came there,' said Gray, 'from Alice Waters to Wolfgang Puck, Andy Warhol, Tyson... And I just cooked the same food that we cook here now in that little place.' It gave her the taste for restaurants through the American eyes. 'When I was there I thought, this is the best job on earth, I'm never going to do anything else again.'

Stephanie Alexander, doyenne of Australian cuisine, noticed the same thing happening in Melbourne, Sydney and Adelaide. With waves of Italian immigrants in the Fifties, then Greek in the Sixties and Vietnamese in the Seventies flooding into Australia and bringing their comfort food with them, it was the blandness of the Australian food culture pre-1950 that allowed it to grow into one of the most exciting national cuisines in the world by the Nineties. But, she says, convenience food is still the biggest evil for the majority of Australians. 'It's a Celt thing,' she told me. 'We are still the dominant tribe here. It came from Protestantism and Puritanism, and the industrialising of food, but there is still the feeling that going on and on about food is obscene. It is always much more important to have cerebral thoughts. We are concerned with our heads rather than our bodies, and food is still seen as fuel. We're supposed to get on with it and then read a book. It's not about being around the table or about celebration; it's about renewing your energy.'

Women would become some of Jamie Oliver's most influential mentors. He gave his list to Simon Hattenstone: 'Alice Waters in

San Francisco, Rose Gray and Ruth Rogers, Stephanie Alexander in Australia, Sally Clarke and Elizabeth David.' Hattenstone wanted to know what it was that he got from them. 'Just not a sense of testosterone, cock first… it was much more maternal cooking. Simplicity, the brief to not try and touch it as much as possible before it reached the plate. I think the woman thing is much more about feeding families and common sense and what's growing.' Alice Waters has said she couldn't be more thrilled by this. 'He has a sense of taste and style that reflects all the principles that I represent – purity, pleasure of eating. He has this set of values and that to me is tremendously important.' She says that she met him 'way back when at your farmers' market, I think,' referring to London's Borough Market, where Jamie still takes his children most Saturdays. 'We've talked on the phone so much that I can't quite remember when.'

It was while Jamie was still cooking pizzas at his mother's side that Alice Waters' interest in local, seasonal produce would become one of the most important influences in British food, one that would ultimately lay the groundwork for Jamie's explosion into the public consciousness.

CHAPTER 6

CREATING A SCENE

If The Stones and George Best had created the feel for a glamorous restaurant culture in the Seventies, a recession in 1980–1 – just after the Thatcher reign began – inadvertently kick-started the big change. TV chef and restaurateur Antony Worrall Thompson watched with interest. 'That recession created a café society for the first time that Madrid, Paris, Nice and New York all had. We'd never had that. We ate out for special occasions but we didn't eat out as a matter of course. When prices came down in Britain, a lot of executives traded down because they didn't want their employees seeing them pay lots of money for food, and afterwards they'd say "Actually I quite enjoyed that; it wasn't all stiff and starchy".'

By 1984 London was coming out of its dark days. Margaret Thatcher's Britain was a place where the individual replaced the notion of society, and the 'Me' culture was propping up a new wave of conspicuous spending. Nigel Lawson as Thatcher's Chancellor of the Exchequer (1983–9) had created the yuppie economic climate that sent a message to the world that Britain was having fun, and there was no point in doing it at home where no one could see you. But Britain had precious few places to be seen other than the rather unglamorous local hostelries. By 5pm on Friday evening wine bars were packed as city slickers splashed out on champagne to toast their latest bonus before unsteadily searching for somewhere to eat. Meanwhile, über-trendies settled themselves in Notting Hill's192 Kensington Park Road as Alistair Little and Rose Gray took turns to serve them the first crumbs of London's first major food scene.

Rose Gray met Alistair Little in the 1970s. 'He was the first to introduce Mediterranean food into the London scene and he did it with great skill and great knowledge. I used to look forward to eating in his restaurant more than anything,' she said, referring to Simpsons in Putney, which he ran for a short time in the Seventies before his business partner died suddenly. 'You went to Neal Street for a social, where you might meet people and see people because it was kind of star-studded. And you'd go to Peter Langan's for a really boozy time and something French; it was like going to La Coupole in Paris. And then you'd go to Alistair for the food; just the food and the wine – he was a great wine buyer.' She said that 192 was 'a seminal restaurant in terms of changing awareness where people were starting to feel at home when they were eating out'.

Gray worked there for six weeks when she first came back from New York as she and Ruth Rogers were just beginning to talk about their own restaurant, The River Café. 'There was a group of us who did a stint there,' she said. 'It was a hideous place but the food was good and you had the chance to buy really good ingredients. There were only a few good restaurants at that time. There were some Japanese restaurants around and the Chinese were getting better. I used to eat in the Greek restaurants; if I was going to eat out, I would do it at the ethnic places which were very modest and didn't cost much either. You went to 192 for the fun and for the food.'

Notting Hill was becoming the unlikely birthplace of modern British cuisine. 'I thought they were very brave to open in Notting Hill because there really was nothing,' said Alistair Little about 192 Kensington Park Road. 'There were a couple of restaurants, including Leiths, but mostly it was rough. It got immediately fashionable because the trendies had moved into Notting Hill.' Up the road from 192, Eric Treuille, a stylish young visionary, had just arrived in Notting Hill from south-west France to open a bookshop called Books for Cooks. The shop would at first cater for professional chefs and a minority of locals with a passion for food but would see the interest expand enormously over the next two decades. By 2005 Treuille's shop was packed with books by TV chefs and a customer base spanning age, class and culture. But in 1984, he said, Notting Hill was a very different place. 'I remember that you couldn't find a cup of coffee. But now you can't find a cup of tea. There was no café culture. Now we have to stop people walking into the shop with a coffee as an extension of their hand.'

Alistair Little moved on, this time to cook at L'Escargot, the grand old French house in the middle of London's Soho with uneven floors, an Aladdin's cave of shabby chic mismatched furniture and a maître d' who ran the place like a madam runs her brothel. Jancis Robinson was his wine buyer and, as word spread about the fine food and wine on offer, actors and artists tipping out of West End theatres came to drink and eat Mediterranean food in the new bohemian revival of Soho before going on to Ronnie Scott's jazz club.

They were cultured, well travelled and had high expectations. They had eaten in San Francisco and Paris and knew what good food should be. Even 14-year-old Tom Aikens was blown away when he visited his first two-star Michelin restaurant in France with his family. 'We had driven hundreds of miles and looked scuzzy,' he said. 'And the waiters were in white gloves and white jackets. I remember I had beautiful vine ripened tomatoes with shallots and fresh herbs, and olive oil. Then the tiniest piece of beef fillet that had been larded with beef fat and served with home-made chips. For me it was heaven. It was the taste and the presentation – it was just so clean and so simple. I remember putting it in my mouth and it melted; I hardly had to chew this thing. It was amazing... Amazing.' By 2003 he would win his own Michelin star within ten months of opening his restaurant – Tom Aikens – at the tender age of 33.

Food could be beautiful and the yuppie climate spawned a new breed of beautiful people who would spend hours over lunch and dinner, creating a feeling of lazy elegance around food. Antony Worrall Thompson noticed that women were the main players, preferring small portions of healthy, slimming food that looked good and was suitably expensive. He had opened a restaurant in Chelsea that grabbed media attention for allowing women to eat starters and puddings alone. 'Girls had often just wanted starters and the waiters would say, "No, Madam must have the main course,"' he said. 'There was a huge difference between starters and main course prices so when I started Ménage à Trois the price gap narrowed considerably.' He came up with a radical offer. 'We were just serving starters and puds. Men left my restaurants wanting a pack of Munchies but the girls loved their puddings.'

Women were key to the growth of the new food scene. A restaurant full of red-faced businessmen was less likely to attract the newly hungry fashionistas than a bistro full of elegant women and their handsome dates. 'Men had always paid the bill and women were ignored,' said Worrall Thompson. 'Women were seen in the restaurant business as bad tippers and bad drinkers. If they came in for lunch they would be put next to the kitchens or the loos. I think in one burger bar there was a ban on single women eating together after 9pm. They were basically saying that they were hookers.' But yuppie Britain was being led by a woman who swiped at feminism with her handbag on her way to the top and Worrall Thompson noticed that women were an untapped market, and not just in restaurants. Suddenly you found women flying Club Class. 'I noticed when I was on British Airways that all the magazines were male oriented and all the washbags were for men, so I wrote to Lord King and told him that all the people in my compartment were women. He said, "I pay thousands for consultants and you come up with something like this." He gave me a couple of free flights.'

Nouvelle Cuisine, the trend for tiny portions on enormous

plates, was the way to women's pockets, according to Worrall Thompson, whom budding food writer, A. A. Gill has credited with its British invention. 'Looking back, it was horrendous,' said Worrall Thompson, 'but at the time it was British chefs shaking off the chains of the French. It was a French invention but they went back into their escargot shells when they realised what a horrendous nightmare they created, and the English went on from there.' Worrall Thompson says that he was 'just a tart of the industry at the time. I set a lot of trends – I've always wanted to be a fashion guru of the food world. Even now I'm doing retro.'

Nouvelle Cuisine spread out across London's restaurant scene, feeding the yuppie diet for style over content, and the new female clientèle's hunger for small morsels of something to talk about. Although *The Face* would be the first magazine to target men in 1980, this was still a time when men did not read magazines, and for glossy women's magazines to write about restaurants, it had to be about much more than the food. The press was looking for a scene, a movement. Food as experience was what women wanted, and suddenly there were chefs around who were prepared to bring it on. Alistair Little was the master. 'He was the first Jamie Oliver in London,' said Eric Treuille (of Books for Cooks). 'He made it seem easy and fashionable to be able to cook good food.' 192 Kensington Park Road had begun to attract the press, which had smelt the aromatic mix of new food and supermodel clientèle and had begun to write about a trend. Little recognised it was time to move on up, linking the stylish Notting Hill scene with the Bohemian Soho that still had L'Escargot as its centrepiece.

By the time Jamie Oliver was chopping his first vegetables in the kitchen of The Cricketers, his teenage colleagues would have sniffed the first whiff of a brand new celebrity chef scene as Alistair Little was featured in *Elle* magazine as the chef to watch. 'It came out the week that we opened Frith Street,' he remembers. 'I got more press than Princess Di for a couple of years.' Suddenly chefs were as exciting, young and good looking as their customers. They could be stars, and cook great food, too. It would be a few more years before foreign press would start to write about the new London food scene. But Little was riding a wave of stylish aspiration while consistently putting groundbreaking food on the table, even if some of his customers still preferred to chemically depress their appetites. 'I didn't put my name above my door at Frith Street but it made it look very trendy; it was the restaurant with no name. We were in *The Face* within a week. We even appeared in trendy novels...'

Little and his old friend from Cambridge University, Rowley Leigh, watched as the Beautiful People began to nibble his Mediterranean inspired seasonal produce, the meat from named farms, the vegetables – organic where possible – and noticed this was different. 'It was still only a latent interest,' he said. 'But the food was starting to become interesting. It was always around in London but it was bloody hard to find in the Sixties and Seventies.' Simon Woodroffe, who would later bring Sushi to London in the Nineties with his 'Yo Sushi' chain of restaurants, agrees. 'I'd been through cycles of London from pink pasta and Mr Freedom to Biba in the Sixties. I could see how London was changing from Swinging London in the Sixties to The Sex Pistols on the King's Road, to the whole punk thing and on to drugs. And then London started becoming a cool place for food in the Eighties. Before that you didn't think of London being a food place; food was ancillary to the party before then.' Worrall Thompson adds, 'It was suddenly very glamorous. At 190 Queens Gate the bar was open late and we used to attract a lot of the music set in there. It was an exciting experience.'

Britain was lightening up after its dark days, and making good food and wine accessible. Ruth Rogers also watched the change with interest. 'Suddenly there were chefs like Alice Waters [Chez Panisse], Rowleigh Leigh [Kensington Place] or Wolfgang Puck [Ma Maison, Spago, LA], who said, "I am a chef and you can see what the kitchen is like, and I can come to your table or you can come and watch me grill a piece of meat." That accessibility opened up the idea that you could eat well and still do that.

Restaurants allowed you to eat in an informal situation and still eat really well.' It was a casual trend that allowed the Beautiful People to sit and watch the Theatre of Food without even having to take a bite. The next stage was to encourage women to eat.

While Alistair Little was making food trendy, he was also creating healthy food and a market for locally sourced seasonal produce even if he wasn't going to ram the message down the throats of his trendy young punters. Sally Clarke was on more of a mission, however. She had come from California's Berkeley hippie set to open her own restaurant in the refined streets off London's Notting Hill in 1984 and by the time he made it to London, Clarke's freshly baked breads and homemade pasta would reach the antennae of the young Jamie Oliver. Clarke had spent the last five years at Alice Waters' side at Chez Panisse in California and wanted to bring her philosophy to Britain. 'Sally was someone who got it immediately,' said Waters. 'She totally understood the philosophy of the restaurant.' Clarke joined the small band of brave new chefs in Notting Hill who were changing the menu and widened the offer to those less interested in posing and more into the food and wines themselves. 'When I was looking around for premises,' she said, 'Alistair Little had just opened down the road at Kensington Park Road and Simon Hopkinson was cooking at Hilaire in South Kensington. Rowley Leigh hadn't quite opened at Kensington Place, but they opened about three years after we did. Alistair and Simon were the two most exciting new chefs; they were cooking seasonally and they were cooking food that was from named farms and producers. They were definitely cooking in the Elizabeth David web. The freshness and the seasonality that I'd been cooking in California was something that was so obvious there – and not so here – that it made sense for me to try to do it here.'

By 1987 there were restaurants in London offering variations on this new eating experience. Clarke was attracting the more serious foodies with her Californian wines and generating genuine interest in what she was putting on the table while Kensington Place was the place to be seen. 'When we opened in 1984 we got a typical Kensington brand of customer and melded with that, the Californian set,' Sally told me. 'It was a cross between the American banker and the Kensington local. Now we have artists and writers, and people who come up from the Shires to do their shopping. We've never been a cliquey restaurant – we've never just had the publishers, or just the estate agents, or just the antique people from the street. We've always had a nice mix of everybody and the majority of them have been interested in food or the Californian wines we buy. They're interested in what we're doing here.'

As the decade came to an end the food scene was so established that it even had a magazine of its own published by that bastion of Britishness: the BBC. While the Government privatised school dinners, *BBC Good Food Magazine* filled its pages with chat and ideas from new TV chefs. Among them were Antony Worrall Thompson, Keith Floyd, Ken Hom, Madhur Jaffrey and Gary Rhodes (who, with his spiky hair and tamed-Marco attitude, was reinventing British food with faggots and oxtail at The Greenhouse in Mayfair, winning a Michelin star for his efforts). Perhaps most importantly, *BBC Good Food Magazine* not only charted the success of British food but wove the chefs into personalities the public could aspire to.

Meanwhile, in Clavering a 14-year-old Jamie Oliver was contributing his own talents to the growth of British food without any help from the TV chefs. 'I'd never seen any cooks on telly,' he told *BBC Good Food Magazine*. 'Except for the Roux Brothers, which my dad made me watch. I remember making things like chicken with wild mushrooms wrapped in puff pastry. And incredible but classic passé desserts; lemon meringue pie, banoffi pie, chocolate fudge cake with sponge on the outside and chocolate mousse inside, toffee sauce on top and marshmallow on top of that.'

It was the kind of country cooking that you wouldn't find in any of the new food emporia springing up in fashionable London. Rowley Leigh, like his future flat-mate Alistair Little, would combine style with great food at Kensington Place. 'I brokered that deal,' said Little. 'Rowley was working with the Roux Brothers in the City, and Nick Small and Simon Slater were looking for a chef for this big restaurant that they'd already got on the go.' He took them to meet Leigh over dinner at Marco Pierre White's Harvey's in Wandsworth, south London, and 'put them together'. It was an inspired move. Kensington Place, with its enormous capacity of more than three hundred covers and showy window displays of the Beautiful People at lunch, would take the ingredients of Ménage à Trois, 192 Kensington Park Road and Clarke's. It would season them with a little Neal Street and L'Escargot, and mix in enough Langans to get the press talking. With Terence Conran ready to explode the food scene out to a massive customer base with super-seaters at Bibendum and Quaglinos, the Eighties would close with a food legacy to dangle in front of a new type of young chef hungry for something much more exciting than a béchamel sauce.

CHAPTER 7

THE STREETS OF LONDON

By the time Jamie Oliver arrived in London in 1991, food had too. Inspired by what he had heard about this new exciting food scene and the new breed of superstar chef, Jamie took his two GCSE's (an A in Art and a C in Geology) and dropped them in the first dustbin on the way to London's Victoria station. Scarlet Division may have been creating 'a minor sensation in Essex' according to friend and fellow band member, Leigh Haggerwood, but Trevor Oliver was not about to let his son languish in a garage in the vague hope of hitting the big time. Jamie was to reinvent himself from the dyslexic hyperactive who failed at school into a demon of a cook. But Trevor had taught him well and Jamie knew that good cooking was not a flash in the pan. He needed to knuckle down and learn his skills at the best college in London.

Westminster Kingsway College (WKC) is the oldest catering college in the UK and has an excellent reputation. Its links with associations of chefs in France and the UK were set up with the help of a consultancy panel including a Mr Auguste Escoffier. Escoffier is the undisputed King of Cuisine and his books are staple reading for any young chef. 'That's where the rich tapestry of history started and from there the links with five-star restaurants and hotels in London and the West End,' Gary Hunter, head of Culinary Arts at Westminster Kingsway explained. 'With our students going there and climbing the ladder, and going on to be head chefs and then going outside London into the home counties, it has developed a network. We're nearly 100 years old, and we have a network second to none.'

It was this pedigree more than just the Professional Chef Diploma that he would hold in his hand three years later that appealed to Jamie. Chefs like Antony Worrall Thompson and Ainsley Harriott had graduated from there and inspired a new generation of young cooks. But getting in was not easy. 'We do about 300 interviews a year for 128 places on our Professional Chef Diploma,' explained Hunter. 'The whole mechanism and the whole fashion statement of the megastar chef is the thing that turns these students on. It's not just the blokes; it's girls as well who aspire to people like Angela Hartnett [The Connaught]. And they're very aware of Sally Clarke. I feel that they think that this is the way in. There are others around – Delia Smith is one of them.'

Suddenly it was cool to cook. Eric Treuille, who has been selling books to catering students at Books for Cooks since 1985, is grateful to the TV chefs for widening his customer base: 'When I first arrived in London and you said that you were a cook, no one was interested. Everyone was a bloody designer. Nowadays everyone's a cook – it's trendy.'

Hunter, who came to WKC when Jamie was in his final year, said he would be surprised if he had been through such a rigorous interview technique in 1991, although when Jamie interviewed would-be chefs for his restaurant Fifteen, he based it on the method that WKC does now. 'We don't get anyone who hasn't cooked or been taught to cook by their family,' said Hunter. 'It's a whole day interview. First, we ask them to bring their mum and dad so that they know what their son or daughter is getting into, and the whole day will be about working out where their passion is. You just talk to them about food – what did they do with food at school? Do they cook at home? Have they got a part time job? – if they have, is it as a brickie, or is it in the local pub? What books do they buy? Which food shows do they watch?' Hunter says that you can spot a chef-in-the-making. 'When you walk around the kitchen at 8am and you see students who've been there for an hour before they're due to start – they're walking around other kitchens and they're looking at the menus for the day, you know that they know where they're going.' It would be this kind of commitment that Jamie would look for in a group of fifteen cookery students ten years later.

Jamie had come into catering at just the right time. In the early Nineties, catering colleges were just beginning to wake up to the new demand for hot young chefs, and quickly changed gear. 'It was almost impossible to find chefs at the time who knew how to cook slow food,' said Antony Worrall Thompson. Heston Blumenthal's PR, Monica Brown, worked in restaurant recruitment at the time. 'You just couldn't find the staff,' she said. 'Agencies would charge ridiculous prices for guys that didn't give a damn about food and would work in kitchens for three months and move on. They had all these titles like "sous chef" and "chef de partie", but they didn't have the integrity or the drive.' This new educated wave of catering students had no practical skills, she said. 'It was a nightmare. So the chefs became trainers.' Gary Hunter agrees. 'It was a bit stale then – a bit of an ivory tower. The industry was already changing at about 125mph and the college was moving around 25mph. Our trainee chefs weren't meeting the needs of the industry. The lecturers now are all around 30–35 years old, and they all come from industry and are passionate about the food.'

At college Jamie's dyslexia meant that he had to grapple with classroom science and the enormous amount of reading he had to do. But this time, with a career and a family set in his sights, he simply got on with it. It helped that he had already gained a reputation for chopping faster than his contemporaries, and the skills he had picked up in the kitchen at The Cricketers, combined with his natural role as leader of the gang, gave him the confidence to become noticed by his tutors. If he felt he was learning something that he would never use again, he didn't say a word. 'I remember spending what seemed like months being taught how to make the perfect béchamel sauce,' said Jamie later. 'I've never made it since.' He was taught the classics, particularly in the first year, which would lay down the firm foundations of cookery and allow him to break the rules later. 'He was taught the difference between shallow frying and poaching, and deep frying and poaching,' said Hunter. 'He learnt about roasting, braising, en papillotte – all of the basic techniques, how to make pasta, how to bake, how to prepare vegetables. Once the students have mastered those, they have the knowledge that they can then apply to all the ingredients that we have at our disposal.'

Catering college in the first year was not a place to try out your grandmother's recipes or to experiment with any of the 'bish-bosh' cooking that would soon become Jamie's trademark. This was about dressing up the skills of cookery that he would only a few years later strip down in *The Naked Chef*. Although it was a deliberately constraining process, Jamie kept his head down and, most of the time at least, he watched and learned. 'You have to have learnt those basics,' said Hunter. 'You have to be able to chop vegetables in different ways, you have to know which dishes are going to cook longer than others. We'll tell them and they'll still make mistakes, but we don't encourage creativity.'

By the second year Jamie was spending most of his time in the various kitchens, from bakery and patisserie to butchery/fishmongery, and the cold larder section where he would hone the skills in terrines, salads and starters he had learnt at The Starr back in Great Dunmow. He was also trained in front of house, just like the current students in the Brasserie at WKC, as well as in silver service at the college's Escoffier Restaurant, both of which are open to a very discerning public.

Placements in five-star establishments such as Claridge's, The Savoy and The Dorchester in Years Two and Three sort the chefs from the cooks, although for Jamie it wasn't the first time that he was subjected to the adrenaline of a real kitchen. A five-star restaurant in London, though, was a far cry from The Starr at Great Dunmow, and Jamie's placement was tough. 'It's inevitable that students find the placements tougher than here,' said Gary

Hunter, not without sympathy. 'We look after them here. But Gordon Ramsay' [who offers WKC students placements at all his restaurants, as well as sharing his suppliers with the college] 'will also look after them although there's a different philosophy there. The head chefs in his restaurants are by and large like him. They're going to follow his philosophy. Someone like Jason Atherton at Maze is very quiet, very intense, and the kitchen is very quiet but it's very motivated. Our students like that – they want to go into a kitchen where they know what they're supposed to be doing, and get their heads down and just get on with it. I think if the kitchen was rabble rousing and it was like a blur, the students wouldn't learn anything.'

For Jamie Oliver, whose brain fires on all cylinders, whose dyslexia and hyperactivity had him looking around for other stimulation at school and branded him class joker, the challenges of coursework weren't always enough to keep his head down. 'Jamie was lucky because there were a few lecturers around who spotted the spark in him,' said Hunter. 'Jamie was a decent student. I won't say that he was outstanding but we have a great regard for him. He was always a team man and everyone liked him. He would never turn up late, and he always loved the food. The fact that he chose to specialise in bread and pasta shows that he loves the food.' Jamie always appreciated the fact that he was privileged to be there: 'I knew one kid who couldn't afford to stay there because his family went bust in the first term,' he said. 'He had to leave and I thought that was desperately unfair at the time – I still do.'

Jamie has a penchant for mentors, and he has been lucky to find some of the best. Lecturer Peter Richards was one of the first. 'Peter Richards had an influence over him and since – they're still in touch with each other,' said Gary Hunter. 'He was very good at looking through to the potential. Perhaps if Jamie was messing around, a couple of the lecturers would say "he's going to amount to nothing, I'm going to wash my hands of him". But Peter was a little more involved and would look at the reasons why, and he saw that potential in Jamie and took him under his wing." Jamie would later invite Richards to use the same skills to spot the potential of the students he took under his own wing for the Fifteen project.

After ten years of sharing his discoveries with the greatest chefs in the world, it took Giovanni, the Italian fisherman who handed Jamie his kitchen in Channel 4's *Jamie's Great Italian Escape*, to remind him that all the teaching in the world can't give you the real passion for food that allows you to make something wonderful out of nothing. Gary Hunter says that Jamie would never encourage a young chef to bypass a formal culinary education although it may not be necessary in order to cook really well. 'Jamie is saying that there is no formal experience required for great cooking. He's extolling the virtues of the fresh ingredient when he says that,' he told me. 'He's saying that if you have the freshest of ingredients you're going to come up with a masterpiece. That fisherman will have been taught – he will have watched his mother and his grandmother cooking.'

If working in the kitchens of the most demanding chefs in the world was hard, leaving his girlfirend, Jools was harder. By now the two had become inseparable but Jamie was already thinking of laying down his roots with her, of getting the kind of qualifications they could build on, of the training that would one day allow them to set up their own restaurant in Essex and have that football team of kids. He found an early compromise; it might mean leaving home at 5.30 every morning, but at least he would be able to sleep in his own bed. And if he was lucky, Jools might be waiting. But there was another reason why Jamie Oliver, the Jack the Lad, the leader of his country-boy gang who could silence bullies with a few words, wanted to come back to his own bed: he was terrified of London. 'Coming from a village where there were so many white people, on my first day at college,' he said, 'I thought I was in New York. I had never really been to London before and I was really pent up about it. I had one of those leather pouches hidden under my shirt with my money in it. Every day I thought I was going to get mugged.'

Soon enough, though, the Oliver spirit of adventure overcame any reticence and he was to find just how exciting London could be. The capital was already growing into a foodie city that would be compared with New York and Sydney within a few years. Victoria is one of the less salubrious areas of London, although the college is tucked away on one side of one of London's enormous squares, and is a walk away from Pimlico, where cafés throw their tables and chairs onto the wide pavements as soon as the sun shines. Its theatrical population has been patronising restaurants and shopping at the local market for generations. Restaurateur Sally Clarke remembers Grumbles as one of the few places where you could buy really excellent food without it costing a fortune back in the Eighties. Even though it is less than five minutes' walk from WKC, Jamie would have been unable to afford to eat out anywhere at the time other than China Town or the kind of Italian restaurants where Gennaro Contaldo was working in the Seventies.

Unlike the streets of New York, San Francisco, Melbourne or Sydney, there were no noodle bars at the time in London, and sushi had yet to hit British shores until Moshi Moshi first opened in the city in 1995. Simon Woodroffe, who would take this healthier fast food into a chain of 'Yo Sushi' restaurants in 1997, had become addicted in Los Angeles. 'I'd got sushi in LA in the Eighties at Sushi on Sunset,' he told me. 'I was out there doing rock shows with Ozzy Osbourne and although I was never a foodie, I loved eating out. I'd come back to London and find nothing like it here, and it felt that there was a cult of us into sushi and that no one else had discovered it.' London was looking for new ideas. 'You kept hearing about these odd bars that were opening,' he said. 'There was a bar in Spitalfields [East London] where you could only buy cans, which you extracted through a tube. But of course that didn't work because only boys like cans, but boys also like girls and girls don't go where there are only cans.'

The mid-Nineties was the era of Pret a Manger and the birth of coffee shop chains. 'They were all opening and they were on the tip of everyone's tongue,' said Woodroffe. 'Belgo had opened in 1992 and it was something completely different. It was like woah – this is not just about food! This is about experience.' It was the time of the entrepreneur. 'Sahar Hashemi [now at Coffee Republic] went to New York and said, "God, I wish that there was something like this in London" and suddenly coffee was everywhere.'

John Major's British government published its Health of the Nation report into levels of obesity and food related diseases in 1992 and it was regarded as the first real attempt to tackle the burden on the National Health Service (NHS) of diet related illness. Olive oil, red wine and garlic, it concluded, the diet of the Mediterranean (which remained largely unchanged for 2,000 years), was the way to reduce cholesterol and weight and introduce some of the best flavours in the world into the British diet. 'That's when it changed,' said Gary Hunter. 'Yes, there were health campaigns behind it, but most people focussed on the vibrant and colourful part of cuisine. Healthy fresh ingredients were becoming available, and customers were becoming more focussed on flavours and colours, and they were beginning to understand more about what they were eating. We were moving away from the snobbishness around haute cuisine.' It was a wave towards a simpler and cleaner, Italian inspired diet that Jamie would learn to ride.

Jamie was profoundly impressed by the endless variety of restaurants, and would walk the streets of London looking at the menus and through the windows at the rich and stylish clientèle, and imagine one day all this would be his. Leaving college with his Professional Chef Diploma, he had just one more stop on the way to where he wanted to be, and with distinction in his exams, he set off for France. Chefs have always been trained in French classical traditions and through the contacts at college, Jamie secured a job in a grand old conference hotel in Pas de Calais. The nineteenth-century Château Tilques, with its manicured lawns and four-poster beds, might have been a hop and skip across the Channel, but it was a world away from the familiar countryside around Clavering and the inner city streets of London town. Jamie was homesick. For the three months he was there, he missed Jools and his family terribly.

According to journalists looking for evidence of any extracurricular activity, part-time waitress Elaine Fournier, who was entranced by the shaggy haired cook, invited him home to see if she could cheer him up. Jamie, glad of the female company, apparently took no time in whipping out his snaps of the lovely Jools and talked long into the night about their dreams of opening a restaurant in the country and having kids together. By the time he was back in London, it was time for Jamie to get straight down to the business of making his mark. He was to do this first at The Neal Street Restaurant in London's Covent Garden, where he met a man who would become his soul mate.

CHAPTER 8

MEETING HIS MENTOR

Gennaro Contaldo had taken the long way round to the best Italian restaurant in London. From the fish and chip shops and bad trattorias of the Seventies to the bread and butter puddings of the Midlands, he finally made it to chef at The Neal Street Restaurant under Antonio Carluccio. There he could indulge his passion for making bread and pasta. With some of the finest olive oils in London on the table, Carluccio needed little more than bread and pasta to make his customers happy.

By the time Jamie joined his kitchen Antonio Carluccio had been quietly cooking the most authentic Italian food in London for 20 years. Sourcing his ingredients seasonally, his white truffles from Umbria and venison from Piedmont were securing him a reputation in a city still on the brink of its culinary makeover. But it was Gennaro Contaldo of whom Jamie had heard on the grapevine. To howls of derision from his fellow students he had told his tutors at Westminster that his ambition was to make great bread and pasta, and Gennaro, word had it, was the man. Today he remains one of Jamie's closest friends and mentors, and still sits in on as many edits of his shows as he can get to. 'They're more like family to each other,' said a friend. 'Jamie's always been interested in Italian food, but Gennaro sealed his passion for it.'

'He came as a pastry chef and he was unbelievable,' Gennaro said in an accent still as thick as pasta fagioli after 35 years of living in England. 'When he came in and asked for a job he was ever so small. He was tiny, tiny but beautiful.' Gennaro talks as he cooks, with a passion for his subject that could be mistaken for hyperbole by anyone who doesn't understand Italians. 'He was someone who, when you see for the first time, has something warm, something nice about him.' He compares their relationship to a marriage: 'Perhaps after a little while you forget and after a few years you say, "Do you remember the first time I saw you? What were you thinking? Oh my God, I fell in love with you the first time I saw you." We keep it close to our hearts.'

Actually, their relationship is more like father and son. Gennaro is his 'London dad' as Jamie once described him on the stage they shared at the 2005 BBC Good Food Show. 'I'm very protective,' says Gennaro. 'It's not in case someone says something, but for me it's like having another son.' (When asked how many children he really has, he puts his hands in the air and asks a higher power for the answer – which doesn't come. His youngest, however, are twin girls of five; his eldest is a son of 35.) In the final episode of Channel 4's *Jamie's Great Italian Escape*, Jamie returns to Gennaro's home town near Amalfi and tells us he has come home. He calls Gennaro's 96-year-old father 'Nonno' (Grandpa). After meeting him for the series, Nonno told Gennaro that Jamie looks just like him. 'He says, "He talks like you, he cooks like you, his hair is like you." I say, "Papa, he's blond." He said, "So were you."'

The two men speak every day on the phone and Jamie pops into his kitchen at Passione in London's Charlotte Street whenever he's passing, or needs some advice from his old mentor. It sounds just like the episode of Channel 4's *The Naked Chef* when Jamie jumps on his scooter to get a heart-shaped bread that Gennaro has cooked for Jools, and in which, just for a second, London could be Rome. It feels like an intimate city where it's possible for superstar chefs with schedules from hell to pop in on their busy mates without booking five weeks in advance. 'He comes down early in the morning and knocks on the door and says, '"Open up, open up!" I say "Hold on, hold on!" That's what he does.'

Under Gennaro's tutelage, Neal Street was where Jamie learnt to fly. More than ten years later, he still credits Gennaro for his bread and pasta, and more importantly, his interest in Italian cooking. Upbeat and endlessly interested in getting things just right, Gennaro was just the kind of teacher Jamie was looking for. He brings food to life, telling yarns about every ingredient, every technique until cooking becomes as enchanting as a bedtime story. During the course of my research for this book he showed me how to cook risotto all'onda, moving the pan back and forth like a wave instead of stirring it with a boring old wooden spoon. We cooked rabbit with garlic, wine and rosemary, and he explained why the heads are kept on at market: 'A skinned rabbit looks exactly like a skinned cat,' he said. 'Except for the head.' He never stops talking; he tells tales of foraging for mushrooms with his twins in Epping Forest as he searches for truffle for the risotto and about picking herbs in hedgerows. He makes it fun, whisking eggs for our hazelnut torte and holding the bowl upside down to show just how stiff they are. It's a trick, I point out, Jamie Oliver did on his *Happy Days* tour. 'Ah, Jamie,' he laughs. 'I taught him that one.'

Gennaro introduced the country boy to hunting and foraging. 'He told me how he killed his first deer,' said a member of Jamie's crew. 'He went to the Highlands of Scotland, shot it, gutted it. He's that kind of guy. He doesn't mind cutting his meat – he has that warrior trait to kill the beast.' Gennaro also taught him to taste. 'At the beginning, the chef will tell you,' he said, 'but over time, experience tells you what to do. Everyone knows that if you have three tablespoons of olive oil and one of lemon, it goes cloudy, and that it will go with fish and salads, meat as well – but it depends on what type. It's the balance that you look for. If you're a traveller like Jamie is now, and you cook so many different types of foods with different chefs, you have to ask people how they do this and that. Then you can create your own.'

Dorset farmer Denise Bell remembers when Gennaro took his partner Liz Przybylski to stay with them at Heritage Farm. 'We went mushrooming together,' she said. 'Liz and Gennaro gathered sea spinach off the cliffs at West Bay and we cooked up a feast with our pork and fine ham. He used his hunting knife and cut fine slivers, and with our wild garlic from the woods made us sandwiches that will stay in our memories forever.'

Jamie describes Gennaro as the man with the kind of passion to light anyone's fire. 'Gennaro is a fantastic guy and I loved watching him work,' he said. 'He has this brilliantly positive attitude to every single thing he does – he always wants it to taste perfect and he never tires of trying to improve things. I loved working with him and I learned so much about cooking.' Gennaro also taught him to love ingredients. 'I bring my little girls to visit the markets,' he said. 'For me, it reminds me of where I come from. You meet the cheese maker who comes from so far away; you have the fish man who goes fishing himself. A good friend of mine, Darren, goes diving for scallops and netting for fish the day before, and by the middle of the night, he will travel 400 miles and sell his catch. There's always a story behind it. He showed me this red mullet the other day and he was telling me the story of when he saw this nice fish in the net, he took it out and selected it. When you buy that fish, you cuddle it all the way home. You will cook it in a nice way because you care about that fish – it's like the fish says, "Hey, what you going to do with me?"'

For a teenage chef straight out of catering college with a fire already in his belly, meeting such a man was a life-changing experience. Gennaro says the inspiration worked both ways. 'You need a young boy half your age to remind you of who you are. He would say, "You're not just a great chef, but you're a nice man." I need someone like Jamie to remind me of that. I work and work, and stress and stress. I have an argument with my suppliers every day but he reminds me of what I am. To catch an old dog from the streets of Naples like me is really something; chefs are very hard in the kitchen, but for me to actually fall in love with someone like Jamie, it's because of his pure honesty and love. He is warm and genuine, and the boy transmits it to anyone he meets. This is what he would be like if you'd met him if he wasn't famous.'

For the young chef on a mission to find out as much as he could, cooking all day with Gennaro was a dream of a first job and Jamie's enthusiasm burst into passion under Gennaro's spell. He couldn't get enough of him. By 1995 Jamie and Jools had settled into their first flat together about a mile away in Fitzjohn's Avenue in Hampstead, a tiny little rented studio flat with a bed on a gallery above the sitting room. 'We had to literally crawl up a step ladder and could only crouch on the bed as it was so close to the ceiling,' Jools wrote later in her book, *Minus Nine to One.* From here Jamie could get into work for 4am to watch Gennaro bake his bread. 'I'm sure I love bread so much because I played with playdough so much as a kid,' Jamie would tell us later in *The Naked Chef.*

With the importation of cheap Canadian wheat in the nineteenth century transforming the art of British bread making, and supermarkets removing most traces of goodness from the average British loaf, Jamie caught the whiff of revolution in his nostrils and resolved to bring real bread back onto the menu. At the time he thought it would be in the restaurant in the countryside that he and Jools spent hours dreaming about. He had no idea that by the end of the century the power of television would turn the Brits back into a nation of breadmakers. Jamie learnt his art well. Coming in to make focaccia wasn't part of his duties, but he would be there nonetheless, and Gennaro was impressed. 'I thought, "my God, he's better at this than me!" He's very intelligent – you tell him anything and he'll soak it up like a sponge. He'll say "fantastic – show me how you do that". And he says "thank you" to everyone. He learns from everyone but he always says "thank you" – he's not proud.' To Gennaro integrity is as important a quality as being able to source the best possible products for his restaurant Passione in London's West End. The combination of Jamie's 'heart' that thrills his mentor's Italian soul and the integrity that the 17-year-old brought to the job right from the first is what has cemented their relationship.

At Neal Street Jamie became a born-again Italian with a passion for life already pulsing through his veins. Call it ambition, but the drive that sped him through the next few years was oiled in Gennaro's kitchen and had nothing to do with making millions or holding seats of power. He had spotted something so simple that he was buzzing with plans. With ideas spilling over, he thought he would explode if he didn't write them down. He bought himself a typewriter and began to make notes for what he planned would one day bring him his first publishing deal. But Jamie was also in a hurry to grow into a great chef, and with plans for his own restaurant in Essex, Jools playing hostess and the bambini nicking food out of the kitchen for their mates, he needed to move on from Neal Street. 'I had taught him all I knew,' said Gennaro. But Jamie knew exactly where he had to go next.

CHAPTER 9

THE RIVER CAFÉ

Back in 1989 while Jamie was chopping vegetables in The Cricketers, Ruth Rogers and her friend Rose Gray, who had returned from living in Italy for four years, had opened a works cafeteria on the banks of the River Thames in Hammersmith, west London. An austere building designed by Ruth's husband, Richard Rogers, architect of Lloyds of London and the National Assembly of Wales among many others, the café had principally been somewhere his wife and her partner could make lunch for Lord Rogers and his colleagues in the offices next door. But The River Café was already making the headlines for its new approach to Italian food and Jamie Oliver had set his sights on a job there.

For Rogers and Gray, good food was about using the best ingredients, and at first they had to be imported from Italy. 'We sat and looked at each other, and decided to cook the kind of food that you eat in Italy,' remembered Rose Gray. 'I got the feeling of seasonality there, how you cook with what you've got, how you don't have to cook with the most expensive ingredients to create something wonderful.' For Jamie Oliver, fresh from the kitchen of Carluccio and Contaldo, a job at The River Café was about raising his game. Rose Gray spotted something in him from the first. 'I would say that Jamie is majorly ambitious, and always was from the moment I first interviewed him sitting exactly where you're sitting right now,' she told me. 'He kept ringing us up and eventually I said "Oh, come on down then."'

But it wasn't his background that impressed her; she doesn't remember him even mentioning the fact that he'd been working in his parents' pub. 'I don't think that if you're a chef applying for a job that you would,' she said. 'What he did tell me was that he really loved pasta and baking, and that he had spent time at Neal Street watching Gennaro make bread and pasta, and he was keen to do it with us.' Jamie had devoured whatever knowledge he could about Italian cookery, even books, which he claims he never reads. 'We had Jamie here as a customer for years,' said Eric Treuille of Books for Cooks. 'He would be looking for a famous Italian classic or something like that, and we had to order it in for him.' Rose Gray was impressed with his eagerness to learn. 'The thing that I liked about him was that he recognised that wasn't the place to continue if he wanted to take it on. He wanted to come here because I think he knew that we were using the best ingredients and we want to make the best pasta.' For Jamie, it was a clever move and one that would seal the credibility for his next move, even if he wasn't aware of how stratospheric a leap it would be at the time. They were the teachers he needed now. 'I think that Jamie was very lucky in going first to The River Café,' said Gary Hunter. 'If he had ended up going to somewhere like the Savoy, not that he would have got on particularly well at somewhere as staid as the Savoy was at that time, you wouldn't have heard of Jamie Oliver now. The River Café really opened up his eyes to that kind of style and that kind of food – and that fashion of food.'

Ruth Rogers and Rose Gray had already also started a brand new trend in cookery books with their first book, *The River Café Cook Book* in 1995, and Jamie was a fan. 'That was the first really successful domestic cook book,' explained Eric Treuille of Books for Cooks. It was a revolution in terms of presentation and price. It was the first to sell for £20. After that, they all did. Ruth and Rose were the first ones to tell the publisher what they wanted and they did a fantastic job.' 'The first book was a mould breaker,' agreed Rose, 'and we had a hell of a lot of chefs wanting to come and work for us at that time because of that book.' Twenty years later, cook books are an important style feature in most kitchens. 'There's a new generation of cook now,' said Treuille. 'I think that when people design their kitchens now, they design it with the space for cook books in mind; it's a design for living. And that's really cool.'

Jamie was thrilled to be given a two-week trial. Ruth Rogers remembers him as 'bright, questioning, curious. He was passionate and professional, and we always knew that he was an exceptional cook. He was here early and stayed late. He wanted to know everything. He asked questions, he was someone who you really felt "yep!".' Rose Gray agrees. 'He was just a charming boy, a positive boy, and he asked lots of questions.' 'My dad always reckoned that the more you put in, the more you get out,' Jamie said. 'If I get a bit bored and start taking things for granted and cutting corners, I soon find that I am not stimulated and I am not enjoying myself. I get like a car that's not firing on all cylinders.'

But there wasn't a chance of that at The River Café. By 1997 it was one of the restaurants on the London circuit, a buzzy, glamorous showcase of the City's new gastro chic, and Jamie and the team loved to show off to the customers in their open-plan theatre of food. It also meant that Ruth and Rose's own staff culture was on display, and this blew a breath of fresh air into chef culture. 'It's the drama of restaurants that is fascinating,' explained Ruth. 'All that used to go on behind the scenes before The River Café. If you were sitting out here and the old fashioned kind of chef was terrorising his staff in the kitchen, you would never know.' That kind of culture would naturally extend sooner or later to the customer. 'Richard and I had an experience in a restaurant in Paris when a chef came out with a knife because we were late,' she said.

Marco Pierre White had been offering the same kind of trick to the tabloids in the late Eighties and early Nineties when he was cultivating his gastro-punk image at Harvey's. Jamie and a new generation of young bucks were impressed with his style, but few were brave enough to chance their arm. At The River Café Jamie was spared the meat cleaver routine in a kitchen run by two mothers. 'I'm not convinced that you get better work out of chefs who are fearful,' said Ruth. 'I think it should be against the law. I do hear stories about how other chefs are in the kitchen, and if they did that to one of my sons who was working there, I'd call the police. If you put a frying pan over someone's head and say "You burn that sauce again..." that's intimidation, that's harassment. It's everything that civilised society is not about.'

The punters too were drinking up the more relaxed atmosphere that dining out was beginning to offer in London. 'People do dress up to come here,' said Ruth, 'and I think that the modernist nature and uncompromising architecture may be intimidating. But people also bring babies in here for a dinner these days. It may be their birthday or anniversary, or they may be in London on holiday or working. People work more and they want to spend time with their kids, and so you see all different people sitting here eating extremely good food because of the pleasure of eating out. Our culture has changed.' Ruth and Rose pumped their message into the team of waiters and chefs. 'Everyone always feels a bit nervous when they walk into a restaurant,' said Ruth, 'but we tell our staff over and over again that everyone should feel welcome.'

Jamie loved it at The River Café. He was a team player in one of the most lauded kitchens in the country, supported by a caring team, encouraged to grow, and he was determined to work hard. 'He was head down and just got on with it,' said Rose. 'But he wanted to be the best,' Ruth added. 'When you work in the kitchen, you're always in a team, but there's always the most important person. It's like ballet; you always have a key person and everyone else dances to their tune. Jamie wanted to be that person – maybe not at first but that was what was so good about him; most truly ambitious people build carefully and solidly, and he was that kind of a person. He was never a grabber; he wanted to fill in his background with us and The River Café. What he got from us was a lot of the basic stuff. He more or less runs his restaurant now in the way that we run ours.'

Ruth and Rose's philosophy extended to taking their staff on the kind of sourcing trips that Jamie now does with students of Fifteen (the restaurant he set up to help 15 unemployed people keen to become chefs). The team went to Florence to source ingredients and to taste the new season's olive oil. The River Café is famed for its use of the most delicious olive oils that they still import especially for the restaurant. 'We have at least three varieties on the go at any one time,' Gray and Rogers wrote in *The River Café Cook Book*. 'We use a lighter one for frying, such as the Ligurian oil. Thick green fruity oils from Tuscany are wonderful added to soups and the dense and fruity oil from Ornellaia is marvellous for salad.'

Jamie's first trip was an adventure into a world of wine, oil and eating around the kitchen table and he was blown away by the simplicity of the food, the white truffles and superior olive oils. He told the press how impressed he was with the way that ordinary Italians would engage in seven-course lunches and dinners, serving wine with everything. He was already collecting recipes. 'By complete fluke I discovered one terrific dish in a grotty little café in Florence. It was a really simple salad with artichokes and shaved Parmesan that is in my book [*The Naked Chef*],' he said. 'The attention to detail was mind-blowing – they would spend three weeks sourcing exactly the right almonds for a particular dish, even when they weren't the main ingredient! And I thought I was obsessive!'

The cherry on the cake at The River Café was getting Jools a job there too. The couple had now moved to Humbolt Road in Hammersmith from Fitzjohn's Avenue so that they could cycle into work together. Jools remembers it as a very dingy, dark basement flat which they made into a little cosy haven with flower pots going down the steps to brighten it up. 'She was sweet,' said Rose, 'a very nice waitress.' She remembered how meticulous Jools was with the way she looked. 'She always tied her apron round so it looked absolutely perfect.' When Jools asked them if she could work in the office as their PA, however, Rose decided that it wouldn't be such a good idea. 'I thought, "Oh no, you'd be hopeless!" She's probably very organised, but it didn't seem right that she would be our PA.'

But Jools wouldn't need the cash soon. The planets were lining up over Jamie Oliver as a production crew moved in to The River Café to begin filming a day-in-the-life documentary called 'Christmas at The River Café'. Sound recordist Rupert Ivey was the first to mic Jamie Oliver up and to record the voice which would become the most well known Cockney accent in the world in the next couple of years. 'I was doing the Italian Christmas documentary with Zad Rogers, who is Ruth's stepson,' said Ivey. 'We spent two weeks at The River Café, and we all became big mates. That's the thing about The River Café; it's like one big family. Jamie was going out with Jools, who was serving front of house and we all used to muck about.'

The River Café is a special kind of place. In 1996 it was making waves about its use of simple ingredients to make fabulous dishes at a time when the EU demanded clear labelling on all modified foodstuffs. The River Café had a clear philosophy based on respect for food and people, and although the crew was there to film a TV documentary, it soon became more than just a job. 'It was the first time I'd come across a place where everyone seemed to know about and love food,' said Ivey. 'You'd go in there as the film crew and do the prep in the morning. You'd go out and sit by the river and grind some pepper. You just felt like you could – everyone who works there is completely involved whether it's prepping veg or grinding pepper. They're all such nice people and that was the beauty of The River Café. At 12 o'clock, we'd all sit down and have our staff lunch, and sit and talk about food. Food was on the agenda for everyone; it was about more than just obeying the bloke who made food.'

Ivey, who would become one of Jamie's close friends over the course of the three series of *The Naked Chef* and the Sainsbury's ads on which they worked together, said that it was The River Café attitude which was the most formative experience of Jamie's career. 'That's where Jamie did the bulk of his learning,' he said. 'He learnt to make food really accessible, about what would happen if you put this with that. For me too it removed the mystique of it all – it was no longer the black art. It looked like anyone could make decent food.'

Ruth remembers the moment when it all changed for Jamie. 'He was frying mushrooms. Rose says she thinks he was doing something else, but I think he was frying mushrooms. He could talk to the camera and be himself, and that's a very difficult thing to do. You're doing two things; you're trying to inform and educate, and you have to be at ease with yourself and the camera in order to do that – and he was there.' Ivey remembers it differently. 'We were doing some background shots and he was cooking one of those long pasta log things, and we just turned the camera on him and he was very funny and brought this dish alive. That's what he's done from day one.'

'They filmed me quite a lot,' said Jamie. 'I think it was because I was really busy. They kept asking me what I was doing and because I was so rushed off my feet, the camera didn't really bother me so I didn't come over as too shy. I never thought that they'd use any of it but they had all these 45-second snippets and they used them all the way through.' Months later when the programme was finally aired his colleagues at the restaurant were among the many that were astonished by this prodigiously talented new TV chef. 'We all watched it on TV and came in the next day, and said, "Jamie, you were amazing",' said Ruth Rogers. 'He was; he was absolutely amazing.'

The story goes that Jamie received fifteen offers the very next day. Pat Llewellyn, the woman behind the success of Channel 4's *Two Fat Ladies* (Clarissa Dickson Wright and Jennifer Patterson) and Sophie Grigson's 1992 series *Grow Your Greens, Eat Your Greens*, said that was news to her. 'He told me he'd had one other call from a cable channel and he never heard from them again. My assistant rang him up and we had a chat,' she said. Back at The River Café, Ruth Rogers and Rose Gray were thrilled for

Jamie and philosophical about where it would lead. 'My chronology was I remember him saying that this woman had called him up and she wanted him to do a screen test,' remembered Ruth. 'He was always open about it; there was never any furtiveness about it. He was just always straight.' As a result she says that everyone was 'incredibly happy' for him. 'We were all rooting for him all the way – oh, you've got a screen test, oh, you've got an agent. Even though we knew we would lose him, we were all there wishing him luck. If you love them, let them go. And when they go, someone else comes.'

CHAPTER 10

TV NATION

In the early Nineties British television was changing as food was pushed into the schedules. Many BBC commissioning editors personally witnessed the new food scene in Notting Hill, a five-minute cab ride from the BBC TV Centre in London's White City.

Food scares played their part in a new interest in what everyone was eating: BSE (Bovine Spongiform Encephalopathy) took beef off school menus in 1990, while dolphin-friendly tuna made its way onto the supermarket shelves, encouraging people to think more about where our food came from. By 1993 the Royal Society for the Prevention of Cruelty to Animals (RSPCA) had set up Freedom Food to implement stringent welfare standards for livestock, while in 1994 Fair Trade woke people up to the bigger picture of food consumption. Food began to drop into TV schedules as soupçons rather than anything meatier. TV chef and restaurateur Antony Worrall Thompson remembers the beginning of the change. 'I did a programme called *Hot Chefs* while I was at 190 Queens Gate,' he said. 'That was a 10-minute slot after the nine o'clock news. Gary Rhodes did his first TV appearance on it, too.'

Bite-sized chunks of cookery classes also came with the birth of daytime magazine programmes such as *Good Morning with Anne and Nick* in 1992, which launched the young Ainsley Harriott. The BBC's Good Food Show had been introduced in Birmingham the year before, and the Corporation was keen to encourage this new trend as the BBC untied her apron strings and there emerged a dynamic business executive. 'Keith Floyd gave birth to that whole style of TV programme in the Eighties,' Worrall Thompson recalls, 'and then we wanted more and more of it. Dinner parties were all carrot and coriander soup, floating nasturtiums and fish that had been cooked to death. We were desperate for knowledge but we didn't put it into practice very often. Suddenly Floyd made everything very relaxed. It was radical – telling the camera to come in and have a look, while Floyd himself was having a glass of wine. Robert Carrier was in a studio, *The Galloping Gourmet* was entertainment but then it disappeared completely, and when the Roux Brothers and Delia came along, it was about education. Floyd was about bringing it back to entertainment again.'

The Eighties interest in 'Leisure' had given rise to 'Aspiration' in the Nineties, and suddenly producers clamoured for role models who could help change lives. Antony Worrall Thompson joined wine expert Jancis Robinson on *Food and Drink* on BBC2 to advise middle class palates what to serve up at dinner parties, and *Ready Steady Cook* took Ainsley Harriot off the morning slot and into prime time in 1993. Within the decade British homes were transformed with the help of a few impossibly good-looking designers and a few sheets of MDF. Bodies were given a rebirth with the help of some carefully chosen trousers and a couple of Sloaney fashionistas and social status boosted with a new confidence in the kitchen, and all through the magic of television.

After 10 years without home economics on the British National Curriculum and the rise in women fleeing the kitchen, convenience food flooded supermarket shelves and junk food began to take the place of many children's main meal of the day. British food campaigners, such as Caroline Walker, Tim Lang and Lizzie Vann, tried to persuade people that food, health and behaviour were interlinked, with Walker's book with Geoffrey Canon – *The Food Scandal* – making newspapers sit up and take notice of an increasingly frightening trend. 'She [Walker] famously said that we know more about the content of a pair of socks than we do about what we are eating,' said food and social affairs consultant Diane McRae, who would work with Jamie on Channel 4's *School Dinners* (2005).

TV companies began to hire people like Walker, Canon, Tim Lang and Maurice Hansen, author of *E for Additives*, to consult on a new breed of programmes. Channel 4 jostled with the BBC for pole position, with programmes like *Food File* as early as 1992 taking serious food issues and making them accessible. The British government's 'Health of the Nation' report, studies linking cancer and diet, the argument for organic farming were all now on a weekly prime time magazine show. The fact file accompanying the programme in which *Food File* put an average family from Worthing on the Mediterranean Diet (which was said to lower cholesterol and reduce weight) was the most requested fact sheet in Channel 4's history at the time. The series launched the career of a young sous chef from The River Café, Hugh Fearnley-Whittingstall, employed food campaigner Tim Lang as a consultant (he would go on to advise on *Jamie's School Dinners*), and hired the services of a young producer, Pat Llewellyn.

By the early-Nineties Pat Llewellyn was working at Wall to Wall Television, a production company known for its serious documentaries on cinema and philosophy. Word came from on high that 'Lifestyle' was the new buzz word in TV, and Jane Root, head of Wall to Wall and future controller of BBC2, sent a memo around the company asking if anyone knew anything about food or gardening. 'I wrote back and said that I knew about food, so we worked on ideas and came up with *Eat your Greens*,' said Pat. 'There had been naff daytime things like *Galloping Gourmet* and Fanny [Cradock] in the afternoons, and then Floyd brought a traveller's spin to that and a kind of post modern thing by calling the camera over. Food became about style and lifestyle, and said so much about sophistication and class.'

Food Lifestyle programmes were about having wine with your

dinner, and knowing which wine to have, about being able to go to the supermarket with confidence and choosing well, and starting to understand some of the issues that informed those choices. The audience was middle class, and the chefs were either upper class or professional – or both. Sophie Grigson came with a pedigree. Her mother, Jane Grigson, was the nearest cook to Elizabeth David that had been seen in Britain, while Delia Smith, if not upper class, was not someone everyone could imagine having a gossip with in the pub. At the end of the twentieth century in Britain TV chefs represented what Britishness was about. From Keith Floyd to Ainsley Harriott and Sophie Grigson to Rick Stein and Delia Smith, it was about aspiring to cook the kind of food everyone had begun to eat chez Antony Worrall Thompson, Alistair Little and Terence Conran, and wanting to make it at home to impress dinner party guests. It was time for a change.

By 1996 Channel 4's *Two Fat Ladies* filled a gap in the television landscape and Pat Llewellyn was looking for a new TV chef. 'Up until then we had had professional men on TV telling you what to do,' she said. '*Two Fat Ladies* were doing dinner party food in an amateur way. They had been about a sense of Britain circa 1950, slightly harking back to good British traditions but not as much as Hugh Fearnley-Whittingstall. They were more stylised than that and they were very into their ingredients.' There was an enormous skills gap, and it was TV's job to fill it. Delia Smith was teaching 20-somethings to boil an egg (*How to Boil An Egg*, BBC1, 1998) after finishing their education without a single cookery lesson. Tony Blair's Britain was a place where 20-somethings would soon make headlines by becoming the dinner party generation with the help of their TV gurus and secretly discarded Marks & Spencer packaging. The first farmers' market opening in Bath in 1997 had given birth to a national phenomenon and the Brits needed to rethink the way they shopped.

With the success of *Two Fat Ladies*, Llewellyn was looking for a new chef. 'The demographics for food programmes were quite old and there was a bit of a gap. Sophie was the youngest person on the block and she was my age. Young people weren't cooking on TV and they weren't in real life either. Women had stopped cooking, which might have been a political statement in the same way as we refused to learn to type. We were all going to go out and get jobs, and convenience foods had allowed us to do that and still eat.' She screen tested 'about 25 people', ranging from chefs to cookery writers to food journalists who were 'friends of friends. I looked at Jason Atherton long before he worked with Gordon [Ramsay],' she said. 'I was trying to find someone who was a bit more informal.' She hadn't given up when she was told by a friend to look out for a documentary called *An Italian Christmas at The River Café*. 'We all used to have dinner at The River Café with friends after work,' said Rupert Ivey, 'and someone told Pat Llewellyn about him [Jamie] and to watch out for him in the background when it was aired.' She might find what she was looking for, she was told.

But Pat was more sceptical about the prospect of finding her man. 'I had been looking for the last year,' she recalls. 'I remember seeing him and thinking "Oh, I didn't go to The River Café. I should ring up Ruth and Rose and ask if I could nose around their kitchen to see if they had anyone."' Pat wasn't immediately sold on Jamie himself either: 'He looked so young; he looked barely legal.' She remembers he was making pasta and she noticed that despite his age he was genuinely accomplished. 'My mother has this thing that you can tell someone who can really cook by the way they use their hands and I've inherited that from her,' she said. 'I don't know what it is. He looked like he'd been doing it all his life – which he had. He had a lot to say. He clearly loved food and it was a big passion of his.'

Although the story has been turned into fairy tale, the truth was a little more prosaic. 'He was very reluctant to start with,' said Pat. Jamie was happy at The River Café. He was doing what he had always wanted to do in a dream of an environment; his girl-friend was working front of house, and his employers were an inspiring combination of entrepreneur and chef. They were following their radical ideals of using the finest ingredients and treating their staff with similar respect – and paying him an enormous fee of £30,000 a year. A TV career was something he had never thought about. His dream was to learn from the great chefs and open his own restaurant. But he made a compromise: he would juggle both jobs.

Jamie was right to be cautious. 'It was a very hard sell,' said Pat. 'People were very nervous because he was so young. Chefs weren't thought to be so young and to get someone so inexperienced on telly wasn't thought to be a good idea. The BBC didn't want him and so I went to Channel 4 and they didn't want him. So I went back to my old boss [Jane Root from Wall to Wall, who was now controller at BBC2] and she was up for it. She said that she'd been trying to poach Hugh Fearnley-Whittingstall from Channel 4 and she was looking for a new chef.' Even with a commission from the BBC, it still was not all plain sailing. The first programme just did not work. 'It was fine, but it wasn't very special,' said Pat. 'His gran was in it and I think we tailored the food for her, and the recipes weren't right, and too complicated and a bit frumpy. And we had to translate every cookery term from the French that he had learnt at catering college. It was hard.'

But Pat believed in her star enough to ask her boss at Optomen Television if she could ditch the programme *and* the format and start again, this time directing it herself. It also meant burying £60,000 worth of costs. 'We'd spent quite a lot of money on it but we thought he had lots of potential and we hadn't quite realised it.' Fortunately her boss agreed. 'So I put the whole series on ice and finished *Two Fat Ladies* and then I did it myself,' said Pat. The success of Channel 4's *The Naked Chef* was due to the relationship between Pat and Jamie. There had been no voice from behind the camera in the first programme, asking polite questions, some of which were met with Jamie's cockney derision and others with a chef's experience. 'We had done that in the screen test, but we didn't do that in the programme,' said Pat. 'We had done it in the pilot with every intention of taking the questions out.' Editing Jamie must have been a nightmare. 'He gabbled so much,' she said. 'He was completely raw and everything came out at once.' The voice off-camera turned into the free flow of conversation that would set the format for *The Naked Chef*.

Matched with Jamie's brash 'cor blimey' mockneyisms, it was Tony Blair's dream, not of a classless Britain, but a Britain in which class was irrelevant on the way to the top. Posh Pat and Jamie the Geezer were the double act for a new century. Jamie's laddism was influenced by the likes of British men's magazines such as *Loaded*, which created an environment in which you could get away with anything as long as you said it with a cocksure confidence and a Sid James wink. Jamie was the chirpy Mockney geezer who would disarm you with an 'alright, darling?' and a cheeky smile. He was Max Miller and Tommy Trinder, The Kinks and The Small Faces, Madness and Blur rolled into one. It was a classic British persona.

When it first arrived British pop culture was still in thrall to the bleak, grey and suicidal nihilism of grunge and Nirvana, while British political life was in the safe hands of the ultimate grey politician, John Major. In stark contrast the Lad was brash, bright and bold. He was confident and self-assured. Life was a laugh and nihilism for losers. As Oasis sang, life could be 'supersonic'.

CHAPTER 11

GETTING NAKED

By the time *The Naked Chef* hit television screens in 1999, Britain was learning to dance to a new soundtrack. Two years out of John Major's Conservative nation into Tony Blair's Britain, there was a younger, stylish society where rock stars and fashion designers were regarded as the nation's main assets. Youthful Prime Minister Tony Blair stood for faith, hope and charity, and an economy based on realising potential. He even played guitar. In an ironic political role reversal, it was Blair who was finally making Margaret Thatcher's vision of a 'Have-a-Go Britain' a reality.

The political climate was such that starchy Delia could happily share TV airtime with Jamie's chunky salsas. His message that cooking, when reduced to the bare minimum of fuss, stripped of all its pretensions and presented as just what it is, could be something that could change the world was just what was needed. Eat well and use the best ingredients to make the simplest of meals for your family and friends. Spend time on and with the people you love, and you've got the Italian recipe for a perfect life. What a gift to give to the world still reeling from the yuppie Eighties and a society in which eating out was a fashion statement.

The British had never seen anything like *The Naked Chef* before. After the posh, pissed gastronomy of Keith Floyd, the bouncy, studio-bound Ainsley Harriott, the headmistress style of Delia Smith and the seafaring Rick Stein, it wasn't that the Brits had been starved of TV chefs, more that unlike any of them, Jamie was one of us, whoever we were. He had the Holy Grail of TV talent – the common touch, the ability to walk, talk and cook, and still make everything look easy. What's more, when we bought his books, and we did, in our tens of thousands, the recipes *were* easy. Jamie's was the life we wanted to live. It was simple, accessible and affordable.

His friends knew the programme would be a success. 'The minute they said he was going to make a series, we knew he had such serious potential,' said Rupert Ivey. 'Little did we know that he had a whole cook book written already, too. It was his communication skills, the way he made it all so accessible. He showed ordinary people how to make food that tasted good. It wasn't about food looking good but about it tasting good.' They weren't worried about the effect that it might have on him. 'He was very ambitious,' said Rupert, 'but it wasn't about being a superstar. His first love is food without doubt – and Jools,' he added. 'He loves his Jools.'

'It's pretty simple,' said Jamie, describing the idea of the series. 'It's me at my house, with my friends and my family, having a laugh and cooking. The Jamie you get on telly is the Jamie you get in real life. *The Naked Chef* is about stripping down complicated restaurant food. It's just a lot of little tricks and shortcuts, and having a good time really.' OK, so it was their flat, but it was Optomen Television who paid for most of it. Pat Llewellyn had wanted to film in Jamie's home. 'He was almost balletic in the way he moved around, and we needed him to be familiar with the kitchen he was working in,' she said. 'He lived in a tiny flat in Hammersmith at the time, and the kitchen was long and skinny, which was impossible for us, so we found somewhere that was better for us to film.' The deal was that Jools and Jamie would put the money they had paid to rent the Hammersmith flat into the pot. 'The rent was four times as much, but our location fee topped that up,' said Pat.

Her location managers spotted the perfect flat in Old Street on the edge of trendy Islington, just before the area became the epitome of Blair's loft style Britain. 'It was stylish and cool,' said Pat. 'It was so grand. I think when we all saw it, we thought "fucking hell, this is alright!" Jamie absolutely loved it.' Jools, on the other hand, hated it there, finding it cold and uncosy, with an awkward spiral staircase – she'd try to slide down the banister to get something from downstairs and do herself an injury. She said she hated having to pretend that she didn't live there. But according to Pat, that was not quite true. 'She didn't like the fact that we were there and filming in her home, and I don't blame her for that, having done loads of filming in my own house,' she told me. But Jools didn't have to pretend that she wasn't living there. Except once. 'There was one thing in the final programme that she was in,' said Pat. 'Jamie was cooking a Valentine meal and Jools had to arrive and ring the doorbell. We weren't asking her to lie or anything.'

From the flat, it seemed that Jamie could pop round the corner to buy his vanilla pods and his fresh fish. London appeared to be a world in which the corner shop was the centre of the community, where cheese shops and butchers lined his nearby streets, waiting for cheeky chappies to stop by for a natter and a slice of something nice. La Fromagerie, where Patricia Michelson showed off her stunning cheeses, was no such thing of course, but Jamie wanted viewers to meet her. 'We wanted to focus on small specialist food shops, and in a way create this network of interesting foodie retailers in London,' explained Pat. With the magic of television making it seem as if Jamie was showing us the contents of his little black book, the result of his continual sourcing around the streets of London, but again, the reality was a little different. 'I make a lot of food programmes,' said Pat, 'and it's my business to know all these people. I don't think that middle-class foodieness was his domain really. He'd be the first to admit it. We took him to all sorts of places that he hadn't been to before. He loves to learn; he enjoys learning about food in any capacity – he clicks with people.'

Jamie showed us how easy life could be, and how much nicer life can be with a bit more of a banter over the shopping. It all seemed very British, but what he was doing was turning the Brits into Italians. London even looked like Rome as Jamie jumped on his scooter to pop over to Gennaro's for a fresh baked loaf. The idea of sourcing your lunch was a novel one and undoubtedly inspired by Gennaro, who would join him on the set and in much of the edits, not just for *The Naked Chef*, but for all his TV series to come.

'In Italy, you buy what you need,' Gennaro told me, flapping his arms around as if to say that Britons are all mad to buy from supermarkets. 'People have allotments or gardens with lovely vegetables. We love our food, but we also want to know who's behind the food, where it comes from. We love the contact with the food – in that way you understand better what to do with it. You want to eat fish? Go find fresh fish,' he told me. 'It's cheaper to cook it yourself, it's healthier – you'll live longer and you'll enjoy your life more.' Gennaro reminded me that we haven't got so far to go in Britain as we might think. 'In small villages around England, they still shop like this,' he said, 'and it can happen in London too; there are so many shops where you buy bread, but people buy a couple for the freezer instead. When we finish work we pass these shops, so why don't we shop on the way home? As long as you've got the best ingredients, you can try. This is what Jamie preached; you don't need big amounts of money. You search it out and then do it. Jamie gives you the confidence to try.'

He watched the relationship develop between Pat Llewellyn and Jamie. '*The Naked Chef* was very romantic,' he told me, referring to the time of their lives rather than the show itself. 'It was at the beginning of everything. With Pat he was a young boy who needed to be directed. She would say, "You're good, you're a natural and this is what I want from you, but let me put you here." And he would listen. They had that relationship right from the beginning. Pat fell in love with Jamie, and Jamie fell in love with Pat.' She is widely credited for what she did with Jamie, not least by his 'London dad'. 'She is the expert,' shrugged Gennaro. 'She's a pure maestro, like Pavorotti when he sings. She recognised immediately that he had what was wanted.'

Over time Jamie and *The Naked Chef* melded naturally into one persona and with Jamie's aptitude to learn quickly, it wasn't long, Gennaro says, before he was almost directing himself. 'But Jamie is very humble,' he said, 'and he would never say, "No, I don't want to do this." He's very polite, but if it felt wrong, he would know and he would say so.' Pat didn't quite agree with this. 'Jamie very, very rarely would interfere editorially in that respect,' she said.

Gennaro watched proudly as what he described as the 'magnetic quality of Jamie's warmth' was brought out and recorded for the world to see. His young protégé wanted Gennaro to be a bigger part of the series, but Pat knew just how much to involve him. 'We were trying to have as many young people on as we could,' she said, knowing how attractive Jamie's laddish lifestyle was to this new audience. 'Pat is a good woman,' said Gennaro. 'I remember when Jamie said, "Let's not forget that Gennaro has been around me all the time. I need to help him – he deserves to be shown. "I looked at her and I said, "He's not a director." So I said, "Don't worry, you'll get what you want from him, not me."' Gennaro was happy to be there in an 'informal way', less Jamie's consultant on the programme than his personal mentor. 'Jamie would ring me up and say, "Big boy, we're going to do this on the programme,"' said Gennaro, putting his Jamie impression through an Italian sieve. '"Yeah, yeah, yeah – why don't you come down?" And I would. I was enjoying being there with him through this.'

Jamie's terminology is infectious. Pat, the posh Welsh TV producer, and Gennaro, the Italian chef, both use his 'yeah, yeah, yeah' when they get excited. Rupert Ivey, Jamie's soundman and friend, does it too, but it was more than the phrases that he caught from Jamie. 'It was around that time that these ghastly buzzwords happened; everyone was saying "I'm passionate about food", but I really believe that Jamie was passionate. He'd been brought up around food and thought it was everyone's right to eat well. And I was on a journey too, and he taught the whole crew that it was easy to eat well and cook food that tastes good. He was on a mission to show people how to do that.'

Making a television programme is often less exciting than the result. There is an enormous amount of down time when the director will consult with the researcher about the next set up or the lighting crew will change the atmosphere for the next scene. 'It's a bit like being at school,' said Rupert. 'You do a little bit of work and then you go off to a corner, and giggle and laugh and talk about things.' While women tend to be more intense with their gossip, boy banter is universal, and in television the crew tends to be male. 'You know what it's like,' said Rupert, 'you'll talk about something and laugh, and then there's a moment of seriousness and that's when you get the little gems. We all felt at the time that we were all doing similar things and cared about similar things, and we all spoke the same language.'

For Jamie the medium was perfect. He could be himself on camera, talking about his real passion with the missionary zeal that lit him up as much as it did his audience. When he wasn't performing to camera, he was hanging out with a bunch of lads who lived the same kind of life, with the same kind of concerns, loves and hates. He could even invite his mates over to join in the fun. 'When I first met Ben,' Jamie told us on screen, 'he was a bit of Don Johnson, a bit swarthy, a bit of hair on the chest.' Ben told us his first impression of his friend. 'When I first met Jamie, he was head down. Then after a while he was gregarious, running around the kitchen.' It gave us an insight into a life well removed from any of the stiff impressions that we may have had of kitchen life.

Jamie showed us what they liked to eat and drink; 'If I give them a nice roast lamb and a glass of wine, they're going to be well chuffed,' he would say of another band of friends coming over that TV evening to share in his programme/life. We met 'the Lovely Jools' and learnt how she had to put up with his food obsession from the first; 'She found me watching the rotisserie going around. She thought I was very odd.' We met Uncle Alan, who 'used to look like Cliff Richard', and his kids, who podded peas for Jamie and munched into roast chicken and coriander wraps without a single grimace.

Jamie introduced us to ingredients, and pushed us to marry those that we thought would never have got on. 'Sometimes flavours have a bit of a ruck, but these two [radish and fennel] are best mates. They get on really well.' Unlike any other food programme on TV in the past, Jamie made us want to cook, and now. Rose Gray watched proudly, although she said he used too many ingredients in his dishes. 'If you look at ours we often only have about four ingredients. That's what the Italians do; they look in the cupboard and if it's winter there might not be a lot around. They might have a bag of pasta and a radicchio, so they could match it with some pancetta and just make a pasta sauce, slicing the radicchio and a little rosemary, frying it for a minute in a bit of butter; adding some pancetta and that's a fantastic pasta sauce using three ingredients. It's a bit bitter and a little bit sweet, all those things that actually make you hungry and make you want to try something again.'

CHAPTER 12

THE SWEET SMELL
OF SUCCESS

The first *Naked Chef* programme was aired in April 1999 and by
the end of that summer Jamie could barely leave his front door
without being bombarded by press and public looking for a piece
of him. With five million viewers watching the BBC2 show, no one
had ever seen anything like it before. Jamie was as amazed as the
TV executives. 'Until I got that phone call from Pat,' he told
Jennifer Selway in the *Express*, 'I had never thought about being
on TV. If anyone had asked me I would probably have said that
there were already too many TV chefs. But when I was asked, I
knew that I could do something that was a bit different – it would
be my kitchen, my mates, my music, my kind of food.'

Playing the PR game was hard, too. 'In two weeks everyone
wanted me on their show,' he told journalist Frances Hardy. 'I had
my head down toilets more often than you can imagine. I was
under huge pressure. It was like [he drives his fist into the palm of
his hand], I've always been a confident person – it wasn't that I
wasn't confident – it's just that it happened like that: thwack! And
it wasn't like being in Hearsay where there are four other people
to fall back on. I was on me own, right? Oh yeah, I was boffing up
in the toilets. It was natural. But then, after a year, I got bored of
being nervous. I realised it was massively unconstructive.'

It wasn't just the paparazzi hounding the couple's private life,
however. 'This gang would constantly bang on the door or the

windows and scribble graffiti on the walls,' said Jamie. 'They were
doing silly things like spray-painting the windows. Then one day,
it got more serious. My computer got nicked from my flat and one
day I found that my car had a puncture. I took it to be fixed and
the guy said I had six huge nails in the tyres. It was just 13- and
14-year-olds who were bored.'

With Jools' safety on his mind, it took a young girl to be
attacked at the end of the road to finally drive the couple back to
the leafier and more affluent streets of West Hampstead. Sumatra
Road was buzzing with café life. Just off the beaten track, this was
as much of a village as London offered with a large transient
population piling into the bagel bakeries and sitting out in the
streets munching brioche with their cappuccinos. It was less of a
celebrity hangout than the nearby Hampstead and Primrose Hill,
where they would soon make their homes. West Hampstead was
the perfect neighbourhood for a soon-to-be superstar chef and his
wife-to-be.

For Jools it was her favourite of the many pads in London
they'd moved through. 'It was a cute little one-bedroom flat with
a garden that backed onto the railway,' she wrote in her book
Minus Nine to One. 'It felt like a real home, apart from the rats in
the garden and the drunk man in the basement flat downstairs!'
Rose Gray's earlier instinct not to employ Jools as her PA was to
be proven right when Jamie gave Jools her first break as his
personal assistant after the first series of *The Naked Chef*. Jools
thought it would be fun and that she would be able to see him
more often. 'He had been organising his entire diary in a battered
little notepad with various scribbles about meetings and appointments,' she said, 'so I decided the first thing to do was to organise
everything.' By the following day she had organised their small
space in the hallway of their Sumatra Road home and was
wondering what else was required of a PA other than chatting to
her friends on the phone and doing the odd food shop. 'I was also
getting fed up with constantly fielding calls from a persistent journalist who wanted Jamie to pose naked, but for a few strategically

placed grapes, for the centrefold of a girls' mag!' She was summarily dismissed by her husband, and replaced by her best friend Nicola.

By the autumn juggling a life as a chef on and off TV was taking its toll, not on the 23-year-old superstar, but on the rest of the team at The River Café. Rose and Ruth realised the time had come for Jamie to move on. 'Pat wanted him and he was working less and less,' said Rose. 'He worked for us for about three to four months after that but he would ring up and say, "I can only work on Monday and Thursday" and I'd say "Forget it, Jamie – I can't have a chef like that," and in the end he left.' She was sorry to see him go, but was as thrilled as they all were that his success had been so immediate. 'I must admit I thought it was fantastic,' she said. 'It was so amazing that it happened to him so quickly. If you're not someone like Pat Llewellyn you don't really see someone with those kinds of eyes.' I asked her if she thought that becoming a TV chef had been part of his game plan, that writing the book, learning the skills had always been something that he had been hoping to take to a wider audience than the customers of The River Café. 'It must have been,' she answered, 'because that's what he's doing. In some ways he could have done what Sam and Sam Clarke did after they left here, which is run a really good restaurant [Moro in London's Exmouth Market].'

Although many young lads in Jamie's position might have flung themselves into a new career in television, *The Naked Chef* was not enough for Jamie, who was not at all happy to leave his day job. 'I feel at home in The River Café,' he said. 'I can be the real me here. If I go, I feel like the television me has taken over and I never really wanted that to happen.' But he had a plan and was already charting its course by working with those he had chosen as the best teachers for what he wanted to achieve. From Gennaro's pasta and bread, to the simple but beautiful Italian cuisine of The River Café, to the tricks of TV under the guidance of Pat Llewellyn, Jamie was learning quickly. But he needed to keep his foot in the door if he was to secure his career in the food industry, learn more about restaurants and, most importantly, keep the regular pennies rolling in just in case this TV malarkey spoilt the broth.

The answer came in an offer to be consultant chef at Monte's, an Italian restaurant in Sloane Street, London. Bang in the heart of designer London, with Knightsbridge's haute couture flanking one side and the fickle fashion of the King's Road stretching out in front, this was also where the kings of cuisine reigned, and where the customers had money to burn.

CHAPTER 13

THE CHELSEA SET

For decades the smell of change had been in London's Chelsea air. The King's Road that stretched from Montes to Fulham was where hippie had given birth to punk after a trippy one-night stand. This was the vibrant heart of faddy London, where style was tried on and discarded for the Next Big Thing. Back in 1987 Terence Conran's art deco food emporium Bibendum had opened just around the corner from Monte's, bringing the culinary revolution out of Notting Hill into its enormous market hall and spreading its influence into Knightsbridge and South Kensington. The former home of the Michelin Tyre Company was filled with colourful fruits and vegetables, and oysters perched on crushed ice in the foyer seduced the beautiful people into an exciting new foodie experience.

Jamie knew that while Londoners were now coming out to eat at night, this was also where people like Pierre Koffman, whose boots Gordon Ramsay had just filled in his first restaurant on Royal Hospital Road, had been slowly building the City's fine foodie reputation for the past 15 years. While New York and California still laughed at British cuisine, it was here that Antony Worrall Thompson made the front page of the *Sunday Express* in the days before newspapers featured food. In the early Eighties his starters and puds-only restaurant, Ménage à Trois, launched Nouvelle Cuisine in the UK. Since his early teens Jamie had been reading about these food heroes and now he was part of the industry, sharing newsagents and dry cleaners with some of the culinary greats.

The gentle giant of London's culinary makeover, Pierre Koffman, inspired a new generation of young chefs, from Marco Pierre White to Tom Aikens. 'He is one of the last true greats,' Tom Aikens told me at the Anouska Hempel designed restaurant just around the corner from Montes, which he opened in 2003. 'He's had a lot of good chefs through his kitchen like Eric Chavot [now at The Capital Restaurant, which was awarded a second Michelin star in January 2001, and formerly at Chavot, The Restaurant (Marco Pierre White), Chez Nico and Le Manoir aux Quat' Saisons]. Paul Rhodes was there too and he became head chef at Nico at 90. It was a shit hot brigade. If you fell on the wrong side of him, you knew about it. But he only had to tell you once – that was it. If you didn't watch or concentrate, you'd had it. I worked my arse off!'

With its gentleman's club atmosphere and old mahogany doors, Monte's seemed an odd choice for the young buck to move into at the end of 1999. But Jamie filled the place with impossibly good-looking young Australians who, of course, would appear alongside him in *The Naked Chef*, and his by-now renowned Essex banter. The food was delicious. Hand-made capellacci stuffed with roasted onion squash, baked ricotta, pancetta and mostarda di cremona strewn with sage leaves crisped in butter and sprinkled onto golden pasta, pork chops baked in the bag with shallots and thyme, sautéed girolles and spinach… This was the kind of menu that Jamie had been dreaming of for years.

But Jamie was on a different mission now; with the lovely Jools on his arm, he was the celebrity party-goer. The restaurant suffered, with Fay Maschler, the undisputed Queen of Food Reviews for the past 30 years, noting that a meal of Jamie Oliver's at Monte's was 'gauche' and 'joyless'. 'He'd gone from being golden boy at The River Café to being The Naked Chef, and I don't think he'd been criticised before. A mutual friend told me he was really upset,' said Fay later to Louise France in the *Observer*.

If he was upset, he didn't show it. The press could barely get enough of Jamie and Jools. They were love's young dream, fit, rich and good-looking, an icon for modern Britain, out on the town, suited and booted and ripe for the covers of celebrity magazines. *The Naked Chef* programmes were bringing in six million viewers a week, with videos and books to accompany the series, and although he might have been only making eight 30-minute programmes a year, Jamie was everywhere. The shows were being broadcast around the world, his books translated into 16 languages and he had been awarded a BAFTA in 2000. It was not just the programme either; Jamie was the undisputed star, with the Elle Style Awards crowning him Most Stylish Male TV Personality in 2000 and *GQ* awarding him Man of the Year Award in the TV Personality category in the same year. A year later their American counterparts hailed him GQ Best Chef, and the WH Smith Book Awards gave him their Home & Leisure Award for *Return of The Naked Chef*.

Gennaro says success doesn't go to Jamie's head. 'I don't watch a lot of TV and I don't read the papers much, but someone told me about an award he got for the work he did on school dinners,' he said, referring to a 'special recognition' award he had won at the National Television Awards in late 2005. 'You know, he never told me. He calls me most days but he didn't tell me about it. So I went to see him and he was showing the students something about salads, and I asked him about the award and he said, "Yeah, that was nice" and got on with what he was doing. I know he really appreciates it but it doesn't fill his head. If it was me I'd put the flag out everywhere!'

By the summer of 2001, after a ramshackle organisation of his publicity between the BBC, his publishers Penguin and Pat Llewellyn, it was time to take on a proper PR company, and where better to go than The Outside Organisation? With clients like David Bowie, Naomi Campbell, Paul McCartney, The Who,

Usher, Craig David, the post-Simon Fuller Spice Girls and Westlife, surely Alan Edwards could make Jamie the biggest TV chef we had ever seen? But it turned out that he wouldn't need much help.

CHAPTER 14

SWEET AND SOUR

Jamie was having the time of his life. He was one of the most well known young men in the country and living the high life. Jools, his perfect girl, was on his arm and the pennies were rolling in. He was an icon for a generation: happy in work, ecstatic in love. The work that Pat Llewellyn was doing with Jamie was hitting all the right buttons and the huge BBC2 audience was flying through the supermarkets after work to buy ingredients for that night's dinner. The impact the two of them were having stretched right across the food-associated industry.

Pat Llewellyn had a 'vast effect on popular culture', according to journalist Howard Byrom. 'She's shaped the way we think about food, the way we treat the people who cook it, and by proxy, the way it's marketed, from the barrow boys to supermarkets.' He called her the 'Scullery Spielberg, the Culinary Cecil B. de Mille' and said that, 'thanks to her, mild-mannered housewives now smash garlic with their fists, toss salads with their bare hands and taste the dressing by dipping in their fingers and slurping rather loudly'. But it wasn't just the food industry that was benefiting from all this. *The Naked Chef*'s food was about making it now rather than aspiring to make it one day. A book of the series is par for the course with cookery programmes, from the Roux Brothers through to Madhur Jaffrey, but Jamie's flew off the shelves. 'He makes cook books move,' said Eric Treuille of Books for Cooks, who employed Jamie's future manager Louise Holland at the time. 'He put us on the map. We were always known by professionals but since he came on the scene, we're now a tourist attraction.' Treuille attributed the success equally to Jamie and to Pat. 'She is very clever; she comes up with the ideas. Everything she did worked.'

It's a shame then that the first book deal was to sour the special relationship between Pat and Jamie, and show a side to Jamie Oliver that we would see again later on with ownership issues over the origins of the *School Dinners* project. The way that Jamie tells it is just like something out of *The Galloping Gourmet*: he had a book that he had made earlier. The scribbled recipes and splurged thoughts he had been compiling since his first days at Neal Street would, he told us, form the basis of his first book. 'I remember him saying that he'd started writing a book,' Rose Gray told me. 'He came to my house and showed me, and it was quite formed – it was even in chapter form. I don't know if it was the book that he eventually published – I suspect it wasn't.'

'He hadn't started writing his book although I'm sure that he was collecting recipes,' said Pat, who introduced Jamie to five different publishers for the book of the first series. 'It was a toss-up between Ebury and Penguin, and Jamie felt most comfortable with Penguin so that's what we did. He would come into the office and dictate his ideas to my assistant, who typed it up downstairs.' For a dyslexic with two GCSE grades to his name, having a book under his wing was a serious achievement. 'At 23,' he told the press, 'I had a best-selling book for half a year from a cook book that I'd written when I was 17–18, which I never actually thought would get published. When that came out, it was amazing but it was just like, "God, I'm lucky!" Then the second series comes and it's like, no, it wasn't luck – you're doing really well now. Fantastic! I don't want to mention names,' he said proudly, 'but you see a lot of books that are supposed to be "written" by celebrity chefs. They're very thin and glossy, and you can just tell they're not written by the people they're meant to be written by.'

Jamie has told the press that the deal he signed precipitated his need to get a tighter hold on his fortunes. He put it down to experience and bears no grudge, but says that the cut was not fair. 'He got the same as the Two Fat Ladies did, and all the authors of those BBC books we did,' said Pat. 'It was always split in their favour. Our MD always does those deals and it's always the same.' Pat thinks it was 'the first agent phenomenon' that caused the problem, the need for a new personality in the mix to show off her negotiating power, and the inexperience of the new star being told his fortune. 'I think we renegotiated for the second book but with the third, they cut us out altogether,' said Pat. 'It wasn't Penguin – it was Jamie and his agent. They said to us, "Fuck off! We won't do a series with you otherwise."'

It still upsets her; the integrity of their relationship was the driving force behind the success of the series and she feels let down. 'I suppose it's when you hear things about what he's said about getting a bad deal on the books,' she told me sadly, 'and you know he's made how many millions out of his book? It was a matter of a 2% difference. His first book made him a fantastic amount of money.' She says that it was a long time ago and it's 'not an issue any more'. But she understands how these things happen: 'I think it was a way for the agent to cook up to try to get the business for herself, for her to say, "Hey, I can improve that deal for you."'

Since his early hubris, Jamie is now more tempered about presenting the way his books are produced although he is still proud of his achievements. He told his Fifteen students that, despite his dyslexia, he had written four books although he confessed that he dictates his ideas into a tape recorder. His editor at Michael Joseph has now gone to work with him at his own company, yet he has said that he covets the ability to craft words like Nigel Slater does: 'Nigel's romantic, he gets into contact with all the right emotions.'

Jamie went straight to the top of the British bestseller list with his first book and things stayed that way as the books accompanied the success of the series. The third in the trilogy – *Happy*

Days with the Naked Chef – became an immediate bestseller and was the official Christmas No.1 in the British non-fiction chart in 2001. 'It's hard to get to number one in the non-fiction charts,' he told the press after 'working his arse off' at book signings. 'I put a lot of effort into trying to get it right, but it is all wonderfully well worthwhile when someone who has appreciated it comes up to say thank you. I just love it when they tell me how a particular recipe went down well as a particular occasion. It gives me a huge kick – that's why I do the job.' Rupert Ivey hopes Jamie changes his signature for the punters. 'Most of the books he's autographed for me are pornographic – he does have a cock obsession. He just loves nothing but drawing cocks.'

With the success of *The Naked Chef* assured, and already screened in 12 different countries including France and Italy, Jamie could begin to relax a little about his future. First things first though: it was time to propose again to the lovely Jools. 'I love Jools very much, and marriage means a great deal to me,' he said. 'It is a very special thing and we're both ready to take our vows. Jools and I both come from good solid families who believe in marriage and it makes perfect sense to take the decision now.'

'I think she's wanted to marry him forever,' said Rupert Ivey. 'They're very happy and they're very linked,' Gennaro agrees. 'If Jamie was not famous, he'd be the same person and Jools knows that.' Rupert says he envies him – 'I don't see him as ever having a drugs problem and he's not a womaniser, and those are two huge advantages.' If it is his celebrity status that makes him think twice about revealing his lack of experience with other women, Rupert is still envious of his self control. 'When you indulge in that kind of thing, you don't care whether you're any good or not. You enjoy it, so you think, "fuck it!"' I asked Rupert if Jamie's self control was more to do with deciding not to jeopardise what Jools calls their 'perfect family'. 'Yes,' he conceded, 'but again I don't understand that one. Most men would jeopardise anything for a shag! He genuinely loves Jools. They've been spoken for for years even before they were married. I don't know why it works, but it does.'

Getting round to signing on the dotted line was simply a case of finding the time and the money to do it their way. The Olivers are both extremely close to their families and chose to get married from Jamie's parents' home in Rickling, with its thatched cottages and village church providing a very English backdrop for the occasion. 'I can't wait to see her walk down the aisle in a wedding dress and veil,' he said.

Despite her father's early stroke Jools' parents had been very happily married. Maurice Norton had been a highly successful 'stockmarket person' (as Jamie described him) before a stroke left him paralysed when Jools was only six. Before he became disabled, the Nortons had seemingly had it all. Jools' mother Felicity was a model and, with their three beautiful daughters, big house and flashy cars, they lived the Essex high life. But Maurice's disability affected the entire family and with the City bonuses gone, they were forced to move house and change their lifestyle. But Maurice did learn to walk and talk again, and Jools' and Jamie's early relationship was cemented as Jamie grew to know and love her father. He asked for Jools' hand when she was 20 and he was just 19, and although Maurice suggested they were a bit young, he gave them his blessing. It would be another four years before Jamie decided the time was right and proposed again, this time at her father's graveside. In 1997 Maurice had another stroke, which was fatal this time. 'It was as if Jamie was asking her father's permission,' Jamie's mother, Sally told the Biography Channel.

Jamie himself organised the food for the wedding in Rickling in June 2000, getting up at 5am to bake the bread, which he planned to serve with antipasti and 'really good olive oil'. With a main course of roasted fish, his dad's 'ratte pataters' with dill from the garden and a cake, which had received alcohol top-ups for weeks on end, the team from The Cricketers and few of 'the old boys' from Montes would be in charge of the wedding banquet.

Jamie was dressed in a £2,000 baby blue corduroy Paul Smith suit, a pink, open-necked shirt and grey snakeskin loafers. The brief to Paul Smith was, 'Sixties pimp, sky blue corduroy, mate, with turn-back cuffs. It sounds weird, but looks absolutely pukka. No tie, very *Quadrophenia*.' Jools arrived at the thirteenth century village church in a 1951 Cadillac in strapless white designed by Neil Cunningham with Jimmy Choo white stilettos. Her sisters, Lisa and Natalie, as well as Nix, the best friend who had taken over her job as Jamie's PA, followed behind in the bridesmaids' 1955 pale green Buick Roadmaster. With Ben O'Donaghue, the Aussie chef from Monte's who had become a regular on *The Naked Chef*, standing beside him as best man, it was Jamie's father Trevor who gave Jools away. An apple was placed on every plate to mark how her own father had called Jools 'the apple of my eye'.

Jamie's grandfather Ted had also died from a stroke and instead of wedding presents, the guests were asked to donate to the Stroke Association. 'We already have enough pots and pans,' said Jools. They continue to raise awareness about strokes, and in October 2000 Jamie opened the Stroke Unit at Addenbrooke's Hospital in Cambridge.

Although the guest list illustrated their early celebrity credentials, with the cast of 140 including DJ Norman Cook and Zoe Ball, and The Chemical Brothers, whom Jamie flew in from Glastonbury to play DJ, the couple refused enormous cash sums for a *Hello!* magazine style wedding. Jamie said he had been offered 'loads of cash, around £250,000. It's an immense amount, obscene money. I'll admit we find it tempting to take it. We probably can't afford it, but we're going to say no on a moral basis because it's tacky and naff.'

Treating it like an Italian knees-up, the meal was a mix of the best seasonal ingredients and close family and friends. It was the kind of informality that encouraged the guests to tear off pieces of Jamie's bread and dunk it in the baby artichokes with boiled lemons, honey, roasted almonds and smashed thyme. Jamie couldn't have been happier. 'It was all in bowls, and when I was sitting at the top table, I looked around the marquee. People were pouring stuff, ripping bread, passing olive oil and every table was like that, which is how I wanted it to be.' 'The marquee was filled with fairy lights, and they had a string quartet and fireworks and everything,' said his old friend Leigh Haggerwood. 'It was a really emotional day.'

As they honeymooned in Italy, Jamie and Jools had time to talk and plan their future. Television might make household names out of ordinary Joes, but a cookery show alone – especially on the BBC – would never make Jamie his millions. His books would, however. But although Jamie has always maintained that he is not driven by the sight of a cheque, Jools, the little girl whose riches were taken from her when her father suffered his stroke, was keen to maximise the potential of their situation. 'I think she's got a lot of ambition,' said Rupert Ivey. 'I think she likes the reflected glory and she's very conscious about what's going on.'

CHAPTER 15

THE DEEPEST CUT

By 2001 there had been offers of big money already; they could have sold their wedding to a glossy, and Jamie could have agreed to pose naked for a celebrity magazine. His mentor Gennaro Contaldo was amazed that he had turned it down – 'I said, "Blimey, I'd do it for nothing!"' But the couple knew that there was now the opportunity to pay outright for their new home in Hampstead, a home for the kids for whom Jools was desperate to start planning, and decided they would not turn the right offer down.

Jamie's second book, *Return of the Naked Chef*, had knocked the first off the British bestseller list and by October 2001, with his third series of *The Naked Chef* still bringing in unprecedented audiences, it wasn't just the paparazzi who were knocking on his door. When the 'right offer' came in the form of an alleged £¼ million deal with the supermarket giant Sainsbury's, he jumped.

For an Essex lad raised on Tory ideals the landscape was rolling with pastures new. Food was abundant in a world in which super-markets dominated distribution and dangled exotic fruits from faraway lands in new, more open layouts for us all to see. Olive oils covered shelf after shelf, offering flavours, colours, pedigrees we hadn't known existed only a couple of years before. Deli counters, butchers and fishmongers all under one roof, with free parking and even somewhere to buy our stamps on the way out gave us the impression we could have whatever we wanted. But Jamie, by now a frequent visitor to south London's Borough Market and

Gennaro's weekend forest forages, saw a way of making things fresher and more seasonal – getting named farms to supply meat and Italian-style recipes to make food simpler, more fun and more accessible to the average family. Sainsbury's and Jamie Oliver, he decided, were the team that could put the finishing touches to British food.

'A lot of the stuff we did at Sainsbury's was about the food of love,' said a friend who shared the late-night shoots. 'It was about what to cook for your girlfriend; it was about entertaining your best mates. There were a lot of TV chefs around then, so when he burst through he was the one for the lads. Before Jamie blokes in their late 20s lived in a tip and relied on their mothers to do their cooking and laundry. But here was a guy who looked cool – his hair and his clothes, the whole lifestyle was cool. Suddenly it was about energetic guys doing something. And he was so into food, that's what was making him high. It was inspirational for young men who wanted to pull women. It definitely made sense for Sainsbury's to get hold of that energy.'

The commercials presented The Naked Chef that we knew and loved in the now familiar context of Jamie surrounded by his family and friends, and offered tips to bring out the best in the kind of ingredients sold in the supermarket. This wasn't about posh food; it was a series of foodie affirmations from the self to trash those TV dinners and get cooking.

Jamie's job was to do more than simply poke his nose into our sitting rooms and laugh at our meals for one. Sainsbury's was initially after little more than a sparky lad to put a little spice in their image and even suggested he might be filmed naked in a bathtub alongside Jools. But Jamie had bigger bubbles to burst; he was on a mission to retrain the British palate, to change our minds about cooking. With Sainsbury's bosses lapping up his ideas, he relaunched Sainsbury's herb section with new names from English country gardens, such as lovage and orange thyme, and encouraged them to stock bigger bunches of basil for us to tear up and scatter over our pasta. He made sure that Sainsbury's preached the seasonal message; he even wanted them to put farmers' markets in their car parks.

But he was criticised for selling his soul to the Devil, for sleeping with the enemy; he maintained he knew what he was taking on. 'My relationship with Sainsbury's is really honest,' he said. 'I tell them the way it is – no prisoners. I want those pre-packed aisles to get smaller and smaller, but they are getting bigger and bigger. But I have re-launched their herb range and sales are up 40 per cent. We have introduced five new herbs around the whole country, for crying out loud! Summer savory, golden marjoram, lemon thyme, lemon basil and purple basil. Right? Don't tell me that is not an amazing thing!'

The Sainsbury's work, like his TV programmes, was inspired by his own frustrations; his local Sainsbury's hadn't provided the ingredients he needed to cook for his mates, and he saw his involvement as a way of raising standards. 'What do you expect me to say when I bring an Italian friend back and I have to make pesto for four people, and I have to buy 14 packs at 89p each of average basil?' he asked journalists. 'What people don't know is that I actually spent hours going into board meetings with their vegetable and herb buyers, and basically abused not just their herbs, but herbs in general in supermarkets.'

But if Jamie was fired with the enthusiasm of a missionary, those who were still working with him on *The Naked Chef* were less chuffed. Pat Llewellyn was terribly upset. 'He did the whole deal with Sainsbury's after the second series,' she told me. 'He did tell me about it but only when the deal was about to happen the following day. What was hard about it was watching on TV what we had created – the informality, the eating with friends, people coming together and eating together. It was a bit annoying but it was a long time ago.'

In addition, while Optomen Television had been jointly credited – and Pat personally thanked – in *The Naked Chef*, the book that accompanied the first series, there is no mention of Pat or Optomen in the credits of the second book, *Return of the Naked*

Chef. And when Jamie was commissioned by Michael Joseph to write the third book, *Happy Days with the Naked Chef*, to accompany the last series, Optomen Television was completely cut out of the deal.

To make it worse, this independent producer found herself in a difficult position. 'We did the third series while he was doing the Sainsbury's deal,' she told me. 'I felt I'd become less of a producer and more of a gatekeeper between our production and Sainsbury's. The BBC asked me to police the relationship. Creatively it became very difficult. There was a paranoia about it all.'

Pat says she holds no resentment against Jamie. 'He rang up the other day and invited me to his restaurant,' she told journalist Frances Hardy. 'Of course I'll go. I do have an immense sense of pride for what he's achieved.' But it's clear that it still hurts. 'I feel that the whole thing about the books was unbelievably unfair,' she told me. 'And I think I personally gave him a lot. But what can I say?'

She tells me, almost as an afterthought, that the last cut was the deepest. The BBC had not renewed the *Naked Chef* contract, beyond the third series. With Pat reeling, Jamie set up his own production company, Fresh One, and he took four members of the production team with him. 'He behaved rather badly actually,' said Pat in her understated way. 'I was the last person to know that he was setting up a production company and that he was doing it all himself.'

Maybe the lure of working for an impulsive maverick after the comforting apron strings of Pat Llewellyn was too much for the young researchers on *The Naked Chef*. The life of a TV freelancer can be flighty and insecure, and most, given the opportunity to work with a major new talent, would think little of the trail they might be leaving behind. 'The impact on a business like ours at the time was awful,' said Pat. 'It takes years to train a good production team. But there wasn't much I could say. By the time I heard about it, it was a done deal.'

One of his recently sacked consultants said that this is what he does. 'He shakes things up every couple of years,' he told me. 'He has a habit of it. But we all stay friends. You'll rarely find anyone, even those caught in the crossfire, having anything bad to say about him.'

With his new production company Fresh One, Jamie tried to pitch a new show *Oliver's Army* to the BBC but talks with the BBC broke down. Jamie was not deterred. With three series of *The Naked Chef* under his belt, his books vying with each other for the number one spot and a golden handcuff in the offing with Sainsbury's, it took less time than it takes to cook his homemade pasta for Jamie to decide to punt his wares to Channel 4. But that's not quite the way he put it to the press. 'I've had an amazing two and a half years but I need to take some time off and step back from the spotlight for a bit,' he said. 'I think people are getting sick of me.'

Pat, too, says she is reconciled to what happened. Her career is unscathed; she went on to make *Return of the Chef* with John Burton Race and *Kitchen Nightmares* with Gordon Ramsay. Optomen Television has won numerous awards and also has an office in New York, where it produces programmes for US networks including PBS, Discovery, HBO and APT. She watched her *F-Word* with Ramsay go out to rave reviews on Channel 4 from 2005 and the *Great British Menu* feature the nation's finest chefs competing to prepare The Queen's 80th birthday feast! TV land is a small world and the finale of Posh Pat and Jamie the Geezer is a well-known story. 'I make food programmes and that's all I care about in the end. Professionally it hasn't hurt. It's a long time ago. So... yeah,' she sighed.

Perhaps it was the smell of the cash that drove Jamie out of the cosy BBC nest, or a sniff of the impact he might have on our food culture through his new job with Sainsbury's. His crew members spotted it early. 'We were sure that he would change it from within,' said one of the camera team. 'And they've taken on board what he says. They know that he's the voice of the nation.' Or maybe he was beginning to piece together the jigsaw that would find an outlet for his missionary zeal and recognised that with the

Sainsbury's millions, he would have the cash to make a difference. 'I didn't really think he was the sort of guy to go for the money, but obviously he's fidgety enough,' said a member of his Sainsbury's crew as he looked back over Jamie's career, 'but what's been amazing is watching him do all these other things like *Fifteen* and *School Dinners*, and seeing him have the will to make a change.'

CHAPTER 16

SPOILING THE BROTH

Call it Karma, but Jamie was about to get his comeuppance. If Jamie and his Sainsbury's bosses were in it for the long term with a genuine mission to change the way we shop, cook and eat, the press were not so long-sighted. The clouds were darkening as Jamie bounced across our TV screens in a relentlessly upbeat celebration of his 'beautiful' lifestyle, and it wasn't long before the knives were sharpening. The press pack laughed like hyenas when Jamie let slip that he didn't actually shop at Sainsbury's, even if he was referring to the ingredients he bought for Monte's when he said, 'I buy from specialist growers, organic suppliers and farmers. It is completely about non-compromise.' He had fallen into his own trap. Set yourself up as a man of integrity, the press was saying, and it's only a matter of time before you are hoisted by your own petard. Integrity is the Holy Grail, sneered the press. You can't get paid a fortune and keep your ethics intact. You can't sip from the cup of celebrity and not get a little tipsy. Drink too freely and you're bound to wobble. Jamie had become an easy target. In the world of newspapers integrity is a rare commodity. I asked a reporter how she justifies the inevitable shafting she sees as her stock in trade. 'After the first couple of times when you've believed a celebrity and found they've been lying through their teeth to you, you begin to find it easier,' she said.

But Sainsbury's stood by their man. 'We have an excellent relationship with Jamie, and we don't usually supply restaurants,'

said another spokesman. 'So there's nothing unusual going on.'
But Jamie had referred to supermarkets as 'factory operations'
and when Jools was spotted shopping at Waitrose, 200 yards
down the road from their local Sainsbury's in north London, it
was clear that they were about to be called in. The glamorous
wife, the house in Hampstead, the celebrity friends, it was all
becoming a bit too much. Jamie and Jools were now well established on the celebrity red carpet and regularly rubbed shoulders
with the likes of Norman Cook and Zoe Ball, Ronnie Wood and
Chris Evans. Brad Pitt and Jennifer Aniston would soon become
mates when Jamie was invited to cook at Brad's fortieth birthday
although according to press reports Jools would soon afterwards
be spotted comforting Jen in the booths at Fifteen. 'Jamie
Oliver's restaurant Fifteen is fast becoming east London's
outpost of the Ivy,' wrote Lydia Slater in the *Sunday Times*. 'Not
only do Zoe Ball and Sara Cox come here every week for a girly
lunch, it's also frequently played host to a distracted Jennifer
Aniston, over here unburdening her relationship angst into the
sympathetic ear of her new bestie, Jools Oliver... but not, so far,
smashing any plates in her anguish.'

The Jamie image everyone had bought into was of an ordinary
bloke. The integrity he had shown in his love of food and ideas
to bring a revolution into the supermarket aisles was at odds with
the megabucks in his pocket and his sexy London lifestyle. But
Jamie still couldn't see what all the fuss was about. He passionately believed he could make a difference through the
Sainsbury's ads without being compromised in the slightest.
'Yes, they're a company and their mission is to make lots of cash,'
he explained. 'But their strategy for the next five years
completely encapsulates everything that I do – bringing interesting products to the nation. I go to Borough Market every
Saturday – I love it. But even the people there can't feed a nation.
They never will. I'm cool about that.'

By 2001 Jamie was everywhere and the press began to prod his
cheeky chappy image and test to see if it had become overcooked.

The tabloids had created a monster, hyping him to saturation point and pumping up his ego until he impaled himself upon their spikes. 'Just two years ago, when asked about designer clothes, he said: "What do I know? I'm just a chef,"' one of the papers reminded us. 'Now he and his wife Jools are fully paid-up members of the celebrity circus. They sit between It-girls in the front row of London Fashion Week. Matthew Williamson is one of Jools' favourite designers. At his last show Jamie and Jools sat next to Jerry Hall and Minnie Driver.' They even poked fun at his hair, once barely touched as he slid down his spiral staircase on *The Naked Chef* and now styled by leading London hairdresser Charles Worthington.

'Jamie Oliver has always divided the nation down the middle, just like Jeffrey Archer books and Marmite. But at this rate, the danger is that the half who didn't think he's a smug little twerp are going to join those who did,' wrote one hack. He was 'a figure of scorn and overpaid supermarket poster boy', proclaimed one website. 'Apart from being intensely irritating, he's intensely irritating.' 'Watching him slide down the banister and dunk a basketball was charming at first,' wrote journalist Andy Kellman, 'and so were his random outbursts of "Yeeeahh", "Pukka" and "Whack it in the ol'..."' But after several hours it became irritating.' Even Jamie's public were turning against him, saying they found it difficult to recreate his recipes. 'I'd rather go down to Burger King,' said a former fan. His latest book, *Return of the Naked Chef*, was even leaked on the internet, depriving him of thousands of pounds' worth of sales. Co-band member and childhood friend Leigh Haggerwood said that it was horrible: 'People began to hate him with a vengeance. There were death threats on the internet, and all sorts. They even tried to break his bike cable.'

A 'big fat fib' to Jan Moir in the *Daily Telegraph* in July 2001 didn't help and its headline – 'I Don't Want People To Think I'm a Prat' – set the tone for what was to come. 'Jamie Oliver strolls through the restaurant in his sparkling chef's whites,' wrote Moir, describing the scene at Monte's that led to his most serious downfall, 'looking for all the world as if he has spent a hard morning thrashing and bashing at the coal face of haute cuisine. "Yep, phew! I been makin' bread, general bits and pieces. A bit of prepping, a bit of butchering, all that malarkey," he says, without even a hint of a blush.' The truth was, as she pointed out, she had seen him with her own eyes 'slipping into his white jacket and being tied into a white apron in the corridor' as he raced to meet her, probably direct from a Sainsbury's or TV meeting. 'At a push,' she wrote, 'he may have been discussing new breads with the member of staff he refers to as "Jethro, my pastry boy", but he certainly has not been rattling pots and pans in any real and meaningful sense'.

It got worse. In the interview, he proudly declared himself 'The Ambassador of British Cooking Across the World' and it seemed that the Naked Chef had trumped himself up in the Emperor's New Clothes. 'I am the first cookery programme ever to be sold to France, Italy, Spain,' he boasted. 'I'm in 34 different countries on 60 channels. I do all the big-name chat shows in America, and I have a lot of sweeping up to do when I get over there. They think the British are a bunch of ******* heathens who eat greasy old toad-in-the-hole, with mad cows and BSE and salmonella. They think we eat slop, that our produce and our meat is crap, and it rains all the time.' It may have been true, but the chefs he had worshipped, and the press that had worshipped him, went in for the kill. Antonio Carluccio, his former employer, was one of the first: 'He has turned himself into a star and the cameras now focus on him and not on his food.'

'My homage for contribution to British food goes to the Roux brothers,' said Gordon Ramsay in a vain attempt to balance the debate. 'When they opened Le Gavroche in 1966 they changed the future of British cooking. What Jamie has done is take away the intimidation of cooking. But there is the premier league – the serious chefs who cook serious food for a fully booked dining room every night. And then there are TV chefs – and we all know which is which. Jamie's a talented guy, but he's got a lot to learn.'

Henry Harris, now chef at Racine in London, said Jamie's

cooking is not even English. 'If you look at the menu at Monte's, it's almost exclusively Italian. The books of Elizabeth David, Jane Grigson and Delia Smith did more than anyone else to raise the standards of British cooking.' Jamie's erstwhile hero Marco Pierre White commented, 'I've only seen him in the ads.' One chef who didn't want to be named told a newspaper, 'We're all sick of those ads. The only good thing about him is that to us chefs he's not quite as embarrassing as that other prat who did *Can't Cook, Won't Cook* – Ainsley Harriot.'

'These people don't really know who I am,' said Jamie defensively. 'I've got a great job, and a lovely wife, and a baby on the way. I know I'm a populist and that chefs like Marco [Pierre White] or Gordon Ramsay are in a different league. I make a point of never saying anything against them, and as for Antonio Carluccio... well, in the past he has been very good to me. I know I could be a great chef too but at the moment I'm choosing to do something else. That's the point about cooking as a career. There are just so many directions that you can go in. I'm moving out of television now, and in a couple of years I'll be doing something quite different.'

Telling the press you're the Ambassador of British Food is undoubtedly naive, and it was Jamie's greatest sin at the time. The great British tradition of inflating your celebrities only to pop them when you please means that we can read whatever we want into anything the press chooses to write and idle hacks made it their business to have a go. With the campaigns of Fifteen and School Dinners safely behind him now, the same journalists – many of them paid to poke fun at public figures – would these days probably colour with shame, but only slightly. Looking through the press cuttings now, it's hard to believe that Jamie Oliver could ever have been so vilified. What is now seen as integrity and authenticity was then regarded as self-important aggrandisement. 'Only last week his series of television ads, which feature Oliver, his family and friends, was cited as one of the primary factors behind the recent rise in Sainsbury's share price,' wrote Jan Moir in the original *Telegraph* article. 'Remarkable, really,' she continued, 'as most people I know have to flee the room when chortling Oliver appears on the small screen, slapping his belly, cuddling his Nan, dropping olives into his scooter helmet and generally annoying all and sundry with his man-of-the-people patter.'

'The pictures that illustrate the books have an unmistakable trace of self-satisfaction,' sniped the *Daily Mail*. 'There is Jools wearing a T-shirt that says "Tuck In" across her breasts. There is Jamie on his Vespa, Jamie bantering with market traders.' He was accused of being 'a television court jester, a national village idiot... It's Greystoke syndrome, with Oliver a modern-day Tarzan: a semi-trained primate who can make soufflé'. In the *Daily Mirror* Jim Shelley was astonishingly unkind: 'Watching the way he zooms around on his Vespa, or genuinely enjoys bashing things, making things dirty and having a go on the Magimix ("mixing the little bits of fine stuff with the little bits of big stuff"), you realise he's not an over-excitable kid. He's actually just retarded... He's Benny from *Crossroads* does cooking.'

He was even accused of being a 'Mockney gobshite', an Essex boy whose consonants had acquired a bit of seasoning since he'd left his nicely spoken parents for TV Land. 'For Oliver, if a recipe is not wicked, then it's pukka,' wrote Brian Viner in the *Independent*. 'His new cookbook, *Happy Days with the Naked Chef*, which is already roaring up the bestseller lists, contains recipes for "my old man's superb chicken" and "wicked baked sardines". But his Essex boy spiel, considered so beguiling by some, has started to grate on others. It is even said, as it is of Bob Hoskins, that his accent is manufactured, that his vowels were a sight plummier until, as he sought increased street cred, he marinaded them in estuary water.'

Even 'serious' journalists like Mark Lawson joined in, describing some of the ads as 'the most revolting scenes of broadcast mastication since John Gummer force-fed his daughter a hamburger to demonstrate the safety of British meat – were as thin and tacky as a supermarket plastic bag'. Lawson's criticism was more measured than that of the British tabloids, and he pointed his finger at other notable celebrities who dropped an 'H' or a 'T' in a culture 'which equates being nicely spoken with phoniness. You are more likely to seem real if you fake how you speak,' he wrote. 'Fifty years ago media celebrity often necessitated losing a regional accent; now it is clever to gain one, even if, in Oliver's case, his verbal tricks are more complex, restoring, for example, the old upper-class colonial word "pukka". But, if you tried to draw up a formula for success in modern Britain, it would include an egalitarian manner and a social conscience, and Jamie Oliver has now perfectly accomplished both.'

Jamie was stunned and said he didn't live anywhere near an estuary. 'I'm a country guy and my friends were country people and like me, they were as common as muck. My mum used to tell me off for being common and say, "Why can't you speak properly?" and I would say, "Introduce me to the Queen and I'll be polite, but when I'm relaxed, I drop a couple of aitches."' What was seen as arrogance in the tabloid telling could be forgiven as the temporary ego of a supercharged ride to the top, but Gennaro Contaldo said Jamie was never any different: 'Unfortunately people took him the wrong way – they think that he's got some other interest. But he's just normal. What you see on TV is what he's really like.' Rupert Ivey watched him close down. 'He got very paranoid about those things on websites. They referred to him as a fat-tongued wanker or something. I think that if someone was making fun about a bit of me I'd probably laugh, but he was shocked. He did get really upset for a time.'

'If someone thinks I am a prat and annoying, I kinda wanna know why, really,' Jamie told the press, amazed at the power of the venom. 'But if people don't like me for just being me, then fair enough. Christ, I'm sure everyone doesn't like them as well. At the end of the day, they can always switch over·or not buy the book.' 'It was a shock,' Jamie told journalist Miranda Sawyer. 'Because I thought it would never happen. It was all golden bollocks before that. And it's not like I got caught smoking joints or doing cocaine or anything. I'm quite boring – I've been with the same girl for nine years, I work hard, everything I do is positive, so I couldn't see any reason why the press would aggro me. But then it did.'

Jamie felt that the press that had created him had now turned against him and he couldn't understand why, particularly as 'a lot of it wasn't true, they'd just got me wrong'. He said he didn't care what was being said about him, but it was friends like Gennaro Contaldo who expressed his anger on Jamie's behalf: 'One or two people criticised him and I went over there and told them to piss off. He didn't care. He said, "Don't do anything; it doesn't matter. I've got a lovely life and lovely friends and a great job, so don't worry about it."' More importantly, at the time Jamie had plans to move out of TV and into setting up more important projects, and he was worried that bad press would slow him down. 'I'd got to the point where I could really make a difference in my area and I was worried that all the potential would slide away,' he said. But with book sales hitting the five million mark at that time, he could afford to be balanced. 'I'm 26 and I've made a lot of money, and you know what? It pisses a lot of people off!'

CHAPTER 17

SUPERMARKET SWEEP

Jamie pretended not to care: he was at the top of his game, the Sainsbury's ads were fun, effective and they paid him a fortune. The day job at Montes, the meetings at Sainsbury's and the shoots may have been pulling at the seams of his family life, but he could always do what he had done on the set of *The Naked Chef* and bring them all along. 'They always involved his family,' said one of the crew. 'I think he always wanted to find ways in which his mates could get paid, like Jimmy, but he also wanted to hang out with them – there was always someone in it.'

He even brought his Gran along. 'We did a night shoot with her,' said the friend. 'Sainsbury's by definition was always open and the only time we could get to shoot in the shop was in the middle of the night. So we'd do three days in the studio and one on location, and his 78-year-old grandmother would be up all night, as fit as a fiddle. He called her "Tiger". She was a lovely woman and you could see that he had such a great relationship with her. There was always such a lot of humour between him and his family. You can see that his energy is based on his humour and he keeps everyone sweet that way.'

Jamie told the *Telegraph* that his family and friends love being part of his TV world. 'Everything that I do just makes them smile and is exciting to them. To be honest, what is everyday and boring for me is absolutely dead interesting to them. My Nan does the Sainsbury's adverts and she is almost reliving her youth. She is famous, she opens fêtes.'

The BBC had cancelled his show and Channel 4 were cool after the ferocious press response to his over-exposure, so Jamie had an idea. With the burgeoning trade in the new DVD market, he was no longer confined to TV. *Pukka Tukka* would give Sainsbury's new front man an opportunity to turn up the campaign for cooking simply, with mainstream ingredients from the local supermarket. Asking people in the street as well as some of the market traders featured in *The Naked Chef* and his best mates how often they cook, he took us by the hand and showed us how to cook a fabulous meal for next to nothing.

Jamie took us to market, not just to Sainsbury's but to Berwick Street market in the middle of London's Soho, just as he had done in *The Naked Chef*. He shopped locally and talked to producers. He took us back to the land to markets in the middle of our own cities. 'Jamie's ideas are not just about the recipes, but the way he cooks,' said fellow chef Jean-Christophe Novelli (The White Horse, Harpenden). 'He made the connection between the producers, the growers and the food he cooks – that's the difference. Whatever he takes out, he puts back. I like that. Most people don't do that.'

It was also an opportunity to have a laugh. Picking on his best mate Jimmy, who at the time was at university in Coventry, he took his favourite crew with him to make an episode about cooking on a student budget. It was a ruse for a good few nights out with his best mate. 'I got debagged by Jamie and Jimmy in a hotel in Coventry,' said sound man Rupert Ivey. 'Jimmy's a bright boy, very hard-working, but very funny and the two of them together are great.' With the negative press campaign at its height, Rupert said Jamie felt the knives were out. 'He could just about get away with it with a bunch of mates around him at the time, and we had a blast. They're all very loyal, those mates. But he did protect himself a bit more afterwards. It didn't change him, though. That's the thing about him – he's never changed. From the time when he was in the background action of The River Café documentary to if he walked in right now, he'd be exactly the same.' Ivey says that although they are still very good mates, 'you don't see people when they become superstars – I think their lives are just so full. I used to go to his birthday parties and round for tea and all that, but I think we like to hang out with people that are similar to us.'

Working with Jamie was a breeze. Unlike many of the celebrities the crew worked with, his fame appeared to be a by-product of what he was doing and he wins friends every time he goes on location. 'Every time, it's straight in – "How you doing?"' said one of his crew. 'He's completely in your face first thing in the morning. He gives people nicknames; he refers to his mates as "Jimmy the Pig Man" or "Andy the Gasman". But he does it to everyone, probably because he never remembers your real name.' 'He gets bloody bored quite quickly,' said another crew member. 'He's very fidgety and we do long, long days with him.' Jamie passes the time by telling little anecdotes and gives the crew some ideas and recipes he's just come up with. 'He does go to his Winnebago for a rest,' said a crew member, 'but not for long; he needs other people. He doesn't want to separate himself; he'd get bored by himself. He loves being with the boys, and loves to talk titillation and childish stuff.'

By the beginning of 2002 independent research had shown that the Jamie Oliver Sainsbury's advertising campaign had been one of their most successful to date. The supermarket giant was said to have offered him another £2 million for the next year, a drop in the £740 million ocean of extra revenue towards which Jamie was supposed to have contributed. For Sainsbury's, whose fortunes were sliding, compared to the might of Tesco in the lead and the positioning of Waitrose on one side and Asda on the other, Jamie was an unprecedented marketing phenomenon. In just six weeks his first-ever ad for a lads' night prawn curry rocketed the sales of prawns by 900 per cent. The British larder was bulging with whole nutmegs after Jamie suggested it was just the job for a pukka Spaghetti Bolognese. Weekly sales of jars of nutmeg rose from 1,400 to 6,000, prompting Sainsbury's to order in two years' worth of stock. Buyers were even sent out into the field to source new supplies to meet demand. It was the same with vanilla pods after Jamie told us he popped them in jars of sugar, and even gave them away as presents to his mates. 'We haven't seen anything like it since Delia and the cranberries,' said a Sainsbury's spokesman.

'Jamie Oliver has had an amazing influence over the way that food is being chosen and eaten,' said David Lewis of Green Core Foods, which supplies Tesco, Waitrose, Somerfield, The Co-op and Morrisons with chilled foods. 'Delia did it with chicken livers, too. The week after she used them in a recipe, they had sold out in stores.' Ann Taruschio, who with her husband Franco (godfather of Italian food in the UK and previously of The Walnut Tree, Abergavenny), is now a consultant for Tesco, is less than impressed: 'Tesco love him because everything that he cooks on TV, they have to copy in their chilled foods. No one actually cooks what he tells them to.'

Tom Aikens wants to see Jamie use his influence to get rid of ready meals completely. 'It breaks up families,' he said. 'There's no centre of the home if you watch TV with a ready meal. What about people cooking, laughing and enjoying themselves together? We've got four or five aisles of ready meals in our supermarkets, but if you go to France you won't see any except for a few by Rubicon and Ducasse, and that's it. Europeans are brought up with food since they were toddlers. They don't rely on the supermarkets like we do.'

But David Lewis says the slow food movement is beginning to have a place among the aisles of packaged goods and chilled foods. 'There are big projects under way to capture better meat quality and better meat cuts, and to show off and be really proud of what they're offering the industry,' he told me. 'Historically a lot of the retailers were slaughtering animals and packing it, and getting it onto the shelves within 14–18 days. Ideally they should be more matured and tender, and had more time to relax.' 'Take pork belly,' he said. 'We developed something in the "Finest" range that was using pork belly. There's always going to be the odd person who doesn't like fat in their food, but on the whole people are becoming more aware of the natural attributes of their ingredients. The problem we have had with convenience foods taking over our lives certainly stems from the lack of food education in schools. There's a whole generation who have grown up without cooking or even seeing meat, or using it in Home Economics. People are working more and buying more convenience offerings, and retailers have cashed in on that and not offered it as a whole food.'

I asked him whether the Soil Association's campaign to encourage us to buy locally could ever influence supermarkets. 'That does happen to a certain extent,' he said. 'There are regional offerings sourced from local suppliers, like Devonshire Clotted Cream in Devon and Cornwall and Somerset, but not in Scotland. There's a big push on us to do seasonal food and fresh food without so many air miles. People do want that. But we have to be realistic. We produce 1.3 million meals a week. Can you imagine getting enough local carrots to meet that demand? Most local farmers wouldn't be able to meet that.'

Craig Sams of the Soil Association disagrees and says it's all about consumer demand. 'At the moment, big supermarkets operate on a colonial basis where they're sucking more of the local money out of the areas they serve than they put in. But all the supermarkets are looking over their shoulder at Wal-Mart. Asda is the only supermarket that's in trouble at the moment and they're the ones who've been most resistant to organic.' (They don't even sell Sams' Green & Black's organic chocolate.) 'Lee Scott, the CEO of Wal-Mart, gave a speech at their last AGM and said, "We've got to take the environment into account and set up targets. We've got to have a minimum wage." He didn't say anything about the minimum wage in China, which is where their stuff comes from,' he noted.

Lizzie Vann, author of *Food for Life*, notices the changes occurring in the way supermarkets source their foods. 'Sainsbury's has worked hard to enable it to know where, for example, its beef comes from. The public can trace from a label via a website to the name of the farm that the animal was raised on. And Waitrose is able to grow some of what they sell on their own farms.' But to be able to supply local meat to local stores is a much harder task, she says. 'Supermarkets are built to be efficient in the way they buy and sell food. They amalgamate large quantities of food and they get it out to their stores, and by being superefficient, which means they can sell it at the lower prices that people want to pay. Once you start changing that supply chain to supply local produce to local stores, it creates a lot of cost in the way the supermarkets operate.'

She says Asda has made a lot of progress in the way that it buys. 'Asda is making a big effort to work with the farmers. Supermarkets have been accused of exploiting farmers. As a result they have decided that the best way to counter that is to have better relationships and long-term contracts. I'm not saying it's the answer to "buying local" but it's a start. Asda should be applauded. And the more the public recognises that, the more that they'll do it because they just want to satisfy their customers.'

With Foot and Mouth Disease robbing the British economy of billions of pounds in lost farming and tourism revenue by 2001 when it was discovered in an Essex abattoir, the British began to study where their meat was coming from. Ian and Denise Bell of Dorset pig farm Heritage Prime say that the culinary revolution, although still very much in its infancy, was, in no small part, ignited by their own efforts. 'We set out first to restore the true value of "eating quality" and secondly, to prove how this was only possible if true value was given back to the livestock whose flesh we eat, this value being both morally and spiritually correct,' said Ian Bell. 'We set a higher benchmark than ever set before in all of these areas. What became very obvious was just how little experience even some notable chefs – to say nothing of Joe Bloggs – had had of what should be normal but is in fact exceptional meat. Their generation was the first to be deprived of it due to the advent of the supermarket culture. Novel at first, but destructive in the extreme in reality.'

Jamie's mission with Sainsbury's may be about making good food more accessible and encouraging us to take our time to cook and eat, but he hopes that as we fall in love with food again, we will become more interested in where it comes from and the kind of people who dedicate their lives to their passion for good food. Sally Clarke is one chef who thinks Jamie has achieved what he set out to do. 'Jamie, more than most, has made the fishing rod easier to use,' she said. 'It's not just the lucky ones in the South who can find the decent cheese or lamb, or duck. It's throughout the land now, and I'm sure that he's been instrumental in that.'

The Bells say that it is virtually unheard of in today's world for a farmer to breed, rear and finish his livestock, 'still less to do it according to bio-dynamic principles and without ever using even the merest chemical or pharmaceutical substance. What they get in return is food that imparts discernible health and vitality, courtesy of some very noble creatures whose immune systems are remarkable and whose resilience, nurtured by the farmer's very presence and commitment, is astonishing. Clearly, although the supermarkets may use the same language, they would never countenance the idea of doing things this way; the reality of supermarket sourcing, especially and particularly in meat, is that "Every Little Hurts!" 'It may be Tesco's slogan,' said Sams. 'But in fact, saving those last few pennies is what causes so much pain to producers, with a knock-on effect on animal welfare.'

Sally Clarke thinks that Heritage Prime is out of most people's league, although she backs them on their commitment to their pigs. 'That's the higher end of the market,' she said. 'There's no middle ground at the moment. I would like to see the Jamie Oliver vein extend to the concentration on the product and its provenance. I'd like to see the growers and the farmers themselves have the sales that they so desperately need.' She said we only need to look to France to see what is possible. 'People buy their food at market – they create the need. And in Italy and probably in Spain, it's the same to a lesser degree. Our climate isn't that different to France.'

David Lewis commented that Jamie's campaigns to push us to stock up on basic cooking ingredients are something that companies like Green Core (which have to list the ingredients in their convenience foods) are also responding to. 'Most certainly there has been a massive push within the business to store cupboard development. Twelve months ago you would have looked at the back of a pack of a ready meal and there would have been emulsifiers and all sorts of stuff that you wouldn't recognise. We made a conscious decision whenever we made a sauce that needed thickening to use cornflour instead of using a modified starch. There's nothing wrong with a modified starch – it's only modified to make it heat stable. There's nothing sinister in it. But that's what's happening; we're reacting to what Jamie is doing to encourage us to be more aware of what we're eating.'

Farmers' markets, says Jamie, are where we should be taking our custom every weekend. 'Markets can sell more cheaply because they don't need to have chiller lorries going up and down the motorway, or have to negotiate with companies like mine [Baby Organix],' said Lizzie Vann. 'They just don't have those overheads; a farmer gets in his lorry from 20 miles away and sells his produce. And you can educate people about where their food comes from.'

Chef and food writer Stephanie Alexander looks on from Melbourne with interest at the changing food scene in Britain. 'As an observer, the supply of ingredients is better in London now,' she said. 'It's not as democratic as it is in Australia, though. You can shop for amazing ingredients now in Notting Hill but it is still based on class. In Australia there are markets in all the city centres except Sydney. We have fabulous fresh food markets in Melbourne. It's a phenomenon of our capital cities.'

With sales of organic food in the UK topping £1 billion by 2003 and three out of four babies eating organic foods regularly, Gennaro Contaldo is proud of his 'London son'. 'I can actually stand back and say to Jamie – "Fantastic. Well done!" He made food easier and more accessible. In ten years' time I can see a new generation will lead a better life. Food *is* life and now we are beginning to appreciate good food that is accessible. Let's see what we can do to find good food for lower prices.' He says that it is Jamie who introduced the idea of local and seasonal produce to supermarket shoppers. 'If you're Scottish, you'll begin to buy in Scotland; if you're in Wales, you'll look for Welsh. I see it growing magnificently. We'll try things out – we're so much more broad minded than other cultures.'

CHAPTER 18

HAPPY DAYS

While Jamie was sitting in board meetings and taking his crew out on the road, his confidence after the press bashing may have been knocked, but it wasn't down. He had reason to feel on top of his game: *The Naked Chef* was the first British cookery programme ever to be sold to France, Italy and Spain. By 2001 the programme was broadcast in 34 different countries on 60 channels. Jamie was doing all the big-name chat shows in America and was about to tour New Zealand and Australia.

His arrogance might have been raising the hackles of the press pack, but he was right: the idea of a British chef teaching Italians, Spanish and French to cook is unheard of. Even Jean-Christophe Novelli's mother is a fan. 'She told me, "That James, he's very nice,"' said Jean-Christophe. 'I thought James? James who? Oh, please not that James Martin! But I knew she meant Jamie Oliver because he was on French TV. He's fantastic. Jamie is a modern Marco Pierre White. He's got that smile, that charm.'

In a country known for its own hubris, particularly around cooking, Jean-Christophe says this is praise indeed. 'In France the press always reports on the chefs who have the Michelin stars, not people like Jamie. They have no interest in imaginative people like him. But French people watch him on TV and they like him because they think he's cute, but also they like what he does with food. French people really know what to do with food but they love him there. I wouldn't have thought it could happen.' A good

PR company perhaps? I asked. 'French people don't give a fuck about PR!' said Jean-Christophe dismissively. 'If you're in business and you succeed in America, you can succeed anywhere, but if you're a chef and you succeed in France, you've really made it.'

It seemed that Jamie had a touch that was more than common; it was universal. But we were beginning to learn that Jamie Oliver was not just a real talent but someone with communication skills Tony Blair would have killed for. As more people came across the real thing, word spread that this man had charisma the size of his global market share. The performer in Jamie had been hindered by the process of television. Endless takes and new set-ups, tape changes and lighting being re-jigged are the reality of the glamorous TV presenter's day at work. While the BBC licked its wounds and Channel 4 held a cool distance, Jamie's energy bubbled like a pot waiting for fresh pasta. He had an idea. The pop star drummer in him ached for a live audience, while his hurt inner child begged public adulation in the wake of the stoning by the press.

'*Friends* meets *Naked Chef* live' was the 'dream' he sold to Mark McCormack's International Management Group. This would be much more than a Good Food Show style cookery demo and would feature his supporting cast – the Boys from Montes – going out on the town and The Lovely Jools, on a vast video screen with bun in the oven, apparently calling him via 3G to ask him to whip up a little something while she scooped up another tiny top at Agnès B.

When Jamie came bouncing onto the stage of the Hammersmith Apollo in September 2001 with his signature 'Oy oy!' anyone in the audience would have been hard pushed to believe his star had even so much as wobbled in the past year. Bursting through a screen onto the stage on his scooter, he invited members of the audience up for a bit of 'champagne, white wine, beer, whatever you like, love'. He showed us around his comedy kitchen, opening a fake window to tear off some herbs from his rainforest of a window box, and proving his bread in a mock airing cupboard until it grew to panto-sized proportions. Here was Jamie Oliver putting his popular touch into fifth gear, cruising through the show as if born to be on stage. As members of the audience donned their pinnies to help him with his pasta challenge, he was as effortless with a four-year-old boy as a Spanish housewife. Bashing the digestive biscuits with the four-year-old and making gags about wrist action with a 30-year-old bloke, this was *The Galloping Gourmet* mixed with *The Generation Game*; even Jamie's asides to camera were straight out of presenter Bruce Forsyth's notebook.

The 'Happy Days' show would have 17,000 people packing into theatres in Cambridge, Bournemouth and London to experience Jamie live in the kitchen before touring in Australia and New Zealand, where he played to sold-out crowds in seven cities. Up until now, his experience had been limited to playing the Ugly Sister in a school play and the drums in his band Scarlet Division. 'They were like my second family, really, the band,' said Jamie. 'It was an excuse to get great people together and create something from nothing, even if it was a sack of shit.'

While Jamie went to catering college, his fellow band members, Leigh Haggerwood and Louise Brannon, had gone off on their own world tour and even appeared on Canadian TV as part of an Amnesty International concert. By the time they came to London, Jamie was already working at The River Café and with Hammersmith Apollo only down the road, he began to dream again about being a rock star. They started to rehearse again, this time with a guitarist and bass player with track records and contacts, and even as Jamie morphed from sous chef to TV's Naked Chef, he boasted he never missed a single rehearsal.

While Jamie was sliding down his TV spiral staircase and leaping on his scooter in search of a bit of banter with a market trader or a fishmonger, it was Sony BMG who spotted the lucrative potential of the young chef's connection with a rock'n'roll band. The £100,000 two-CD deal in 2000 would be kicked off with a compilation of the soundtrack of *The Naked Chef. Cookin'* featured Jamie's favourite band Toploader's 'Dancing In The

Moonlight', his mate Fatboy Slim's 'Right Here Right Now' and Nineties classic bands like Sneaker Pimps, Manic Street Preachers and The Wonder Stuff. It was music to cook to, but when the second album was released and Scarlet Division's single 'Sundial' reached only number 42 in the charts, they were unceremoniously dropped. Jamie blamed himself and the media backlash for halting them in their tracks.

But the friendship lasted, particularly with his childhood chum Leigh Haggerwood. 'He is amazingly generous,' Leigh told the Biography Channel. 'In 2001 I was diagnosed with Hodgkin's disease, a cancer of the lymphoma, and I told Jamie that I had to wait six weeks to have a CAT scan on the NHS.' Within 24 hours Jamie had arranged for Leigh to see a specialist in London's Harley Street and paid for seven months of chemotherapy. 'He didn't think twice about it,' said Leigh, now fully recovered.

A year later Jamie was still banging his head in London's sweaty underground venues, but Jamie Oliver, The Naked Chef, was live on stage at the Apollo Hammersmith, playing his drums between dishes as if his life depended on it. 'My dad would never have let me be a rock star, to be honest,' he said as the performer in him took a bow.

CHAPTER 19

FAITH, HOPE AND CHARITY

Taking the 'Happy Days' tour on the road was a chance for Jamie to get some perspective. As he crossed New Zealand and Australia, he knew better than to worry too much about idle hacks looking for the next celebrity to expose a weak spot. His is a rare breed of man whose energy is irrepressible. Jamie's altruistic spirit is, according to personality experts, often driven by the need to please a parent, and he has always attributed his drive to the influence of his father. He had also spent his formative years pleasing Gennaro Contaldo, and at The River Café learning about the greater good of Italian food culture. 'I would like to think that a good meal makes people happy,' mused Ruth Rogers, 'and we have a better society. What Jamie did was that he took it into a different social consciousness.'

Given the strength of the venom thrown in his direction now, it was time for Jamie to rise above pleasing his dad and go straight for public adulation. He had an idea. 'About seven years ago, when I'd just started working at The River Café,' he wrote in *Jamie's Kitchen* (although he later said the idea came to him at The Neal Street Restaurant), 'I was having a cup of tea with a friend, Kirsty. At the time she was working with problem children – aggressive and bad-tempered, they weren't fitting into their school or home environments very well – and she was explaining to me that the main thing was to inspire and empower them, and to give them some hands-on responsibility. She said that cooking classes had been going really well with them because they could feel, smell and create things, and above all it was fun. Plus they could eat what they'd made! I realised that my biggest weapon in life was the determination, enthusiasm, hands-on and "actions speak louder than words" approach my father taught me, and I wanted to get this across to others, especially those interested in food. Having had five really great years, I felt it was about time to give a little back and help inspire others.'

The idea was sound, if ambitious. Jo Bates works with young offenders in Brighton. 'If you stick beside someone who is dysfunctional or damaged,' she told me, 'and you consistently give them the same message, they will eventually come round. But they need a lot of time, space and dedication. Very often there's just not enough time to invest in young people.'

Jamie's idea was to train a team of unemployed kids from inner London to become chefs in his very first restaurant. Rather than looking for slave labour as some early critics suggested, this was an opportunity to take learning to cook to a new level through the magic of TV as Channel 4's cameras recorded the entire project. The idea had first been offered to the BBC and titled *Oliver's Army* but it was rejected. After the break with Pat Llewellyn, Channel 4 offered Jamie a new start, and with average weekly audiences well over five million, *Jamie's Kitchen* would become one of the channel's top two shows of the year in 2002 and be shown in 34 countries.

If Jamie Oliver could offer hope to kids whose personal problems had prevented them even finding a bed for the night, how easy would it be to persuade the rest of us that cooking was a life-saver? Food was the medium that would transform their lives, as it had for those gypsy friends of his in Clavering who sniffed the pickle in their baps for the first time and decided there was more to life than jam sandwiches. 'He couldn't think of a business idea,' said a member of the crew. 'That wouldn't be the way he thought up Fifteen. It's a heart-felt thing that he did without a doubt. It was a gut reaction and not a business plan.'

His vision was wildly optimistic. He would open a first-class restaurant in a London now rich with good restaurants and run it as a charity with profits poured back into scholarships to send graduates off to work with some of the best chefs in Britain, Italy, France, Australia and Japan. 'Just look at the difference that the Roux brothers, Marco Pierre White and Gordon Ramsay have made in such a short period of time,' he said. 'They are all incredible chefs and we should aspire to be as good as they are. Together they have broken the mould for British food and now their protégés are continuing in their footsteps and cooking to a brilliantly high standard.' With his trainees going into the restaurant industry, their cooking skills honed by some of the best players in the game, and a track record of changing their own lives through his influence, what contribution would Jamie have made to the greater world of food, not just in Britain but across the world, too?

He would call upon the people he had already worked with like Gennaro Contaldo, Rose Gray and Ruth Rogers and a team of people who had taught him so much about food in the short time he had been in London. They would offer his trainees work placements and, if they were good enough after the course, a job. Even the doyenne of the Californian food scene, Alice Waters, agreed to take part. Patricia Michelson, whose cheese shop La Fromagerie he had visited during *The Naked Chef*; David Gleave of Liberty Wines, who had taught him about olive oil and wine; Peter Gott, whose farm in Cumbria would be used to demonstrate to students how to cure the best pigs and wild boar; and Ruth Watson, food writer and chef/patron at his mother's favourite gastro pub, The Crown and Castle in Suffolk, were all on board to act as mentors as he put the last pieces in place. All he had to do now was find the students. Sending 10,000 letters out to job centres and putting out an APB through London radio station XFM, Jamie called upon his old catering college, Westminster Kingsway and Hammersmith Catering College, to help him sort the wheat from the chaff.

Fifteen hundred people came to the interviews, leaving Jamie feeling simultaneously chuffed and overwhelmed by the responsibility of offering these kids a new life only to dash their hopes by the end of the day as he whittled them down to an initial 60. Jamie loved playing to the crowd of youngsters, who loved his bish-bosh TV persona, but little did they know that his success was based on the philosophy that in order to break the rules, you had to learn them first. Their interviews revealed a desperate lack of awareness about food among 16–24-year-olds on the streets of London. Mashed potatoes and pizza were their favourite food, and most showed almost no interest in cooking. Those who were chosen were the ones whose game was raised if only slightly. 'Spaghetti Bolognese' – 'In'; 'Rice and peas' – 'We'll have him'; 'Sunday roast' – 'Yup'; 'Moussaka' – 'Sign her up!' As the rejects burst into tears, Jamie hugged as many as he could. 'We'll get you on the course you want,' he said. 'Come and see us next year. Promise?' It was *Pop Idol* all over again.

With a group of 30 potential chefs to shape into a cast of 15, Jamie set them to work in the kitchen. They would have to watch, learn and copy a simple salmon dish and then perform a taste test. For most, the salmon was a disaster and the taste test a depressing revelation about the palates of the young and dispossessed. There was also the reality of their situation: 'I've got a problem with cooking for myself at the moment,' said one. 'I'm living in a hostel.' Jamie was undeterred. 'I want to know what you're feeling,' he said as he popped oysters into their mouths. 'Go on, my son,' he said, offering various morsels up to the 29 other mouths. 'Try that, gorgeous.' Not one could come up with the 'sour', 'sweet', 'crunchy', 'silky' that he was aching to hear. As 17-year-old Michael Pizzey, a hyperactive dyslexic from Middlesex, spat his oyster straight into a napkin, he wasn't the only one who was astonished. 'But he was the one who was passionate about food when I talked to him on the phone,' stuttered associate producer Zoe Collins.

Her confidence was vindicated by Pizzey's enthusiasm as he produced the salmon dish that would earn him a place on the

A Huckleberry Finn childhood in the Essex countryside.

Alistair Little, the Jamie Oliver of the Eighties.

Marco Pierre White, gastro-punk role model for a whole new generation of chefs.

The River Café family: Jamie with Ruth Rogers.

Jamie and Jools
move into the
limelight together.

Jools with her new father-in-law, Trevor Oliver.

'Like swans', the lovebirds finally get married in a thirteenth-century church in the heart of the Essex countryside.

Jamie and his 'London Dad': Gennaro Contaldo
of Passione restaurant, London.

Fifteen: Playing Dad at work, as well as at home.

Changing the world, with a little help from dinner lady Nora Sands in Channel 4's *School Dinners*.

Discussing revolution over tea with the then Prime Minister, Tony Blair.

Life's a beach: Jamie opens Fifteen at Watergate Bay, Cornwall in 2006.

Growing his own: Jamie promotes copies of his new book *Jamie at Home* at Borough Market in London in 2007.

Cooking with the big boys: with Tom Cruise and David Letterman in 2006.

'We represent two pieces of a puzzle that fit perfectly together' – Alice Waters of Chez Panisse on Jamie Oliver and their plans for a revolution in American food.

course. 'It's indescribable how I felt,' he told the camera, shaking. 'I loved the way everything had to be done in time. I'm well chuffed.' But the panel were divided; 'He's a nice boy,' said Gennaro, who sees the best in everyone. 'I worry about him,' said Ruth Watson, concerned that Pizzey was typical of those in thrall to Jamie the famous chef and whose commitment to the project was based on the desire to be on TV. 'He's enthusiastic, but he needs support, and it would break him if he was abandoned later on,' she warned. 'I think we should give him a chance,' said Jamie, following the line of his mentor. 'Let's do it.'

The tabloids were typically sceptical, and as Jamie's credibility was still in the dock, they played dirty. The *Daily Mirror* was among those who sent undercover journalists as potential trainees to see what dirt they might bring home, but they could find nothing to report. Reporter, Stephanie Young was chosen as one of the final 15 and remembers her experience with nothing but genuine fondness and respect for Jamie's commitment. 'After barely two minutes in the company of Jamie Oliver, I found myself swept up in his arms,' she reported later. The reason for this spontaneous display of affection? 'As part of the selection process, I was performing a taste test to identify different flavours under his close scrutiny and I was very nervous. So violently was I shaking that Jamie stopped me, reached over the counter and hugged me, reassuringly. To him I was just another young hopeful from a disadvantaged background whose dreams of being a chef were on the verge of being realised, someone for whom he could make a difference.'

If Young was impressed, Jamie was appalled. 'There's me trying to fuckin' train 15 underprivileged kids and one of them's a fuckin' blagging journalist. It was sick. And at the end of the day, she was never going to find me fucking a receptionist or doing lines of coke because I'm not like that. I'm quite boring in many ways.' Other critics were quick to point out that of the underprivileged youngsters providing the drama for the series, those who survived were mostly from a middle-class background. Nineteen-year-old Johnny Broadfoot's father owned an apartment in Kensington and a restaurant in Sydney. Ralph Johnson, a 20-year-old 'A' level art student, had opted out of his foundation course, while 22-year-old Roberto di Mambro had been a wine-taster for Marks & Spencer and was considering his options, 24-year-old Turkish born Elisa Roche was a drop-out of Edinburgh University.

By the third intake, Jamie said, 'About a third are on loan from prison so they get out early, a third are post-prison and a third homeless, so give or take a couple of students, that is it.' At least this is what in 2005 he told journalist Simon Hattenstone, who found that this was not quite true. 'His press officer tells me that, of 21 students, six were homeless, six had a record, two of whom had been in prison, and nine were relatively normal,' wrote Hattenstone in the *Guardian*. 'Some of the students in the original series complained that they were presented as a bunch of miscreants when they'd led perfectly decent lives. Oliver may not have much of a head for figures, but he has always known the value of a good sell, even if that occasionally means economising with the truth.'

If Jamie wasn't going to spell it out, it was an opportunity for the rest of the world to see that it's not just the disadvantaged who can't find their way, that there are more complicated reasons why young people end up on the streets. 'I've had lots of different jobs,' said Elisa, who would quickly rise to prominence in *Jamie's Kitchen*. 'I've worked in a fish and chip shop, been a researcher at a newspaper, an air hostess and worked in pubs when travelling.' She dropped out of her degree course in French and Art History at Edinburgh University, and when she came home from a year out in Martinique, she found it difficult to get a job. 'Things got difficult for me at home and I ended up living in various hostels for seven months. It was hard looking for work. I didn't have much money for clothes for interviews and I'd go to Internet cafés or the Job Centre to use their computer to apply. It was hard to remain persistent. A lot of people in that situation get despondent. My friend heard about the course and didn't want to do it, but I applied. I had a group of friends from the hostel who were all rooting for me to get through.'

Even Kerryann Dunlop, who stole the show for her ballsy 'Am I bovvered?' attitude, had worked in a kitchen before, and knew enough of the ropes. 'I did a year at the Butler's Wharf Chef School, which went bust halfway through,' she explained. 'I'd already done my NVQ2 [National Vocational Qualification] for front of house and for the kitchen. When it closed I was very disheartened and got quite down in the dumps. I worked in a baker's for a while and thought about going back to college to do social care but I knew I really wanted to be a chef. Then I heard about this course, so I went for it.'

In terms of television, it meant that a tight band of educated middle-class kids would provide the rock solid brigade that would underpin the success of the project – and Jamie's future restaurant. With only £40 a week plus travel expenses, it was inevitably those who had had a better start who would last. It was enough for Ben Frow, commissioning editor at Channel 4, to give Jamie his break from *The Naked Chef* and the BBC, and cast him into the rough seas of reality TV.

CHAPTER 20

THE PARTY'S OVER

After the happy days of *The Naked Chef* under the direction of Pat Llewellyn, Channel 4's *Jamie's Kitchen* was a darker beast with Jamie using the F word within the first couple of minutes. His bouncy enthusiasm ('I haven't been this excited in I can't tell you how long') was an edgy presence against the realists from industry who made up the selection panel. Even the title sequence had the e's falling off with a clatter. The party was over, it was saying, and Jamie's work was cut out if he wanted his passion for food to really make a difference to the students themselves, his TV audience and the wider food industry. 'I'm proud of all the *Naked Chef* stuff,' he said. 'It was all about a young chef cooking good food at home for his friends and family. It was a very happy, upbeat thing and it did well. But this is a different animal.'

Jools, meanwhile, was heavily pregnant and with Jamie immersed in his new project, she was becoming increasingly upset at the amount of time he was spending away from home. From the silent doghouse treatment in *The Naked Chef* to the ditzy pregnant shopaholic begging to be fed on the 'Happy Days' tour, Jools' TV presence to date had been a side show. With Channel 4's reality theme, hers was now the supporting role. 'We just don't get any quality time,' she told him in the back of a cab, the director choosing to position her in the background while Jamie sulked in the fore. 'You may come in, but you jump straight on the computer,' she hissed. 'I get weekends off,' he protested. 'No, you don't!' she retorted. 'I get Sundays off,' said Jamie, refusing to roll over, and dismissed her with a wave of the hand and a lack of respect that couples would recognise as the privilege of intimates. The next shot showed them back to the camera, Jools obviously in tears, Jamie's arm around her in a placatory gesture.

The use of the scene caused consternation among critics and fans. With his own cameras filming his real life drama, the thin line between telling it how it is and exploiting his nearest and dearest became frayed. For the first time, the public sided with Jools, until now represented on impressionist shows as the wife sidling into the limelight and basking in his reflected glory, with pages in the tabloids dedicated to the debate. She even consulted lawyers and tried to get the scene cut. Simon Hattenstone raised the subject in his interview with Jamie for the *Guardian*. 'She never signed a release form, which every production company in the world is obsessed about getting, which is full of shit,' Jamie told him. 'Now I say to her, don't bother getting a release form. They don't mean shit!' Hattenstone, like the rest of us, felt his indignation appeared disingenuous: '*Jamie's Kitchen* was co-produced by his own company, Fresh One productions,' he wrote. 'If he really wanted the scene cut, surely he could have insisted?' 'No, because whenever you hire a producer or director, if you want anyone that is good, I've always handed over complete editorial control.' Jamie is right; the scenes at home were more memorable than some of the social politics he brought to light and any director worth his Maldon Sea Salt would have pushed to include the scenes – but at what personal cost?

Jamie's lack of diplomacy was becoming hurtful as Jools reached the end of her pregnancy. Her obsession with reading up about the process and her preparation for the birth were not something she had been able to share with him as much as she would have liked with him. His misplaced priorities meant that they would almost always arrive late for the Monday night ante-natal classes that she found so supportive. For him, his work was his passion, and while both of them were thrilled with the prospect of becoming a family, Jamie was proving not to be quite the New Man that he might have been.

With a week to go before due date, they were set to move to a new flat. As Jools cleaned and bleached their new home to prepare it for their new baby, Jamie decided to organise a photo shoot featuring him cooking sausages on their new Aga. 'As my sister and I were grappling with the baby's cradle in the nursery, surrounded by screws and instructions, something boiled up inside me and I just exploded with anger,' she wrote in her book *Minus Nine to One*. 'I stormed down the stairs and into the living room and raged as I watched Jamie and about seven other media magazine types mmmming and ahhing like spectators at a firework display.' She blames her hormones for an outburst she says was out of character. 'I think I shouted something like "Where are my bloody sausages, you selfish *******!"' and then stood back while the entire crew – including Jamie – leapt to her aid. By the end of the day, she had not only got her sausages, but the cradle was finished and all the boxes had been unpacked. Jamie, however, was back at work.

As Fresh One sent its cameras to join the paparazzi at Queen Charlotte & Chelsea Hospital, it seemed that Jamie Oliver had sold himself to the devil. 'The missus is not very happy you lot are here,' he told his own cameraman before excusing himself to watch his baby daughter's birth. What we didn't know when he came back – with the magic of television, only seconds later – to tell us that he was the proud father of Poppy Honey was that all had not quite gone as planned.

CHAPTER 21

BECOMING A FAMILY

Jools had been planning this pregnancy for years. With a history of polycystic ovaries, a condition that can affect a woman's menstrual cycle, fertility and hormones, amongst other things, it had been difficult for her to conceive. With the punishing schedule of her superstar partner, the odds were seriously stacked against them.

Jools had a plan. She had never made any claims to want a career, preferring the retro glamour of becoming a domestic goddess to earning a crust. But back in 2000 her boyfriend was still on the way to making their fortune and the bills had to be paid. Jools had flitted from job to job as a part-time model and a waitress, even trying her hand as a BBC TV researcher, and eventually decided to have a go at organising Jamie's life as his PA in a vain attempt to keep up with his increasingly busy schedule. Until then he had been scribbling down details of his meetings on pieces of paper and relying on an old notepad, and Jools had seen an opportunity to spend more time with her new husband and earn a bit of cash for herself into the bargain.

When being a PA didn't turn out to be quite as easy as it seemed, she was quickly replaced by one of her best friends and happily swapped the job of fielding calls from journalists to lolling away the hours at Harvey Nicks. But although Jools was ready to give up the day job, she was still adamant she would organise Jamie's days for far more practical reasons than simply wanting to wear the trousers. Her wall charts, on which she had carefully planned out her husband's meetings, were also studded with red and white markings denoting 'the good days for a bit of lovin''. If they were to have a baby, it was vital Jamie was around when the going was good.

But it was to be much trickier than they had imagined. Jools chronicled the entire adventure in her astonishing 2005 confessional *Minus Nine to One, Diary of an Honest Mum*, which is either a testament to her perception of her celebrity status, or a fabulously direct one in the eye for the intrusive tabloids. If you can't beat 'em, she seemed to be saying, make your own fortune with a top 10 bestseller. And how she must have relished the fact that some of the details were enough to make the toughest of male hacks squirm.

The tales of the inevitable legs in the stirrups under the guidance of IVF pioneer Sir Robert Winston's team and the race against time to deliver Jamie's sperm from Hampstead to The Queen Charlotte and Chelsea Hospital in Hammersmith are the stuff of girly gossip. It's the kind of chat Jools and her ladies who lunch would have happily swapped over a glass or two. In the book she laughs at the bizarre nature of celebrity as she recalls the moment when Jamie, scooter helmet still in place, hands over the precious phial to the hospital receptionist. As he attempts to beat a hasty retreat, she recognises him and, phial still in hand, calls her colleagues over to get a closer look at the Naked Chef.

She even performed a service to sufferers of the estimated 10% of women of childbearing age who suffer from polycystic ovaries with her intimate descriptions of the side effects of drugs like Clomid, which she was prescribed. The stress was taking its toll, she told us, as she shared her panic attacks and bouts of intense dizziness and nausea with her readers, as well as her stoic demands that they adhere to their rigorous baby-making schedule. Most notably, it's the fairy tale ending, with their two perfect babies in two years, which makes her baby-pink-covered book studded with intimate family photos such a good-time read for women suffering any kind of child-bearing issues.

While it was welcomed by the many sufferers and her account litters the super-highway of the internet, the press reaction to the exclamation marks, capitals and italics as Jools nudged and winked her way through to their happy conclusion was inevitably mixed. Janet Street-Porter was less than impressed. 'As her husband's fame receives the ultimate accolade, an endorsement from Prince Charles, Mrs Jamie Oliver is the focus of much media attention as she promotes her new book, subtitled *The Diary of an Honest Mum*,' she wrote in the *Independent*. 'Jools Oliver is the Jade Goody of the moment, an engaging "ordinary" person we have only ever met through television, but who many people still find extraordinarily interesting.' Street-Porter felt that the project was 'less a useful guide to having a baby in modern Britain and more a marketing opportunity on a par with Jamie's Sainsbury's ads, cookery books and restaurant'.

It was Jamie, Street-Porter concluded, who had encouraged his wife to bare so much more than her soul. She felt they had missed an opportunity. 'If Jools and Jamie really wanted to help young women who are considering having a baby in Britain today, then perhaps he could make another television series in which he sets out the best environment in which to procreate. I don't mean sea-grass floor covering or linen sheets, but the necessity, whenever possible, of having two full-time committed parents, a stable relationship and a total commitment to nurturing your offspring morally and spiritually.'

The pair were terribly upset when the tabloids broke the news of the pregnancy before they could tell their nearest and dearest. 'What I can't understand is how the papers found out about it so early,' Jamie told them in his by now co-dependent pact with the press. 'Jools was only five weeks pregnant and we ourselves had only known about it for five days.' But their euphoria was greater than their disappointment. 'We don't know if it's a boy or girl. I wish I did,' he said. 'Nobody seems to like my choice of names though. If it's a boy I'd like to call him Elvis. I think Elvis Oliver sounds really good. And if it's a girl, I'd love to call her Honey.

I've never liked my name much. I think Jamie's a bit nancy sounding and I've always wanted to be called Seamus – that's classy.' He was thrilled at the prospect of becoming a dad. 'I'm good with kids, me,' he had told us in *The Naked Chef* when he was looking after his nieces for the day. 'I'm on their level – we all talk rubbish!'

By March 2002, with the *Jamie's Kitchen* camera crew sitting patiently in the hospital lobby, it was the moment they had been waiting for, for the last two years. But for Jamie, the anxiety was unbearable. 'I tried to reassure him that although it looked like I was in hell, really I was OK,' wrote Jools in *Minus Nine to One*, 'and he said, "Babe, I'm not worried about you – you are doing brilliantly. It's just that my chicken is in the Aga and it looks like we're in for a long night. Shall I go home and refuel so I can support you later on when you need it?"'

Jamie told journalist Miranda Sawyer that while Jools had wanted him to sit and hold her hand, he couldn't keep his eyes off the other end. 'I didn't want to miss a thing,' he said. 'And when Poppy was born I started telling the consultant what to do. I know now he wanted to tell me to shut up, but I was saying, "Shouldn't she be on all fours now, using gravity?"'

Forty-eight hours later Jamie was telling the *Jamie's Kitchen* cameras that Poppy had been born three minutes earlier. 'Now I've got to tell the mother-in-law,' he said in a hushed voice. Jamie had learnt by now that sleeping with the enemy was the smart move. 'The hospital offered to smuggle us out the back, but we knew that as well as all the mob out front, there were already five paparazzi outside our house with long lenses that could see in through the windows... So we said, "OK, we'll be out around 3.30 tomorrow. And when we came out, they were the politest I'd ever seen them – they kept saying, "Congratulations!"'

If it seems that his willingness to bow to the needs of the press is often ill-timed, his friends are not surprised. 'He will never say "no" to anyone,' said one of the crew. 'Any time the paparazzi want a picture, he'll say "yes". He'll go into bookshops and sign all the copies of his book – all the booksellers have got his mobile number. I've noticed that with all the successful people I've worked with – they always give that extra minute; they do so much PR. If you're not willing to give it 24/7, there's no point. It's not about giving up so much of what he is – maybe that's *who* he is.'

CHAPTER 22

BECOMING A DAD

Life with a newborn had all the drama and euphoria parents will remember well, but which neither Jamie nor Jools had fully anticipated. At the same time, his young charges in the kitchen were also calling more on his fledgling paternal skills than those of an employer. Although some of the trainees were the unsung heroes who kept their heads down and got the job done, *Jamie's Kitchen* preceded Channel 4's *Supernanny* in providing the kind of reality TV which concentrated on the bad guys, where the drama was in the transformation of truant into trainee chef. While those who would be sent to work at some of the world's best restaurants were almost ignored on screen, the cameras spent most of their time in the naughty zone.

They were stroppy, unable to work as a team and, to the endless frustration of teachers Mark Gautier and Peter Richards, persistent truants. Jamie's tough love didn't appear to be enough to keep them clocking in, and his decision to stick by them was the clearest sign that he had grown up. After the happy days of *The Naked Chef,* the scooter-riding Sainsbury's superstar had become a daddy and a social worker in a matter of months, and it was taking its toll.

He was withdrawn, angry and sulky but unfailingly clear about his intentions: 'I want them to be employable. I'm not doing them a favour; I'm not laying down a red carpet,' he said as Kerryann Dunlop, Nicola Andronicou and Nicola Smith consistently stayed away, blaming their personal situation on their inability to get into college on time, or even at all. Jamie took them all to task, hugging the sobbing Kerryann and Nicola 'Blonde', while begging Nicola Andronicou to explain to him how she could allow this situation to happen. 'If I'd known that I was going to get a rollicking,' he told her, 'I'd be embarrassed and I'd get my act together.'

Jo Bates explained what it's like to be a truant. 'Often they won't have any self confidence or belief in themselves, which means that they're very unmotivated.' Nicola Andronicou's glazed expression as she took Jamie's dressing down showed the chasm in understanding between mentor and trainee. 'For some young people there is an aspect of self-sabotage,' said Jo, 'they've never been offered anything before so their heads are all over the place. They don't think that they're worthy or able, so they crash before they can fail. They're not used to being in a structure; a lot of them don't know what it's like having to get up every day. I've worked with lots of people who've been offered great opportunities but they just can't do it. They don't have the internal resources. They've had too much chaos in their lives to be able to deal with a structured environment, so even if the will is there, and they're desperate for this opportunity which they know can change their whole life around, it's like a barrier is there to moving their lives forward.'

But, she said, there has to be a cut-off. 'You've got to think of the group dynamic. Working in a kitchen is a team dynamic and if one person isn't there, he's letting down everyone else. You have to look at the whole picture. For young people who have been disaffected, you have to give them a degree of opportunity to fuck up and then say, "Come on, let's try again", and then give them a lot of bolstering and it has to be very slow, very gentle. Some kids we've worked with for years. It takes them a long time to even sign on.'

But Mark Gautier and Peter Richards were shocked when Jamie gave second and third chances to the truants. 'He mollycoddled them too much,' agreed Gary Hunter, Peter Richards' former boss as head of Culinary Arts at Westminster Kingsway. 'He was almost apologetic when he got them in the kitchen, he said, "I'm sorry you're here and I do understand what you're going through, but we've got stuff to do here and I am going to try and make you a chef."' Hunter told me that they would not have been given such chances in a real education environment. 'He acted like he owed them a living,' he said.

Jo Bates explained that this is the crux to making the charity work. 'The main thing to remember is that they don't owe us anything. You don't do this work if you think you're going to get thanked. Why should they thank you? Other people get great opportunities without being beholden to their tutors and teachers all their lives.' Gennaro Contaldo, who was on the selection panel, agreed. 'It's like being a mum or a dad. You do things for the children because that's what you do. You don't want them to clap their hands and say, "Wow, Mum and Dad!" but you do it anyway. You don't do it to show them what you can do – you do it because it's natural.'

Jamie's Kitchen was filmed at Westminster and Hammersmith catering colleges, with Peter Richards teaching in the former and Mark Gautier in the latter. The gossip in both canteens was at fever pitch for the nine-month training period. 'We heard some things that were going on off-camera,' said Gary Hunter, 'and believe me, those kids had a lot of problems, a LOT of problems. Jamie just jumped off the deep end where I don't know if we would have done. I know that we're a bit elitist, but a lot of these guys have been rejected from school with all sorts of hang-ups to do with family or no family, and that's not who we look at here.'

Hunter said that at first, the infrastructure that colleges like Westminster would have was not in place. 'We have counsellors here,' he said. 'We have people to help with financial stuff – the whole lot. Jamie was lacking that in the first instance. Maybe he thought he could tap into that through Hammersmith or Westminster but he didn't use that facility.' Hunter, who watches some students – among the many more who leave with flying colours – let themselves down every year at Westminster Kingsway, believes it was the infrastructure that failed them. 'His [Jamie's] retention rate wasn't great,' he reminded me. 'I can understand why he was disappointed, but instead of him mollycoddling them, that should have gone out to an expert wing. He should have had that safety net there.'

Jamie's answer to the truancy was to ring the girls at home, or in Kerryann's case, during a shopping trip with her mum to Kent's Bluewater Shopping Centre. He wanted to give them a chance to explain, to tell them he hadn't given up on them. Sticking with them, whatever the excuse, is, according to Jo Bates, the answer. 'Some people say that's nannying but if you don't do that, nothing's going to change. A lot of social workers would disagree and say that it's babying, but my own view is that you have to encourage young people; if they haven't had that at all, they're just not going to be able to do it. Having been given a great opportunity, they're going to throw it away, and that will feed into their self-hatred.'

Jamie put his truants to work on the nightshift in the bakery with a last warning to turn up or face being thrown off the course. Despite having a young baby at home, he went too. This was his paternity leave, his self-imposed holiday to spend time with his new family, but for four nights on the trot, he was at the bakery at 2am watching the truants' every move. He was cheering them on as Kerryann developed a real skill and love for baking, and willing them to want to come back for more. 'It's 1.30am and Jools is asleep,' he told us from his cab into the bakery. 'If she knows I'm out doing this, she'll kill me. It's a bit naughty but I have to keep doing this these days.'

At home the reality of family life was kicking in, and perhaps Jamie's stints at the bakery were not quite as altruistic as they might have seemed. Jools was battling with baby Poppy's early sleep and feeding patterns, and deprived of sleep, all three of them were becoming increasingly bad tempered. 'I had started to resent Jamie,' wrote Jools, who understood the irrationality of the emotion, but cared less after weeks of not sleeping through the night. 'God forbid if he started to snore mid-feed; I think I might have killed him.' Jamie tried to help by stroking her back but she knew that by the time she looked over at him, he would already have fallen back into deep sleep. She said, 'When I look back now, I want to laugh just thinking about the dagger eyes I would give him while he made those unmistakable sleeping coos... It's not fair!'

For Jamie the problem was that he was learning to be a father in two brand new families at the same time. 'He cares,' said Gennaro. 'It's like when you have your own children; you have the babysitter, the doctor, the grandmother, but when you're the mama, you're the person who puts the hand on the child when they need you. And when you see them respond, you understand why you do it.' Jamie's loyalties were split between his life-changing experience at home and his fast-track course in looking after teenage truants at work. Michael Pizzey was particularly heartbreaking. Suffering from learning difficulties, his education had been chequered, but Jamie recognised his spark from the beginning. 'A lot of kids with attention deficit disorders tend to be very intelligent, but unable to manage it in a learning environment,' said Jo Bates. 'Their experience of school would have been insular and alienating; they're often restless in school and the cycle begins early. They might have been labelled the "naughty child" with letters home to the parents. Then they'd get ostracised from their peers because they're just too difficult, then they might get excluded. To suddenly become part of a team could just be too hard.'

Lizzie Vann, author of the Soil Association's *Food for Life* report and Baby Organix chief, said that Jamie saw something in them that he might have recognised in himself. 'That's what I think gives him such compassion. If you have something in common with them, you know that it's sometimes harder for people like them to achieve things that a normal person would, and so you want them to succeed more. I think that's what happened with the guy at Fifteen who had ADHD [Attention Deficit Hyperactivity

Disorder]. Jamie wanted to help him succeed. He saw through the problem, and he helped the guy believe in himself. He thought, "I know you, I know you're not a bad person, I'm going to help you achieve because I've overcome it. Maybe you've always been told you're never going to be anything and then Jamie comes along and says, "Yes, you can".' She thinks this happened to Jamie. 'His father encouraged him. It regenerates it, and the more the public reinforces that idea, the more confident he becomes.'

Jamie drove the 20-mile round trip to see Michael at home to try to understand the reasons behind his truancy. But however compassionate he was, however much he could empathise with his inability to concentrate, when Michael's big issue turned out to be boredom, even Jamie was lost for words. 'I don't know what to say,' said Jamie on his way home. 'I thought he was going to give me a whole load of reasons for not wanting to do the course, and all I get is that he's fucking bored!' Within a few weeks, Michael had been suspended for verbally abusing Sheila Fraser, head tutor at Hammersmith, and would not be allowed back on the course until the following year. Jo Bates wasn't surprised: 'The identity of the "naughty child" snowballs, and without it these young people can become lost. It's something that they've created and it's hard to let it go.'

It was the same for the joker in the pack, the kid who would not pay attention and always played the fool. Nineteen-year-old Dwayne Monford couldn't resist it, and it wasn't long before he too was riding for a fall. 'A lot of people get credibility for the first time when they do something wrong, or make people laugh,' said Jo. 'They've never had any status or acknowledgement before from any adult or peer and even if it's wrong, it's going to make them feel really good.'

But for Jamie it was a test of his patience, his professional credibility as a TV chef, and his wallet.

CHAPTER 23

LOVE IS THE MESSAGE

By June, with a couple of months to go before the opening of Fifteen, the costs of the project had escalated from £450k to £1.3 million and Jamie had put his home and office on the line without consulting Jools. Using the camera as his confessional, he knew it wasn't a real betrayal; Jools, like the rest of the world, would realise Jamie had nothing to hide as soon as she saw the programme, wouldn't she? By that time, Jamie hoped, the mess would be sorted and his supreme confidence in the project vindicated.

Jamie vented his spleen to the press and on camera. 'The restaurant stuff is just driving me mad, I mean really mad. It's not my fault and it's my money on the line.' The red tape stopping him from opening the restaurant on time had started when Hackney Council turned down a planning application due to the situation of the kitchen's extractor fan. Months of discussion followed, with both sides blaming each other, Jamie blaming the Council for not doing its job properly and the Council demanding detailed information from the restaurant's architects. 'If they are telling me it can never ever have extraction,' said Jamie, 'it means it can never, ever open, which means I've basically got £1.2m worth of kitchen and decoration in a building I can't use, which then means my house goes. Simple, really simple.'

With the problems piling up, and his students still failing the tests Jamie was setting them, it was time for a break. They would soon be taking deliveries in the new restaurant, if it ever opened, and Jamie needed them to understand the importance of quality meat and produce. Looking to his expanding band of mentors to inspire them, he took his urban posse to the wilds of Cumbria to get their hands dirty with pig farmer Peter Gott. It was Jamie's old mate, Jimmy Doherty, who had suggested the farm. Jimmy was helping out at Peter's farm to learn the ropes and would not only help Jamie with his band of urban campers, but would also meet the love of his life, Michaela, who had come to Cumbria as part of the *Jamie's Kitchen* production crew. 'It was there, both of us standing ankle-deep in mud, that I told her my dream of setting up my own pig farm like Peter's one day,' Jimmy wrote in his book *On the Farm*. Michaela was hooked on this young entomologist, who had hiked through Israeli deserts, trekked through the jungles of Malaysia and dived through the seas of Asia, and followed him to the completion of his dream.

But if the campfire and fresh Cumbrian air were meant to inspire a bit of communal singing and group bonding, instead cynicism was setting in among the students. They took the opportunity to tell Jamie they thought he was using them, putting his own career before their needs. Jamie was astonished, and decided to tell them just what was happening with the finances behind the scenes; they would see it all soon enough on Channel 4 for themselves. When he told them that even Jools didn't know that he had mortgaged their home and office to finance the project, their respect was restored. According to the *Guardian*, the truth is that 'one of Jamie's properties, which didn't have a mortgage, was mortgaged to raise funds for Fifteen'. 'Although he had invested around £1.7m in the project by 2004,' wrote Simon Hattenstone in the *Guardian*, 'he was reckoned to be Britain's third wealthiest chef at the time, worth an estimated £17m.'

But for some students it was more than cynicism holding them back; they felt that the Cheeky Chops Charity support system was failing them. 'Everyone knew I had childcare problems and nothing was done,' sobbed Michelle, who had been one of the few to fail her exams. 'Just because you're a single mother doesn't mean that you can't learn a trade,' said Jamie. 'We want to help, I want to help. Let's look at all the options, sweetheart, and let's talk next week.'

Daily Mirror mole Stephanie Young used to take the bus from Wandsworth to Hammersmith College with Michelle each day, and remembers her as 'a fiercely intelligent and feisty woman, whose teen pregnancy had meant she had been unable to finish her education or make a career for herself. She was ecstatic to have been given the opportunity to make something of herself and talked in glowing terms of Jamie as a mentor and benefactor.' Young said she was upset to learn in a Sunday tabloid that Michelle had quit Fifteen and turned to prostitution. 'In the first weeks I remember him encouraging her to stick with it to make her daughter proud. How devastated he must have been then to read that she'd gone on the game because she "wanted to make sure my daughter gets the best".' Michelle admitted Jamie had 'been on the telephone' and that he had 'asked if there was anything he could do and even offered me my job back'.

Back in London, with students falling like skittles, Jamie had to keep raising the standards if Fifteen, the restaurant, was to open to the rave reviews he planned. It was time to send the students – and their attitude – out into the wider world of top London restaurants to show them just what they would be competing with when Fifteen opened, and what kind of future the restaurant industry offered them. St John, Le Caprice, The Capital, Isola, Smiths, Alistair Little, Vong, The Ivy and The River Café were among the top London restaurants to offer work placements to the students. 'We had Ben with us for the period that they wanted,' said Jamie's former boss, Rose Gray of The River Café. 'We just agreed. I think it was set up through the production company but I think he probably rang up and asked us. But that wasn't important – we just said that's what Jamie wanted to do and we were happy to help.'

Ben had been one of the students who demanded more parenting than even Jamie was prepared to give. When he arrived eight hours late one day, Jamie took him to task. 'I know your situation,' he said, referring to the fact that he was living on the streets, 'but there has to be a point where I stop wiping your arse!' The point was when he sent him to Ruth Rogers and Rose Gray, whose combination of social conscience and mature maternal skills was an unusual mix in the restaurant world. Rose had seen it all before. 'Ben was like any of the juniors we have here,' she said. 'The moment they walk in the door, they leave their baggage behind. He was just a young kid who had had very little training, but that's the whole thing about a kitchen – you train as you go. I always have a junior at The River Café; loads of people just write in. At the moment we've got a girl called Alice and she did a very short course at a private training school, but she's very similar to Ben in a way. She knows no more and she knows no less but she wants to do it, just like he did.'

But Rose admitted that Ben's baggage was a little more than most of her juniors might leave on the doorstep. 'He had a few problems like he didn't have anywhere to live. I was rather concerned that they hadn't worked that one out. They were using them in their TV programme so they could have made sure that they had somewhere to sleep at night.' 'That's madness,' said Jo Bates. 'How can someone be expected to go to work if they haven't got a home to go to? It's all about the support for the individual. To have Jamie Oliver boosting the person is great, but you've got to have the infrastructure to support that person because of that background of disengagement and chaos. These kids are not going to change overnight. Not many people would be able to do that. Even turning up would be astounding for some of them. It's good to have high standards, but you've got to be realistic. They need decent food, and a safe place to sleep and other people around you saying, "You're doing really well", "Come on, you have to get up", "You can do it."'

Passione also opened its kitchen doors to the students. 'Of course we wanted to help,' Gennaro told me, his Italian shrug questioning why anyone would refuse to help. 'But some of them are so hard, it's unbelievable. I'd say that to Jamie and he'd say, "Don't worry, they'll soften up". He really believes it. A good person always believes in good things; they don't believe in bad things. One way or the other, people will always help,' said Gennaro. 'There are so many boys and girls all over the world who need help, and if Jamie can just help one out of the thousands and thousands who need help, he will have achieved something. This is his big reward. He doesn't need people to clap their hands for him; his reward is inside his heart. The biggest pleasure for him is when one of his trainees does well. He doesn't need anything else. But he has to be there to encourage them; no one else can do that. I want to help him more, and in the future I will be more involved because I've learnt from him that the sentimental rewards are the best. No money in the world can pay you for the good things that you do. It took a boy half my age to teach me that.'

Jamie's confidence in the students was vindicated as they came back a more mature brigade with a sense of perspective and respect that we hadn't seen before. 'They've gone from being like Kevin and Perry to being sparkly-eyed, passionate young chefs,' said Jamie. 'It's quite emotional for me. They're by no means all the way there yet – they still have things to learn. But they've come so far. I didn't feel I had to do it, but I felt I could do it. It felt really right, and had never been done before, and that's what excites me.'

Ruth Rogers admired his tough love. 'I think he's very fair. You've got to be very firm and very clear. In the end you're training while you're working in most kitchens. Someone shouldn't have to say, "This food was made by a trainee on their first day at The River Café so it might not be so good." We've had to put chefs in situations where you've looked at the food and you've thought, maybe that's not so good, but we're not a school. You are very demanding and very strict, but within the boundaries of being fair.'

If the building still wasn't ready, and the costs continued to spiral out of control, the students were motoring now. The mistakes they were making still provided the narrative, but as the series propelled itself towards the grand opening via a number of knuckle-biting rehearsals in front of top chefs and discerning guests, we knew by now that Jamie had won. The pale blue wall tiles might have been stuck on with glue, the back rests on the seats might have been bizarrely high, but we all knew that the foundations of Fifteen had little to do with cement. 'I'm definitely extremes,' Jamie told Simon Hattenstone in the *Guardian*. 'I'm incredibly sensitive, but incredibly hard. I do not like bollocks – I'm not interested in people getting pissed like fuckers on a Sunday night and coming to me on a Monday when I'm paying their wage. If you want doors to open, then I'll open them for you, but you've gotta be a rock, you gotta be consistent every day, day in, day out. Y'see, my dad used to fire people like that.' He clicks his finger hard and fast. 'You fuck with me, right, you piss off! You can't do that now.'

'Love Is The Message' his T-shirt reminded us when all looked bleak, and after nine months of depressing reinforcements of stereotypical youth culture, it looked like his consistent hard line had finally won out. Seven out of the 15 took their new skills out to some of the world's best restaurants including Tuscany's Osteria di Passignano, Sydney's MG Garage, California's Chez Panisse and The French Laundry, and London's Nobu and Tom Aikens. Johnny Broadfoot, who agreed to defer graduation until Jamie was satisfied that he had reached his true potential, says that it was worth the wait. 'I never expected to graduate and be working in a Michelin-starred restaurant in central London. I feel so lucky. I've been given the chance to get into the industry two rungs up the ladder. Most young chefs find themselves standing in a hallway peeling mushrooms for two years but here at Lindsay House, I'm really cooking.'

The newspaper hacks were stunned. No sooner had they found a new Jade Goody to burn at the stake than out of the ashes flew a new Princess Diana. This was 2002, and the world had only just witnessed the birth of hatred with the attack on the Twin Towers in New York. Saints were thin on the ground but Mark Lawson recognised the raw ingredients of a new one when he wrote for the *Guardian*: 'An American commentator writing about Mayor Rudy Giuliani's response to September 11 suggested that he had somehow managed to combine charisma, efficiency and compassion, qualities which we usually expect to occur in separate personalities. While the scales of their challenges were in no way comparable, I have thought of that description while watching Oliver running his redemption kitchen.'

CHAPTER 24

THE JAMIE & JOOLS SHOW

Jools was running out of patience. If *The Naked Chef* and Sainsbury's had taken Jamie away from her in the past, at least he would come home with stories to tell and a lightness of being that was hard to find these days. The Olivers were a family now, and although she had the metaphorical roses around the door, she was jealous of the other love interest in his life.

She spotted an opportunity to use the ever-present camera for her own needs. 'I'll see you in an hour and a half,' she said pointedly as Jamie sloped off to the building site during another day's holiday. 'You've got that on camera: 5.30. Any later and Poppy and me will be packing our suitcases.' She wasn't joking. 'He's got to give his mobile to Nicola [his PA] and no one is allowed to get through except family and friends,' she told the camera. 'Otherwise it's ridiculous. His mind is still going even if we're at lunch. He's not listening to a word I'm saying, so it's not fair on either of us really.'

'Everyone around me has no patience with me,' Jamie told the camera, as if it were the only thing that understood him. 'They just say, "Well, get rid of them," but it's all very well for the college to do that. I can respect Sheila and Mark for treating them like normal college kids – what do they owe them? Nothing.' Jamie's commitment to the students was deeper; he needed to know that he was right in believing in them.

'Jools has admitted she has to check his official website to find out where he is,' wrote Hilary Douglas in the *Express on Sunday*. 'Jamie's work commitments mean he leaves home at 7am and doesn't return till after 1am,' revealed Jools, who was due to give birth to Daisy Boo in eight weeks. 'I haven't seen him in daylight hours for as long as I can remember. The other day he was in Scotland and I only found out through the website.'

Antony Worrall Thompson pointed out that Jamie was like a lot of successful dads: 'A lot of company directors go out at 6.30 in the morning and come back at 9pm, and the kids will have gone to bed. They will neglect their family. It's the price they pay for being so successful.' 'It's a classic case of the husband working hard and never getting home, and the wife left looking after the family,' a friend told the tabloids. 'They are a very loving couple, who actually adore each other. But little problems get bigger and bigger if the pressure starts to build up on your family life. Jools' unhappiness has been simmering for quite a while and although publicly she is very proud of him, privately she is frustrated at him being away all the time. She wants Jamie to be a husband and a father.'

It was the one stumbling block in the viewers' love affair with Jamie Oliver. While the affair largely did not extend to Jools, it was Jools that we felt for as Jamie's own TV company exposed his shortcomings as a dad and showed us around his personal life. While the tabloids were carping on about the end of their relationship being nigh, we knew this was a couple who believed in the institution of marriage enough to work it out. A sense of tradition, a deep understanding of what being married means passed down from both sets of parents, and a bond that went back to their mid teens meant that Jamie and Jools were in it for the duration.

But there was a nagging feeling that Jamie had moved out of the reality he shared with us into the warped world of celebrity where normal rules no longer apply. Workaholism may well be a common problem in marriage, but few couples would invite their mates around to witness their rows. Yet this is what Jamie did with his relationship; while we signed up to watch the transformation of a group of homeless kids into five-star chefs, he had sneakily sold us tickets to the Jamie and Jools Show. Even his friends were confused. 'His kids will be 18 and running off before he knows it,' said one member of the TV crew. 'But maybe I don't understand him because I'm such a family man. He might get bored sitting around with the kids – a lot of men are, although he looks great with the kids. I don't know why he doesn't give up if he's got all that money. But maybe my agenda is different.'

But perhaps that is what he needed to do to take *The Naked Chef* into the world of social politics. Maybe after the Alfie persona, the Essex lad who bypassed the apples and pears for a cheeky fast track onto the streets of London via a sexy spiral staircase, he needed to add a new dimension as he took us deeper into the world he wanted to change. Both *Jamie's Kitchen* and *School Dinners* were tricky projects and could so easily have gone badly wrong. With egg on his face, he could still have come back and cooked up a dream, but with the soundtrack of his wife and child begging him to come home as he pursued his mission, he could tear at the hearts and minds of a wider range of viewers. He was right; it was compelling TV, and it meant that the dual dramas in and out of the kitchen were enough to keep us glued to the screen, whether or not we cared about the fate of a disadvantaged bunch of would-be chefs when we first switched on.

'Do I care that it might not be real for the camera?' asked Gill Hudson, editor of *Radio Times*. 'Do I care about his relationship with Jools? Not at all! Whatever you do, no one is 100% natural all the time. You change according to whom you're talking to. What's the problem with that? But ask me, "Do you care about this issue or not?" And actually, yes, I do.' I asked her if she believed in him when she met him in person. 'Yes, I think I do believe in him, but again, whether I do or not simply isn't the point. I think he sorted out a genuine problem and he did it in a winning way.'

Actually it was Ben Frow's fault. As commissioning editor for

Channel 4, he admitted to the Biography Channel that it was entirely intentional that he put Jamie and his marriage under pressure. After the over exposure of *The Naked Chef*, the Sainsbury's ads and the subsequent press fall out, he laid his conditions down. 'I said, "Unless we have access to you 24 hours a day and unless we can film you having the rows with your wife, unless we film you having the down sides as well as the upsides of all this, I don't want to do it." I felt that the only way we could turn Jamie into a hero was to see him struggle.' Of course at home, things were not quite what they seemed to be on TV. 'I think he's authentic as a husband,' said a friend. 'The nuts and bolts of it don't occur to him. I find her a bit odd, though. She's not nearly as approachable – but you find that with a lot of people who are not the famous person themselves. They can be a bit awkward. But she is very sweet, and their relationship is lovely. She finds him childish; he's such a kid that she shouts at him and tells him to grow up.'

The tabloids snapped the two of them looking fed up and at the end of their tethers. Their headlines screamed disaster, until Jamie rang the editors and personally begged them not to attack his family. 'They couldn't have got their relationship more wrong,' said Jamie's manager, Louise Holland. 'They're so devoted.' According to Jools, Jamie is an old fashioned kind of bloke, the kind who doesn't talk about his work to his wife, and she believed that her job was to make their life together 'light and happy' while the pressure was mounting at work. She wanted him to come home not so that he could tell her about his day; she wanted them to play babies.

Jools admitted that Jamie was born to be a dad. As awkward as she was with bathing newborn Poppy, he was a natural. As much as she tried to master changing a tiny baby's nappy, Jamie did it one-handed. It was as easy to him as cracking an egg. As much as Jools fussed and worried about everything being perfect, Jamie took new fatherhood in his stride. Gennaro Contaldo says it's the children that cement an already strong relationship; 'He's a cuddly bear with the children, he's down on the floor with them.

He loves being a daddy – he's like a child with them.' 'I'm good with kids, me,' Jamie told us on *The Naked Chef*. 'I'm on their level. We all talk rubbish.' He told journalist Miranda Sawyer that he swore he wouldn't be 'an idiot parent, but there I am, pretending the spoonful of food is Noddy's aeroplane swooping into her mouth'.

Gennaro says that although Jools might grumble, there's nothing to worry about long term. 'With Juliette, he's fantastic. She cares so much for the family, and she's an unbelievable mother. She's a pure mummy; she's shiny. As long as the children are there, and Jamie is there, and the relatives and the friends are all there, she's happy. She's a very warm person and if she can do something for someone, she will do it. She's like Jamie. The glory and the money came anyway. That's not what they're about.' Jamie responds to the newspaper articles that try to tear away at their marriage with a dismissive wave of the hand. 'She gives me a kicking on a regular basis and I love her to bits so it is weird when people get these ideas that something's going on,' he told journalist Cameron Robinson. 'Basically it's just builders ringing up the papers saying they've seen things, trying to make a couple of quid. Jools and I are really happy right now. She's changed over the years and having kids has made her a really confident person. Whereas once she was really shy – in a very nice way – being a mum has made her blossom.'

Gennaro's partner and mother of his two-year-old twins, Liz Przybylski, understands Jools' position. 'I feel sorry for her,' she said. 'But maybe it's quite good if he's out the way so much. She can get on with it then. But it can't be easy.' She described the two of them as polar opposites: 'She's nervy and stressy, and he's laid back. But they've worked it out.' Gennaro agrees: 'When you get married you become one person. Jamie has so much love but he does worry so much.' 'The Olivers are like swans,' Jamie's father Trevor said simply. 'Once they mate, it's for life.'

Jamie is proud of his family and friends, and shows them off wherever he can. He has taken them with him into his TV world and supported those he can with cash and favours so they can share his stage. Jimmy the Pig Man Doherty is there at The Good Food Show not just to sell his sausages but to sign the book of the series that would probably never have been made without the help of his mate. When Jamie comes to The Food Lovers Fair at London's Covent Garden, Jimmy's sausages sell out within minutes. When the banks refused to lend Jimmy money for his venture because he lacked experience and collateral, it was Jamie who gave him a £55,000 loan. 'I went to him with a proper business plan and everything,' said Jimmy, anxious to prove that this wasn't just a back-hander from his best mate. 'He believes in what I'm trying to achieve. Like me, he's passionate about getting back to producing good, native food in a way that works with nature.' And it works; read Jimmy's book and you might even be inspired enough to change your life; you'll almost certainly never eat a supermarket sausage again.

Jamie's right to drag his old mate Gennaro up on stage with him, too. Gennaro's passion for good food is infectious and when Jamie gave his book, *Passione*, to Nora the dinner lady at the end of the *School Dinners* project, it was as if he were passing on the mantle. Even the book *Minus Nine to One* that Jamie persuaded Jools to write about becoming a mother went down a treat with women who like nothing better than to sift over the tiniest details of pregnancy and birth. She wouldn't have thought of doing it without his help. 'Jools is interesting 'cos she's not like me at all,' he told journalist Miranda Sawyer. 'She hasn't got a mission, she just wants to be married to someone she loves and have a family and that's it, end of story. It's odd for me, because I'll go, what do you want to do? Then do that, I'll help you! Because I believe that anyone can do anything. If I wanted to be a surgeon, then I would be – I'd just have to work my arse off for 10 years. It baffled me for ages. I almost felt she had a part of her life missing, then I thought, it's sweet and quite refreshing, especially in London.'

It was another slam dunk, a bullseye for Jamie, the marketing maestro; Jools was the wife of the man who could do no wrong, who nagged Saint Jamie to take a break from changing the lives of the homeless and come back to Hampstead to play house. Suddenly, with a book on the shelves under the surname of Oliver, she could help the millions who have problems with polycystic ovaries and fertility issues. She could pass hints to those whose babies won't feed or sleep, and offer empathy to the zillions of women who obsess over pregancy and childhood while their husbands leave work too late to make it to the baby class on time. Jools, who never particularly wanted to change the world, had gossiped her way onto the shelves of the nation's bookshops.

CHAPTER 25

A GRAND OPENING

With the kitchen finished just hours before the official opening, Jamie was back on top and Fifteen would soon be packed to the gills with global glitterati, from Jennifer Aniston and Brad Pitt to Terence Conran and celebrity good-timers like Sara Cox and Zoe Ball. 'Gordon Ramsay came back for seconds and Cherie Blair once made me wrap up her chocolate pudding in a doggybag to take home to eat,' said star pupil Elisa Roche. 'We were so popular we had to turn away Jennifer Lopez and Justin Timberlake. Meanwhile, ordinary families took their seats and congratulated the kitchen. I never shook so many hands. Everyone from the pot-washers to the front-of-house staff loved working there.'

The spirit of Jamie was infused into the paint-work although the line between optimism and excellence was still a tightrope for many of the trainees. It wasn't for want of trying on Jamie's part. 'Jamie works his butt off,' said one of the receptionists. 'You can't take it to heart when he swears at you, it's just because he's concentrating on his cooking. Most of the time he's an absolute honey.'

Emma Cox was one of the many tabloid reporters who tried to get a job at Fifteen and one of the few who succeeded. She worked on reception taking 'Three thousand calls coming in every day from people desperate to secure a table – and many spending up to a week trying to get through only to be told there was nothing available – it was no mean feat to keep them calm. Some claimed to be terminally ill, pretended they had already booked or resorted to unashamed begging. One distraught lady phoned to say her son had a "breathing disorder" and it was his desperate wish to go to Fifteen. A harassed man, clearly getting grief after forgetting to book a table for Valentine's Day, tried to blag one by claiming he had booked in September – before the restaurant even opened.'

The reviews were mixed at first, and continue to be four years on. Matthew Fort of the *Guardian* was immediately impressed despite his early cynicism. He wrote, 'Fifteen, tucked away in a cobbled backstreet in London N1, has all the trappings of riotous success – black-garbed minder at the door, large bar packed with long, blonde tresses, three-button jackets with the buttons done up, mussed hair and Brad Pitt stubble, mixologists turning the act of making cocktails into an aerobics routine, and enough energy and noise to fuel a power station. The whole place has a kind of sweet retro quality with something of the sunny optimism and fizz of the 1960s about it.

'And in the kitchen you catch sight of the faces familiar from the TV, so at least some of them must have lasted the course. And among them are one or two battle-scarred old pros marshalling the forces with that disciplined precision that you need to keep a kitchen on its toes. And there is Mr Oliver himself, patrolling the pass, quality-control executive, and wholly involved in getting the food right and getting it out.'

Grasping the 'rock'n'roll spirit' and making the kind of allowances that Jamie said he never would, Fort admitted that the food did not always make the grade. 'It would be easy to make fun of the tendency to list virtually every ingredient, not to mention the Oliverisms such as "kinda sashimi", or the shameless selling of "melt-in-the-mouth", particularly when aspects of certain dishes don't live up to their billing. The oxtail might have been melt-in-the-mouth, but the pasta with it was not – it was undercooked and had a stiff, cardboard texture. The "kinda sashimi" was over-salted. And the pannacotta that Amaryllis had for pudding was stiff with gelatine. But it would be unfair to see these as anything other than minor gripes because the style of the food, and the pleasure it gave, were unmistakable. It was jumbo stuff; British in cast and character, whatever the original provenance of the dish. There are broad, booming flavours; chunky textures; big helpings; generosity in every mouthful.'

Matthew Norman thought that the prices were outlandish, but was so awe-struck by the fact that Jamie himself was in the kitchen that he could barely remember what he was eating. 'Then again,' he wrote in the *Telegraph*, 'perhaps people will merrily pay a premium for seeing the Mother Teresa of the herbs and spices in the flesh. But my friend found the sight of him standing proudly at the front of the kitchen, under what looked like TV lighting, rather troubling. "I thought he just did lifestyle," she said.'

Australian chef and writer Stephanie Alexander said it was the best food she has ever eaten in London. Even the Queen of Food, Fay Maschler, whose good reviews can increase a week's covers by 40 per cent and who has since become a patron of Fifteen, wrote in the *Evening Standard*, 'The food is pretty fantastic – as it should be for the money.'

Victor Lewis-Smith, who makes a living out of hating most things – including Jamie Oliver and his revolutionary social experiments – also had good things to say. 'From first to last, it was exceptional,' he wrote in the *Guardian*. 'The maltagliata alla bolognese was a slow-braised shank of lamb cooked in chianti with "the best tomatoes, orange, rosemary and Parmesan", whose subtle, juicy flavours burst in the mouth. The texture of shredded lamb and fresh pasta was incomparably exquisite. The temperature was perfect – this sort of pasta almost always arrives at table far too hot. It was one of the best starters I've had all year. My guest chose Devon crab, bruschetta di pagnotta with nasturtium leaves, lemon aïoli and red chilli, and pronounced it delicious, though I'm not sure his opinions on food are of much value.'

Lewis-Smith had been one of the only journalists to refuse to review the restaurant when it opened in 2002. 'I'm glad I declined,' he wrote two years on, 'because during those first few months, I hated the circle jerk of journalists who spent evenings there on the falling-down water, then filled their columns with unthinking Gemütlichkeit and sentimental tripe about social responsibility and helping youngsters into work. All declared the food magnificent; one even proclaimed that Jamie should be given the VC [Victoria Cross].' If it didn't come, an invitation from Clarence House for the students to cook for Prince Charles was second best.

The reviews by punters were more mixed, although it's important to remember that most people who can be bothered to write reviews on websites tend to be fans, or very unhappy with their experience. Hugh Peto for LondonView.co.uk wrote: 'Unbelievably rude service, a surly manager, ordinary food, silly menu, broken loos, shoddy decor – all at absurdly hiked prices. It looks like the good cause has obscured the point: to serve good food at reasonable prices in a relaxed environment.' Gaby Huddart, editor of *Square Meal*, wrote: 'We've got page after page of complaints. A main course can cost £27. For that, people expect good quality food and service.'

'Starters were very good,' wrote one visitor, 'scallops crudo and a fig with dolcelatte and gorgonzola. However, the main courses – pork that I could have used as shoe leather and lamb that had been marinated in rosemary from the day it was born – well, suffice to say we did not eat much of either but this drew no comment from the waiting staff. I understand the ethos of the restaurant and know that the chefs have "L" plates on, but really at £140 for two with one bottle of wine and two dessert wines, this was outrageous. The quality of the food was not sufficient to justify the price. Maybe Sunday is a bad day to go but unfortunately, we will not be trying it again.'

But when the 2005 *Harden's London Restaurant Guide* that collates comments from ordinary restaurant goers grabbed newspaper headlines by damning Fifteen 'amateurish' and overpriced, Jamie was incensed. 'Harden is right down there in the depths,' he said. 'As a restaurant guide it's at the bottom of the pile. They were using me to publicise it, press-releasing my gob all over it. If you want to sell something you either use talent or a face to endorse it, or come up with a clever idea. Harden's was "Let's dump on Jamie Oliver from on high". But one of the Harden brothers has never eaten at Fifteen and the other said he had a nice meal there.' If it seemed that he was overreacting to the kind of criticism that he had taken on the chin in the past, it was because this time he had others to think about. 'The restaurant speaks for itself and we are pretty much up there with the best in town,' he said. 'The reason I get really cross is because the students believe what they read in the papers, even if it's rubbish.'

He admitted that charging £8 for the Heinz beans on toast was a mistake, even if it was made with ciabatta bread, olive oil, cherry tomatoes, basil, balsamic vinegar, red chillies and rocket leaves. 'I should have been brighter,' he said. 'Heinz came to us and offered £15,000 for us to put something cool made with baked beans on the menu. That funds one student for a whole year. Am I going to do it? Of course I am!'

Although it's normal for restaurants to still be making a loss until their third year, the press was quick to point out that Sweet as Candy, the management company which handles Jamie Oliver, the brand, had to bail Fifteen out after the losses were becoming unmanageable. 'Someone has got to fund the losses and he will have egg on his face if the restaurant has to close,' Chris Lane, an accountant with Kingston Smith who specialises in the restaurant trade, told the *Independent*. He said it was not possible to tell from the accounts whether the losses were due to a lack of 'bums on seats' or excessive costs.

Accounts published in 2005 showed that Fifteen had made losses of more than £1m since it opened in November 2002, the balance sheet revealing opening operating losses of £611,000 for 2002, falling to £120,500 in 2004. Putting it down to high start-up costs and a staff of 70, accountants estimated the total figure of losses so far to be set against future tax at £1.23m. Amanda Afiya, managing editor of *The Caterer*, put it into context. 'Given its charitable status and the amount they are investing in training, it's hard to compare to other restaurant businesses. It has been criticised for inconsistency and has had to increase staff numbers. People like the fact that it is non-profit making but they expect reasonable standards in service and good food.'

But by the end of 2005 profits were finally being ploughed back into the charity, with figures as high as £600,000 being suggested. The Fifteen concept rolled out around the globe with restaurants opening in Amsterdam in 2004, and Melbourne as well as another in Britain, which opened in Cornwall's Watergate Bay in 2006. It was a triumph in social politics. 'It's about seeing real results,' said Jo Bates. 'It's about young people having something to hold that they've achieved. I think structure is great for guiding young people once they've realised that they can gain something from this. For many of them, they've just never had any experience with structural environments like school, family or youth clubs. They often don't have the mentality. So if you could offer them something with boundaries and outcomes, and high expectations as well, why not? Some of the most amazing people I've ever met have been kids in the youth justice system – very creative, very inspirational young people.'

For the students who had dropped out, it must have been galling to miss out on the finale. Two years on Dwayne Monford was earning £6.50 an hour cooking pizzas in a Pizza Hut in south London and studying for an NVQ in catering at a local college. 'I regret dropping out,' he said. 'I feel like I let everyone down – Jamie, me, the others on the course... I wish I could rewind and start again. I'm vexed. I could have been one of the top kids there; I could have got myself sent to one of those top restaurants, like Johnny. I'd like to be working in a Michelin-starred restaurant but I'm squeezing cheese onto pizza base.'

Jo Bates thinks the work Jamie did with Fifteen is a great start. 'He shoots through the apathy and bigotry. He's got good public support; he's got charisma, but he's also got a strong social conscience and he believes in a fair and just society.' But, as she says, his celebrity status gives him an edge others might not be able to bring to the table. 'Approaching people is going to have a very different effect. In the rest of society it's about naming, shaming, blaming and if you want people to turn their life around, you have to say "Come on, what are you going to do?"' She says that the problem is endemic in society. 'What you've got is a culture about us and them. Adults don't want to take responsibility for young people at all. The media creates a culture of hostility and the Government introduces ASBOs [Anti-Social Behaviour Orders] and says how out of control they are. There's no culture of repairing the damage.'

For Jamie the awards came rolling in. The Time Out Eating and Drinking Awards gave him a special award for 'promoting good food and putting it within reach of ordinary young people' and Fifteen was short-listed for the New Restaurant of the Year in the Tio Pepe Carlton London Restaurant Awards. The project would even earn him an MBE in the New Year's Honours List in 2003. 'Does this mean that I don't get any more parking tickets?' he quipped to the press.

But it was a humbling lesson for him. 'I think the public liked seeing me on the day job – when everything wasn't going sweet and rosy, and I was stressed and getting my backside kicked,' he said. Not only had he learnt how to play the game with his trainees, he had discovered how to play the press. 'Fifteen drives everything else that I do,' he told the *Independent*'s Caroline Stacey. 'It wasn't just a programme; it was a real thing. I wanted it to work like an old-fashioned apprenticeship, with a family aspect and to show there was an integrity about the food and the sourcing trips.' He told Stacey: 'I didn't fucking do it to be a pissy little thang, you know. I did it to make change. That's the only thing that kept me going last year when I was miserable. It was hard; it was frustrating.'

After the battering the press had given him, it was a relief to have his integrity restored and for the press to believe in him again. His celebrity star was shining again and press and public couldn't get enough of him. If it made him cynical, he did not show it. 'When I used to go there [Fifteen] with him,' said Rupert Ivey, 'you were just surrounded by important people who wanted a piece of him, people who see themselves as important in their own world like publishers and company directors. And you think, "You poor lamb!"'

The success of Fifteen meant that Jamie could feel vindicated about his work with Sainsbury's; with Fifteen's bills rising to £2.5 million and his personal assets providing the guarantee at the bank, it was Sainsbury's which had indirectly provided the capital. He was free to make money finally, now that we knew what he would spend it on. 'What I've fallen in love with is social business versus commercial business. For me, that's what makes the world go round. I work to feed the beast.'

CHAPTER 26

SHARING THE BREAD

By April 2003 Jamie was mixing with the big boys. He was even discussing mutton dressed as lamb with royalty at a meeting with the Prince of Wales. 'I thought he was a good old boy,' said Jamie, who sat next to his future king. 'He was very interesting and undoubtedly passionate about nature, organics, self-sufficient farms and small holdings.' Charles even gave Jamie a bottle of champagne to celebrate the imminent birth of little Daisy Boo. 'It's English champagne,' said Jamie, 'so I am looking forward to having a look at that.'

After the success of Fifteen, the press had resumed their love affair with the Olivers and life was sweet again. The papers ran features on the secrets of a good marriage, using Jamie and Jools as their role models, and painted Jamie as a perfect father. At the launch of Gennaro's book, *Passione*, instead of chastising him for not being at home with his heavily pregnant wife, they asked for tips on how to multi-task. 'That's why I've got my mobile phone strapped to my bottom and switched on to "super vibrate"' was Jamie's reply.

What was making Jamie increasingly untouchable was that everyone now knew that his motives come from a good place. 'Jamie will help anyone if he can,' says Gennaro. 'Jamie phones me almost every day. He looks after me. I work very hard and I love my job – it's my *passione*. But Jamie cares how much I work and tells me to have a rest. He rings me up and asks if he should send over one of his chefs to help me. I say, "No, no," but a couple of months ago I was in Italy and I wasn't feeling well.' Gennaro, the 58-year-old father of five-year-old twins, whose restaurant in London's Charlotte Street, cookery courses, book signings and appearances at food fairs throughout the year are a tough work load, looked tired as he remembered how alone he felt. 'I was a bit frightened actually because it wasn't like me to be ill. Liz and the children were in Spain with her family and I didn't know what was wrong, but I was feeling really down. I was in this lovely tiny village in the south of Italy with these lovely trees and a lovely church. It was just me and the cicadas. But I was down – I'd just been overworking.'

He looked at the mobile and saw that Jamie was trying to contact him. 'I didn't want to speak to him because I knew that he would sense something was wrong in my voice,' he said. 'The phone rang again but I didn't answer it and sent him a message saying I was OK, and telling him where I was.' Four or five minutes later he rang again. 'This time I answered it and immediately he said, "What's wrong?" I told him that I was OK, that I was just sitting here thinking about the memories, and he said, "No, you're not OK."' Gennaro was moved again as he told the story. 'I'm a very tough person, but to hear his voice and to have all my worries...'

He confessed to Jamie that he had seen a doctor but stressed that he just was feeling lonely and begged him not to say anything to his family. 'I wish I hadn't told him,' he said, moving swiftly into an impersonation of his friend. '"Stay there, I'm coming!" he said. "Don't move, I'm catching a plane now!" I felt tears; I couldn't pretend any more.' Gennaro managed to persuade Jamie not to fly over, but he insisted on easing the way home and sent a car to the airport to pick Gennaro up and take him to a five-star hotel, where he would be looked after until his family returned from their holiday. 'It was beautiful, fantastic,' said Gennaro. 'I can't tell you much it must have cost.'

Gennaro says Jamie will help anyone if he can and the trainees at Fifteen were the latest in a long line. 'He's not just involved in the restaurant or the TV series; he really cares about every single one of them. They are like his family, and he cares whether they're sleeping well, or whether they're working too hard,' he said. Even Fifteen trainee Dennis Duncanson would find himself given the five-star Jamie Oliver family treatment despite appearing in court for driving without insurance. Jamie was there by his side in court as a character witness when the judge agreed to give him 120 hours' community service and a four-year driving ban while Jamie promised to get him community work in catering. 'Dennis is one of my hardest working trainees,' said Jamie. 'I felt it would be a shame if his training was cut short by putting him in prison, so I decided to do everything I could to stop that happening. I told the judge this is a lad who has finally turned his life around and has a real chance to make something of himself.'

But instead of rapping him over the knuckles, Jamie flew Dennis first class to Hollywood to cook for his celebrity mate Brad Pitt's 40th birthday. 'At Christmas we got a phone call saying, "We'll give a donation to the Fifteen charity if you come and do Brad Pitt's birthday,"' Jamie told Susie Harding in the *Sunday Mirror*. 'We thought someone was just having a laugh, but it turned out to be the real deal.' Brad was reported to have dressed up as his then wife, Jennifer Aniston's, teen idol, Simon Le Bon, and to have sung Duran Duran's hit 'Wild Boys' on a karaoke machine. Jennifer was dressed as Helen of Troy to acknowledge Brad's latest film triumph, *Troy*. 'The pair have long been *Naked Chef* fans,' wrote Harding. 'They became hooked on his cookery shows after watching them on cable TV, and Jamie sends them his recipe books.' The Pitts had decided to fly the Olivers to LA for dinner so long as Jamie cooked and according to Harding's source at the time, 'they got on brilliantly and have become very good friends. Jamie and Jools want to return the favour and have them over for a slap-up meal.'

By 2004 Jamie was getting used to the celebrity scene but he knew what a thrill it would have been for Dennis. Jamie told

Harding that he rang his mentor from the plane. He said, 'Jamie, I'm 33,000 feet in the air, I've just had a massage and I can have as many Jack Daniel's as I like, what's going on?' Jamie was there in spirit with his talented protégé. `I was like, "Yeah, that's my boy – have another massage!"'

Brad Pitt is still waiting to hear whether he will play his idol on the big screen in a film about Jamie's life as a revolutionary chef. Michael Kuhn, executive producer of the project at Qwerty Films, told me that there are 'lots of people' interested in playing the role. 'There have been several big name people who have approached us. I don't want to get into those discussions until we've got a script that's great and you just never know with these things. It could be next week or it could be a year from now, so until then, we're not going to respond to any of them.' It's not just getting the script right that is causing the delay. 'Well, obviously we've had to get the rights from him,' said Kuhn. 'We had to jump through endless hoops – it wasn't just him; it was all the other people involved. It's taken two years so far, and that's what has caused all the delay. Obviously we send him all the stuff to look at, but I think he wants to keep some distance from it.'

The script is based on *Jamie's Kitchen* and *Jamie's School Dinners*, and centres on the process of transformation. It's the story of the mentor who learnt more from the process than his mentees, but Kuhn is still unsure about whether to stay true to the story of Jamie Oliver, or to distance it from him, basing it in New York and disguising the central character. Jamie himself would prefer the latter. 'I think he's very interested in the whole thing,' Kuhn told me. 'But he didn't really want it to be a biopic. The other side of the coin is that the more you go away from his story, the more you get away from the heart.'

He says that the obvious thing is to centre it on the kids who would otherwise be left on the scrap heap. 'Without the coach character, they would have no future and no one to give them something to be in life. It's a *Fame* kind of movie, the coach who comes and whips the no-hope baseball team into shape, and changes more than the kids – that's what attracted me to the story. That's what happened to Jamie Oliver; he kind of fell into it, but somehow he changed more than the system or the kids. Obviously when you meet him, you realise that it's not something that he fakes. He's obviously consumed with this. I think that's what people are interested in. It's not about how he came along and changed the world, it's like the world came along and changed him. There's an element of surprise about it.'

The criticism that Jamie received is also part of the story. 'That goes with fame, doesn't it?' said Kuhn. 'You either respond to it – and do what the press wants you to do – or you do your thing which is more instinctive, and that's what he tends to do.'

CHAPTER 27

PLEASE, SIR...

With the success of Fifteen reinventing him as a modern day Robin Hood, charging the rich through the nose for a three-course meal and pumping it back into the lives of the disadvantaged, Jamie had found that he had a drive to make real change in the world. If Fifteen had been a departure from the laddish image that had him riding around London on a scooter and whizzing up a breakfast for Jools' sleepover mates after a night out on the town, its trials, errors and the transformation of a group of no-hope kids had made him grow up. More importantly, as he zoomed towards his 29th birthday in 2004, it had shown him a power for politics that was as fresh as a Sainsbury's herb counter, and as a father of two small girls he was ripe for exploring it with the next generation.

Jamie was poised to stoke the fires that had been simmering for some time in school kitchens across the UK, and to expose an attitude towards food which had become institutionalised in Local Education Authorities in Britain for 25 years since the Education Act of 1980. In one fell swoop the Act had ended education's relationship with food by cutting Domestic Science from the curriculum. With the privatising of school dinners in 1989, the combined result was a school catering service which believed that putting its customer first meant giving them what they wanted to eat, and a generation which did not have a clue how to boil an egg. By the time Jamie Oliver met their children, they had been feeding them pizza, burgers and chips since they started on solids.

When Jamie addressed an assembly of secondary children at Kidbrooke School in Greenwich, south-east London, in 2004, a cheap and cheerful plate of junk was passing for many school children's main meal of the day. It was seriously undermining British kids' understanding of what real food looked like. Italian children might be able to tell the difference between an aubergine and an artichoke, as we would see when Jamie took us to his spiritual homeland, but British kids couldn't even tell a stick of rhubarb from a stick of celery. With reconstituted meat and powdered vegetables whizzed up into battered nuggets, the relationships between food, the land where it came from and children's taste buds were in real danger of dying out.

But Jamie had a dream. First, he would take a school, then a borough, through a revolution of his own making. With children eating good food out of his hand, he would create a 'cleverer, cooler nation' tackling obesity and the NHS (National Health Service) budget, as well as antisocial behaviour and its related burdens on the State. With the success of Greenwich on a plate, how could the British Government refuse to come to the table? Of course it was riddled with potential problems; working with children and animals is a big no-no in showbiz, but somehow Jamie knew he would have those kids off their turkey twizzlers and onto real chicken drumsticks within a year. It would be trickier than he thought, but he was right.

There had been a precedent in a celebrity chef getting involved in Government business, albeit an unsuccessful one. In 2000 BBC *Masterchef* host Lloyd Grossman had been brought in to lead a team of food experts for a £40m revamp of NHS food. Grossman and a team of Britain's best chefs were asked to create menus suited to individual patients' needs, but while they came up with imaginative and delicious recipes, they fell at the first hurdle. 'Food does definitely need changing within hospitals,' said Mike Stone from the Patients Association. 'Some of the menus actually change the whole mindset about hospital food, but like many things within the NHS they have got to be backed up by money.'

Jamie told the newspapers that he was working on his most important project to date and that it had given him a shocking insight into the nutritional health of our nation's children. 'The country is in crisis,' he told Frances Hardy in the *Daily Mail*. 'We're numb to food and none of us will accept it. We're the laughing stock of Europe and we have a government that should stop making suggestions and actually do a handful of things that will improve our children's health, their lives and their capacity to learn.' In the *Guardian* he told John Crace that it wasn't just Europe either: 'I recently went to a township outside Johannesburg, where the kids and the schools have almost nothing compared with what we have here. Yet the standard of school food there was better than in 95% of schools in England. So we wanted to do something about it. The problem was that we didn't have a clear picture of what the something would be.'

He was preaching to the perfect readership: the *Daily Mail*'s and the *Guardian*'s middle-class outrage was the perfect fuel for his fire. That the Government was poisoning their kids was his first bit of bait. He then went on to hook them with every parent's nightmare. 'No one has proved categorically that the food a child eats affects their intelligence but you have only to ask a teacher what it's like trying to control a kid who's having a hypo because he's just lugged down his seventh can of Coke of the day. Fizzy drinks used to be an occasional treat. Nowadays kids think water is for ponces, fruit juice is posh – and that's only the tiniest bit of what I've experienced. Kids are being fed at school on 36p a day and it's a struggle to provide a nutritious meal on that. You have to be a pretty resourceful accountant and creative cook. So they usually get rubbish and we're wondering why they can't concentrate, and why diet and food related problems are now costing the health service more than lung cancer.' State-controlled poisoning, epidemic levels of behavioural disorder and a nation of fat kids leaning on the buckling struts of the NHS... It was a potent mix for Middle England, and Jamie was offering himself up again as our knight in shining armour.

No one knew what to expect when he rode into the kitchens of Kidbrooke School, but Fresh One's researchers had spotted a lucky find in dinner lady chief Nora Sands, who was to be Jamie's golden ticket. Nora's plucky attitude and tight ship impressed Jamie, although to begin with, the feeling was not mutual. 'When he first came in, I didn't know what his motives were,' she told BBC Five Live, 'but after a while I realised that his heart was in it. We were all just doing our job, and no one likes someone coming into the workplace and telling them what to do, so it was strange at first.' She told reporter John Crace that it was *his* lack of experience rather than hers that was the problem. 'There was just such a wide gulf between what he does in a restaurant and what we do here. It took time for him to understand that if the food wasn't in the hotplates by 12.50pm you might as well throw the lot away. You can make restaurant diners wait a few more minutes to get the food just right but you can't tell 500 hungry kids to come back later because they'll just go off to the chippy.'

As he insisted that Nora and her staff cook from scratch and prepare food that she knew would go to waste (and try to remember recipes he was making up as he went along), she felt she had dived into the deep end on the whim of a celebrity chef. As the project spread out across the borough, the dinner ladies were working harder than they had ever done before with no extra cash. They were not happy. 'We just didn't see an end to it,' said Nora. 'But he has such confidence in himself and a great passion for food. He would pick up a herb and talk about it for a week, whereas we were all looking at the clock. We have to do breakfast, lunch and a homework club too, so weren't thinking about the food in the way that he was.'

But it was Jamie's genuine love of food that would win Nora over. We spotted him kissing the dough in Nora's kitchen: 'If you don't kiss every batch of bread you ever make, you'll never spread the love,' he said in an echo of his mentor Gennaro Contaldo. And he was right; the love spread, slowly at first, but gathering a pace through all the kitchens of Greenwich, past the tears and the tantrums of the dinner ladies ('This is not my life; it's just a tiny bit of my life') and into the dining rooms where the children were facing food that some of them had never seen before.

Customer choice was at the heart of the problems facing school dinners in the UK and Jamie would conclude that depriving children of choice was his biggest challenge. As he watched parents bend to their children's every whim, giving them sweets and fizzy drinks as treats when they could see that they made them bounce off the walls, his mind was made up. When children came home in tears because Jamie had put vegetables on their pizzas, his resolve stiffened. After weeks of providing his dishes as a healthy alternative to the usual suspects, burgers, fish-less fingers and nuggets of sinew and chicken skin were now to be off the menu completely.

Rose Gray, who set up a charity called Cooks in Schools (which offers professional chefs as mentors to dinner ladies), remembers that it was the parents rather than the kids who turned their noses up at her children's tea parties. 'They'd see these pancakes. They were huge things that I'd fold over and cut into pieces, and they'd say, "What's that? I don't know whether Johnny's going to eat that." I find that children will eat delicious food. It can be quite strange but if it looks good and smells good, they'll try it. I think it's the fear of the parents in our culture based on the fact that fast food has become the only food that is presented to children. Parents don't give their children any confidence in food.'

The star of the TV series turned out to be not Jamie or Nora, but the Turkey Twizzler. An unknown before Fresh One's cameras trained down on an unsuspecting school dinner, it was suddenly hoisted onto the public stage in a homage to our make-over culture; this was a product that had almost nothing real in it at all, and our kids loved it. As soon as the programme was aired, two of the biggest school catering companies, Scolarest and Sodexho, announced they were dropping Twizzlers from their menus as if they hadn't read the ingredients on the back of the packets before. Georgina Parkes of Scolarest held her head high and told the press: 'Turkey Twizzlers will be removed from all our menus. Across the vast majority of schools, we have not been serving Turkey Twizzlers for more than three months, but in a handful of cases the client requested the product was kept on. We recognise consumer concerns over the product and, regardless of client preference, will not be serving them any more.' She claimed that they would have removed them without the pressure anyway: 'We don't regard it as a knee-jerk reaction to Jamie Oliver's programme, although he has had some influence in us putting the final step in place.'

David Joll, managing director of Bernard Matthews, which made the product, pouted and accused the press of being mean: 'We have been unfairly treated. Turkey is the least fatty of all meats.' He pointed out that they had created a new version with 7% fat. 'The new Twizzlers have only a third of the fat level of the average pork sausage, yet you don't hear Jamie Oliver telling people not to eat sausages.' What he failed to mention was that the Twizzler was bulging with the kind of ingredients you'd never find in an Essex Pig Company sausage. Turkey accounted for only 34% of its ingredients, with water, pork fat, rusk, wheat starch, three sweeteners (including the controversial additive aspartame), hardened or hydrogenated vegetable oil and colourings and flavourings bulking it up and making it last for months.

The nation was shocked and playgrounds across the country were filled with shoulder-shrugging parents gossiping about how this evil interloper could ever have been allowed into school dining rooms. The Turkey Twizzler became an icon of our neglect, our blind trust in our schools to take good care of our children once the morning bell had been rung. It warned us that if you didn't watch your back, the Government would sell your child's health to the highest bidder. Forget stranger danger; the enemy was already within our schools and furring our children's arteries.

CHAPTER 28

CHILDREN'S CHOICE

Jamie's no-nonsense conservative roots had set the tone for the series, but programme consultant Tim Lang, who had been championing the idea for the last 20 years, pointed out that refusing customer choice was not something that any political party would be aligned with. 'I don't think Government, the food industry or parents recognise yet that it's about not having a choice in what we put into children,' he told me. 'Allowing eight-year-olds unrestricted choice means that they'll eat crap. They'll eat sugary crap; we all understand that maybe biologically there might even be a predilection for such things, but not if it's the sum of food.'

He believes that the issue of choice is an ideological problem of the Blair Government. 'How can children be expected to understand and appreciate the implications of how what they eat now and up to their twenties will impact on them when they're in their seventies? It's the difference between short term and long term, between individualism and citizenship.' But he knew from personal experience what Jamie was up against: 'It hasn't been fashionable to speak about it, and politically it's always been a no-go area. You don't become their favourite person.'

In Greenwich the kids were outraged at having their junk food taken away. 'The kids didn't give a shit about me and who I was,' Jamie told *Education Guardian*. 'Kidbrooke is not a posh school and the kids never once thought they were lucky to be getting the chance to eat some good food.' Primary school children wept at the loss of chips from the menu – and vomited when they tasted real chicken for the first time. With banners demanding that Jamie go home, secondary school children demonstrated in the playground and gangs of girls made angry complaints to the dinner ladies. Those old enough to leave the grounds during lunchtime voted with their feet and nipped off to the local chippy, passing those who were not allowed out packets of fish and chips through the railings. Parents spoilt their already obese children with lunch boxes packed with chocolate bars and fizzy drinks.

With his mobile screaming Jools' increasing frustration at Jamie's latest extra-marital passion, and Poppy sobbing at the news that Daddy had to go back to work after a rare appearance at home, this was not the trip back into the playground he had imagined. He had even piled his cash into the project again. 'I probably did 300 grand of my own dosh on *School Dinners*,' he said. Jamie's morale was rock bottom. 'This project was becoming bigger and uglier than he thought,' said Timothy Spall, the unlikely narrator of *School Dinners*.

Again the cameras followed him into his private life, even showing Jools breaking down as Jamie told her the latest tabloid story. 'Have you heard the latest?' he said as his right-hand woman and manager Louise Holland and the crew watched on. 'I've shagged some waitress in Amsterdam.' Instead of telling her that it wasn't true, bizarrely he chose to prolong her agony with the strange choice of words, 'It's all gone away.' 'What do you mean, it's all gone away? How can it go away?' she screamed until he eventually told her, 'Because there was nothing to it, it's all untrue.' 'Poor Jools,' he said to camera. 'She finds it quite hard.' Ultimately, he trusted the producer and director, both foodies and parents, not to stitch him up. 'I'd rather not film at home, quite frankly,' he said, 'but if you want to touch hearts and souls, and paint a really true picture, how else can you make a meaningful documentary?' as if he were reading a directive from his commissioning editor. '*School Dinners* wasn't just school dinners, it was an emotional thing. I wouldn't risk my family for anything. The point is did it impact upon my family? Jools wouldn't let it and nor would I.'

Using his website again instead of picking up the phone, he posted a message for us all to see. 'I have really missed Jools, Poppy and Daisy. I am so looking forward to this weekend as we are spending time together in the country. It will be great as I have not seen them all week. Jools works so hard running my family life whilst I am away. In fact tonight, my darling, I will massage your feet for more than three hours.' Whether she got the massage or not, we didn't find out. But judging by how often he let her down throughout the series, it's unlikely. He was working late on the recipes Nora insisted he write up, taking the dinner ladies off to boot camp to teach them to cook and off on location for weeks on end. It was only the previous year that he had told the press, 'For the first three or four years of my career on telly, even though I enjoyed it, I was pushed around quite a lot. But in the last couple of years I've learnt to finally take control myself by saying no. I'm just going to be working at Fifteen, doing some charity work, a bit more travelling, some reading, cooking and having a bit of fun for a change. Jools deserves a medal for putting up with me.'

But he had discovered a monster, and he could not walk away until it was slain. The figures that Fresh One's researchers were feeding him were stacking up to provide an appalling picture of British children's health and Jamie realised the success of this project really could change the nation. Fifty-seven per cent of children, he was told, had a totally unbalanced diet. Constipation clinics were dealing with children whose fibre-less diet had left them bunged up for six weeks at a time, with a real risk of colon cancer later in life. He heard about eight-year-olds vomiting semi-formed faeces. As Jamie's jaw dropped, the paediatric dietician told him, 'It has to come out somewhere.'

Jamie knew this was no longer just about being a good dad: 'I'm not doing this because my kids are going to state schools, because they ain't going to state schools, let's be honest.' In their little blue-and-white dresses and boaters, Daisy and Poppy were already among Hampstead's celebrity infants. They were spending their days at Devonshire House prep school, where the idea of a Turkey Twizzler finding its way onto the menu is as preposterous as the concept that any one of the children at Eden Primary in Peterlee, County Durham, might afford the fees.

It was at Eden Primary School, though, that Jamie found the missing piece of the jigsaw. Taking a group of 10-year-olds to cook freshly picked asparagus in a billy can at a special Year Six picnic, he spotted the first crack in the children's armour. Noticing that 10-year-old 'Chocolate Boy' seemed to enjoy his first bite of asparagus until he turned to see his mate Liam spitting it out in disgust, Jamie saw that for children, the experience of eating was as a pack. He came up with an idea; those who wanted to get involved in cooking their dinner with him would have to eat it, and those who did not would have their packed lunches outside the class. It was a divisive measure and one that alienated the picky. When pushed outside the pack, the shock was sure to bring them back to eat their home-made Jamie Oliver lunch – and love it.

Praise the good and ignore the bad; it's the mainstay of good parenting and the philosophy of Eden Primary, and it worked. With another trick plucked from his childhood, the Cub Scout's armful of badges, Jamie gave stickers to the children who had tasted his parsnip chips and kept off the sweets at home. With parents and teachers reporting calmer behaviour and higher levels of concentration in the classroom, Jamie left Peterlee, statistically the most unhealthy area of Britain, and went back to Greenwich with a resolve to step up the experiment.

Improved behaviour and concentration were clear evidence of the impact of nutrition on the brain, but Jamie's School Dinners were also having an effect on the body. In one school, there were no requests for asthma pumps at all after junk food was removed from the menu. This was the cleverer, cooler nation that Jamie had dreamed of. After six months of children filing in to complain to Nora, now there were only two. 'We can deal with those,' she said as she sat down again to cajole and calm another of the 800 children she had persuaded to eat Jamie's food. A year on, 600 kids were using the canteen regularly, with another 100 buying the healthy packed lunches Jamie designed to counter the choco-late and fizzy drinks packed by anxious parents.

With a template emerging for success in every school, a bible of recipes and ideas for ways in which food could be integrated into the curriculum, food weeks and tips from Greenwich schools were printed off and distributed across the borough. The 'Feed Me Better' campaign on Jamie's website meant that anyone could do it. It was time to call on the Government to take it to the country. The then British Minister for Education, Charles Clarke, was impressed as Jamie and Louise Holland met him for dinner at Fifteen. When Jamie first told the press of his plans, the Government response had been swift. 'If Jamie's got views on school meals then we would be very interested to hear what he has to say,' a spokesperson from the Department of Education told the newspapers. Charles Clarke was said to hold Jamie Oliver in high regard after he lent his support to the Government's 'Get On' literacy campaign in 2000.

Now Clarke was coming to his table and Jamie was determined to deliver the message clearly. If the Government had been clear about the impact speeding and drinking could have on our lives, thought Jamie, why would they refuse to use the same kind of shock tactics to link nutrition to poor health and behaviour? Clarke was easily convinced, and confessed that he was surprised to find there could be such a difference in quality for so little extra cash. He promised then and there to take junk food off school menus, providing no choice for a healthy lunch. He would find the money to pay for the better ingredients and for dinner ladies to be trained and properly rewarded for their longer hours. He was talking about a mere 15p per child, but it was what Jamie, Louise and the team had worked so hard for.

'In the haze of it all I knew what we were doing was important,' he told the press. 'I knew that I should feel good about it, but I felt shit every day. But in the way it was edited, those four programmes – fuck it, I'll be big-headed – were brilliant and clever and honest.'

CHAPTER 29

WHEN JEANETTE MET JAMIE

Jamie's School Dinners had been a triumph of TV and a victory for food campaigners. But to begin with, Jamie hadn't had a clue. He was relying on his relentless optimism in the human condition, and his own charisma and passion for food to inspire the school, the Council and the dinner ladies to change their menu, and the children to try it. Television production teams work hard to make a journey like this into the unknown as gripping, as elating and ultimately as hopeful as the audience needs it to be. Fresh One had done it with *Jamie's Kitchen*, again another potential disaster which Jamie's unique energy and commitment had turned into a dream of a series, giving life to a real charity which would spread out across the world.

Gennaro Contaldo watched Fresh One line up a group of experts for both *Jamie's Kitchen* and *School Dinners*, and says that it is Jamie's instinct for choosing the right people that makes his projects work so well. 'He delegates well and he trusts everybody,' he told me. 'But he trains people and he's very intelligent at choosing the right people to work for him.' Louise Holland, his right arm, is one of them. 'She manages him,' said Gennaro. 'She is another Jamie. He finds amazing people to work with him, but she's another one of him.'

This time Louise was on screen throughout the series, steering him through meetings with politicians and behaviourists, nutritionists and campaigners. She broke the news to Jools about the latest tabloid smear, wiped the tears of the dinner ladies when

Jamie threw his early strops and planned his itinerary like clock-work. 'Right,' said Jamie to camera, 'I'm off to Germany!' The director asked him why, and Jamie was momentarily silenced. 'I have no idea,' he eventually replied. 'Louise, why am I going to Germany?' he asked as he got into the car and drove to the airport.

Fresh One also worked with Fiona Gately of Prince Charles's Duchy Originals. 'She is a very cool customer, a very clever woman,' said food consultant Tim Lang. 'She's an astute woman with a strategic brain. My take was – and is – that we're halfway towards recognising the challenge in what needs to change in our food culture. I encouraged them in what they wanted to do, but I am very sober and I don't think that school meals on their own can do it because it wasn't school meals that caused the problem in the first place.'

The Soil Association was supplying Fresh One with information about alternative ways of providing food to schools and Tim Lang prepped them on the politics. 'I'm a great fan of what they did and how he grasped it immediately,' said Lang. 'He went into dangerous territory.' Fresh One was dealing with a political no-go area stretching back 20 years. 'It started with the 1980 Education Act under the Tories,' said Tim, referring to the years of Margaret Thatcher 'the Milk Snatcher' and the farming out of school meals to the private sector. With business targets and profits dictating the menu, customer choice became the only way to get bums on seats at lunchtime.

Kevin McKay, chair of the caterer's association, LACA (Local Authorities Caterers Association), whose members received the biggest bruising after the airing of *School Dinners*, says that it was when the British Government introduced competitive tendering in 1989 that it all started to go wrong. 'It happened because the Government were committed to reducing the cost of school meals. They needed to save money. It was front line, blue-collar services that were targeted first. The strong view was that they could reduce the cost of this by opening it up to competition and bringing in the market economics.'

Caterers for schools and hospitals were receiving subsidies of up to 80% for saturated fat products such as full-fat cheese, butter and milk, and with finances on the critical list, they claimed to have both arms tied. Robin Jenkins, Senior Catering Officer at what was then the ILEA (Inner London Education Authority), told me back in 1993, when Jamie Oliver was an 18-year-old catering student, that children's eating standards in school were back to the way they were in the Thirties. 'It's an absolute scandal that they're not getting enough energy or calcium in their food,' he said.

Jenkins explained the institutional lack of commitment to healthy eating. 'The local authorities want to keep the school catering services in-house, and healthy eating is low on the list of priorities while they're struggling against the cuts and closures. Add to that the innate hostility between caterers and nutritionists, and there's not much chance of a change in that direction.' Little did he know what Jamie had been simmering in the First Year's kitchen at Westminster Catering College. 'Staff are employed according to the demands in the kitchen and dining room,' he went on, 'and if children are refusing to eat school meals because chips are off the menu, the staff are going to be laid off, too. The irony is that the only answer is to give your child a packed lunch, and that doesn't require catering services at all.'

The 1992 British 'Health of the Nation' report had gone some way to address the effect that the nation's waistline was having on the NHS. A Mediterranean style diet, rich in garlic, olive oil and red wine, it concluded, was just the job to bring our cholesterol down and turn us into a food-loving band of merry men and women. Even though we had the recipe for regaining control over spiralling diet-related health issues, it would be another 12 years before an Essex boy with the soul of an Italian would bring tuna arabbiatta with penne and tomato and basil salad into the dining halls of British schools.

At that time Tim Lang was a lobbyist at Parents for Safe Food and had already launched a campaign backed by the British Medical Association and the Women's Institute to persuade the

Government, parents and schools to apply healthy eating standards to school meals. 'The good news is that the Government is beginning to recognise its responsibilities to ensure that caterers play their part in achieving national health guidelines,' Lang told me 12 years before *Jamie's School Dinners* had to deal with the legacy of a Government which didn't keep its promises. 'Schools have a huge responsibility to promote public health,' he said. 'The big question is whether these fine intentions will be put into practice at a local level and whether the Government will back its promises nationally. We have to give a priority to giving children good food in school so that they eat well throughout their lives. It's too easy for Government to say that it's the individual responsibility of parents to make sure their children eat properly.'

Spin the clock forward to 2005 and Lang can see that it wasn't just the Tory party who were contributing to the decline of nutritional standards in schools. 'Labour didn't want to debate the issue of choice either,' he said. 'They preferred voluntarism and loose guidelines. It's not enough.' When you start talking about removing choice, the word 'Nanny' is not too far behind. 'You don't become their favourite person,' said Lang. 'But Jamie took that risk and he gained from it. He didn't lose face at all.' But if it seemed that it was Jamie's unique blast of energy and profanity that would have Health Minister at the time Ruth Kelly checking her figures and moving goalposts, in reality the School Dinner Revolution had much humbler beginnings.

Jeanette Orrey, a 'simple mum with three strapping lads', was an unusually imaginative dinner lady at St Peter's primary school in East Bridgford, Nottinghamshire. She was depressed by what her job had become: 'Dinner ladies weren't allowed to cook any more,' she told the *Telegraph*. 'All we had to do was be able to use a pair of scissors. We would cut open packets of orange pulp and bung them in the ovens. Then we scooped out the mush and flung it into plastic flight trays. We might as well have been on a production line.' She seized upon the opportunity offered by the deregulation of school meals services in April 2000 to bring her catering in-house and set about sourcing as much local, organic and fair trade produce as possible from local farmers. 'I got sausages, carrots, broccoli, and I got the kids to try it all,' she said. 'They are your customers; they'll soon tell you if they don't like something, believe me.'

Orrey's vegetables were supplied for the same price as non-organic produce by a local organic grower, her fresh meat by a farm shop that sources locally and uses an abattoir 20 minutes away. 'I can tell you which farm the animal came from and how many miles it travelled to be slaughtered. Being from a village background, BSE and the Foot and Mouth crisis made me want to put beef back on the menu. The only way to do this was to make it fully traceable – so that's what I did.'

The children were having fresh local pork with Bramley apple sauce, but they also had pizza. The difference was that Jeanette would make the bases. She used local milk and organic flour, margarine and sugar, and said that the children's favourite was roast dinner – topside of beef providing the central feast with trimmings from the surrounding countryside. Her costs rocketed to 60–70p a day but she managed not to pass these onto the parents. She was even making money and soon had enough to buy a new cooker. By cutting out contract suppliers and red tape, as well as increasing demand for her roast beef, 80 per cent of the 230 children were eating school meals. Parents were invited to join the kids for lunch, and on Wednesdays – or 'wrinkly day' – senior citizens were offered school dinners, too.

It was sociable and old fashioned, without a plastic tray in sight. 'They talk socially, enjoy food and use knives and forks,' she told journalist Lara Watson. 'Proper cooked school dinners are what I want to see – we need to get away from the fast food generation.' Eating organic and local increased the quality of life for everyone. 'Staff are getting their skills and respect back too,' she said. 'Things are not going to change overnight,' she added, 'but if we all do a little, we can make a huge difference.'

The initiative won her the Local Food Initiative of the Year at the Soil Association Awards in 2002, but although she didn't know it yet, she had barely begun. Meeting Lizzie Vann, a former analyst and product development consultant for large food companies (and the brains behind the Organix baby food company), would change her life. Vann was a governor of a school in Hampshire. 'I asked what the children were eating and because of the poor quality of food, the governors exploded with questions,' she said. 'That began a six-month process of trying to understand how bad the school meals were, why they were so bad, and who was organising them.'

Lizzie went to see the catering arm of Hampshire County Council and their procurement office to see what could be done. She talked to children, and through Organix, analysed the food on offer until a picture began to emerge about widespread discontent among pupils, parents and governors, and a shocking lack of attention to the nutritional values in a basic school meal. But Lizzie and Organix were not the only people who wanted to see widespread change, and it was the meeting of like minds through the Soil Association that inspired her to take the next step. 'I met Jeanette at a conference in 2003 and we agreed to do something together. So Jeanette and Simon Brenman [a specialist in the organic supply chain] and I got together on a motorway service station on the M4 and said, "Right, we're going to launch a campaign."' They called it 'Food for Life'. 'Our aims were based on achieving 100% of the Caroline Walker Trust nutritional standards, and in addition, we targeted 50% locally sourced, 30% organic and four days a week or 75% of meals to be made from unprocessed ingredients – that meant food cooked from scratch. Some schools interpreted this to be one junk food day a week, a Bangers and Mash or Fish Fingers Friday, while others did it on meal components.'

They went to five schools in Devon, Hampshire, London and Nottingham, and asked them to meet these targets and measure the costs. 'We knew that we would be far more successful with the campaign if we could show the practical effect – and the financial cost – of improving the meals,' said Lizzie. 'So Jeanette took it to her school, St Peter's in Nottinghamshire, Simon took it to his in Devon and I took it to Sopley. We also worked with two other schools – one in London and one in Devon. We wanted to see what the consequences were if children would take up school dinners. Schools were running meals at 30% take up; it's like running a school for 30% of the children. It just doesn't make sense. They all wanted to provide good food, but given the budget and the way the procurement chain was constructed, it was a tough challenge. But we were able to show the Government and other sceptics that it was possible and that costs would not rise too much. At Sopley in Hampshire, they went up from 37p to 43p in the first term, but at the same time the uptake doubled from 35% to 70% of the pupils, which brought in more money to pay for the higher ingredient cost.'

They also wanted to measure any change in child behaviour. Lizzie's personal background as a hyperactive meant that she had been studying the relationship between food and cognitive behaviour for years, and this was at the root of her food campaigning.

Jeanette, Simon and Lizzie took their campaign to the Soil Association. 'For a long time I had been badgering the Soil Association to run a campaign about the quality of food fed to children,' said Lizzie. 'We knew that people really understand the benefits of organic food when they have children. Today four out of five parents are feeding their new child some organic baby food in the first year of life, and the sales of organic baby meals in jars outweigh the sales of non-organic baby food. We wanted to take it to the Soil Association and say, "Look, if you want to get involved in good stuff, this is perfect for you." To the great credit of Peter Melchett [policy director of the Soil Association and an organic farmer himself] he saw the strength of the campaign, and got behind it, persuading the organisation to take it on. So we ended up with a great team: Jeanette with her practical and management experience, me with my food campaigning hat, Simon working on the supply chain, Hannah Pearce researching and writing the report and Peter, who is such a persuasive political operator. And the time was right – it was something that couldn't fail.'

What would make it more effective would be a high profile and very public TV series. Jamie had just won over the hearts and minds of a cynical public with *Jamie's Kitchen* and Lizzie recognised that he had an unusual sense of conscience. She personally took their newly published Food for Life report down to Fifteen in October 2003. Lizzie said, 'I put it on the counter. He wasn't there, but I said, "Please give this to him. We've just finished watching *Jamie's Kitchen* and it's a great programme, but this is his next TV series."

'I don't know if that is what kick-started the project. But whether it did or didn't, the work that the Soil Association team had done behind the scenes, understanding the issues and the solutions, meant that when Fresh One started work on the school meals project, there was a lot of very useful thinking to go with.'

The campaigns ran together. 'We were all working in the background,' said Lizzie, 'although they were obviously doing their own stuff and choosing their own schools. We suggested that they work with Thomas Fairchild School that was previously supplied by a private company, but they chose Greenwich so that they could work with more than one school to broaden it out. That was good because they had to tackle a local authority that didn't have to make a profit. If they had gone to Thomas Fairchild, which has been part of – I think – Compass or Initial Catering Service, they would have had different criteria to work with.'

Jamie first met Jeanette at the Radio 4 Food and Farming awards a few months after Food for Life had reached his door. 'I told him how revolting school dinners were and he was gob-smacked,' she told the *Daily Telegraph*'s Alice Thomson. Their shared no-nonsense approach to food was to hit gold for both of them. She even sounded like him when she was quoted in the press. 'I believe in what I'm doing and I can see the difference it makes. I don't need fancy studies. Surely meat that's got nothing on it has to be better than something that's been sprayed with God-knows-what, and food that comes from five miles down the road is better than something that's come 500. It's just common sense.'

'Well done, babe, you're a national hero,' Jamie said to the woman who Patrick Holden, director of the Soil Association, described as 'living proof that one person can change the world'. 'You've taught schools how to change their bloomin' awful rubbish food into healthy food.' He promised Jeanette that he would help – 'He came to our school to cook in our kitchen,' a trip that would lead to the Channel 4 show and ultimately a change in Government policy. 'I never thought he'd be able to banish Turkey Twizzlers for good,' said Jeanette. 'Now even the Prime Minister has become involved in the battle for better school meals.'

With Jeanette's inspiring story and Food for Life's fact file, Jamie was on to a winner. Lizzie provided Fresh One with the Organix surveys on children's food which investigated the extent of mechanically recovered meat, the Dirty Dozen of additives that Organix campaigns against, as well as information on the poor quality of foods such as sausages.

To be fair, it was probably Jools who planted the seed in Jamie, which Food for Life fed and watered. She had already become famously fanatical about the way that she fed little Poppy, and by the time Daisy was toddling, she admitted she took fresh fruit to children's parties for them to eat instead of the usual kiddie tea on offer. The tabloids loved it, and accused her of being a Nazi mother, something Jools found 'extremely offensive'. 'Yes, I *do* do this,' she wrote in *Minus Nine to One*. 'I mean, my girls are only 18 months old and two and a half years old, and if you can't control their eating habits now, then when the hell can you? I know only too well that when they reach four or five they will be eating chocolate and cakes, whether I like it or not.' It was this attitude of 'no choice' that would be Jamie's conclusion to sorting out school dinners.

Jamie stuck to his guns about the source of inspiration of *School Dinners* when he wrote in his foreword to Jeanette's book, *The*

Dinner Lady, 'For the last year and a half I've been working on a project about school dinners; learning about all the deep and mysterious things that go into the feeding of our nation of kids. Very early on, me and my team became aware of the amazing work of Jeanette Orrey at St Peter's School in Nottinghamshire.' Recently, however, he has taken a more pro-active approach and has lent his support on the Soil Association website. 'I support the Soil Association because I want to cook with the best ingredients,' he wrote. 'They're working to ensure that food is the way it should be: healthy, tasty and grown with nature.'

'Jamie is very close to Jeanette,' said Craig Sams, chair of the Soil Association, which employs Jeanette two days a week as School Meals Policy Adviser. 'We gave her the income so she could delegate her day-to-day responsibilities as a dinner lady and embark on this gratifying new role in life that she's been leading as a consultant helping transform school dinners all over the country in the same way she did at St Peter's.'

Jeanette now travels around the country encouraging other schools to implement the Food for Life targets, and won The Observer Food Award for 'the person who has done the most for the food & drink industry' in 2003. Her book, *The Dinner Lady,* with recipes for a family of four or a school canteen of 96, was reaching an Amazon rating of 486 at the time this book first went to press. Compare that with *Jamie's Dinners,* which comes in at 10, and Nigella Lawson's *Feast* at 384, and you can see why she's not complaining. In 2005 she was awarded the highly prestigious Glenfiddich Independent Spirit Award in recognition of her 'outstanding contribution towards widening the understanding and appreciation of food and drink in Britain'. 'Very rarely do I deviate left or right,' she told *The Education Guardian.* 'I just keep going; I believe totally in what I am doing.'

Jamie too has grown with the role of social revolutionary. A delegate at the Soil Association conference thought that Jamie looked uncomfortable when he first addressed them in 2004. 'He was talking to an audience which is also passionate about food but they go about things in a different way. It's a very middle-class organisation and I think he felt out of place. He did that thing that he does, when his collar is standing up and he spreads his legs, and he puts his hands in his pockets and wiggles his chest. It's an alpha male thing with him. He's saying "Here I am." But I think that it was because he was overwhelmed. He was in a sympathetic audience and I think that was quite unusual for him. Most of the time he's been saying a message that people don't recognise or feel comfortable with, and he has to fight with them.' Craig Sams, chair of the Soil Association, agreed: 'He was as nervous as anything. He even called me "Sir."'

As his audience has become more sympathetic, Jamie has grown in confidence. His message about the need for good food is no longer resisted or sidelined. When Lizzie Vann met him a year later, he seemed to have settled into his new role with a new confidence. 'It was at a dinner with Prince Charles – I think it was an anniversary of the Soil Association or something, and he was cooking. He was talking about ingredients and he was on his own turf there, which made him much more confident.' The audience was entranced, she said. 'He speaks from the heart – it's a real cliché but he does, and you get a real sense that he's thought about it and he's really angry about it. He taps into the kind of things that people should feel angry about – every parent feels tremendous responsibility about feeding their children. We send them out into the big wide world and they get corrupted by advertising and all sorts of influences. We get angry that other adults in the food industry and those running the schools are not taking responsibility, but the difference is that Jamie says, "I'm not having it – and let's do something about it." Everyone loves him being the guy at the front of the campaign, and he realises that now. He's a great guy.'

Lizzie Vann has nothing but praise for what Jamie has been able to do to change school dinners. She doffs her cap to Fresh One's ability to see the big picture. 'They made the right decision. We would have had to do it school by school, head by head. But they used Jamie's great personality to make it something much bigger than Jeanette or I could ever have done – it was great.' She is currently using her Goodies brand to campaign for more child awareness about additives and good nutrition, coming up with innovative ideas such as fridge magnets which mark off a daily intake of the five portions of fruit and vegetables currently recommended for a healthy diet. 'You put it out there and then move on to the next thing,' she said. Craig Sams too is more interested in the bigger message but it's clear that a little more acknowledgement of the enormous work at grass roots level would not have gone amiss. 'Lizzie Vann gave a passionate speech about kids and school food, and food in general,' said Craig, 'and we pushed this whole thing, and then Jamie comes along and does a TV programme and barely mentions the Soil Association. I couldn't care less; for me the important thing is goals rather than vanity but there are people who say, "Well, why didn't he mention the Soil Association more?"'

Emma Noble, policy co-ordinator at the Soil Association, recognises the value of Jamie's ego. 'He was able reach a bigger audience than we ever could at the Soil Association. We have to be more careful but he doesn't care who he upsets. I think that there were lots of people in the middle tier at the LEA [London Education Authority] who had been trying to change the issues affecting school dinners for years and then Jamie came along and blew the lid off it all. I think that some people were a bit cheesed-off after not being able to get anywhere themselves but mostly, they were thrilled with what he did.'

She thinks we need more people like Jamie to change our food culture at its roots: 'I think what's really interesting is what he brings to the food discussion. He's made processed food really unfashionable. I hate this reductionist attitude to food where people have to count calories, or eat certain types of food. We need to re-educate people about food culture. We need them to have a relationship with food, to cook it, to know where it comes from, to understand how farms work, how food unites cultures and to really celebrate what food is. It's young mums he needs to start targeting now. Teaching them how to cook would make the real change that we need.'

The Soil Association continues to work behind the scenes to ensure that school dinners comply with the Caroline Walker nutritional standards and Craig Sams is happy with the profile the Fresh One project has been able to give the Association. The Soil Association sat on current Education Minister Ruth Kelly's review in 2005 and their presence now gives them a different role to play in influencing Government policy.

CHAPTER 30

THE POLITICS OF FOOD

The response to the *School Dinners* series was immediate. Jamie
exploded the issue onto the screens, and the media couldn't get
enough. He harnessed our collective outrage by painting a picture
of government and corporations working together to poison our
kids. Parents who knew how bad the food was were suitably
shamed, while those who didn't were equally red-faced at their
negligence. 'Parents wonder why their kids are hyperactive, have
gut ache and stink when they come home,' said Jamie. 'It's
because the food they are fed is made of shit! It baffles me.'

The press was impressed with how genuine he seemed to be.
'He has the figures – "21,000 schools, 130,000 dinner ladies,
£1.4bn spent a year on school dinners" – at the tip of his fingers,'
wrote Caroline Stacey in the *Independent*. 'Nobody pulls his
strings. Midway through transmission of *Jamie's School Dinners*,
Channel 4 had organised a debate between academics, policy-
makers, organic lobbyists and food activists. 'Phrases such as
"devolve responsibility to people who are incentivised by their
shareholders" tripped off his tongue,' wrote Stacey.

The revolution had planted dynamite under the very heart of
the food industry; even McDonald's began advertising a healthier
range. So when Home Secretary David Blunkett resigned only
two days after Jamie's meeting with Charles Clarke, catapulting
the former Education Secretary into his boots, the blow was felt
from Fresh One's offices in Nile Street to Greenwich. Ruth Kelly,

it was announced, would come from the Treasury to take up his position. As the Fresh One team read her report that set limits for lower salt, fat and sugar, but did not propose taking junk off the menu, their hearts may have been sinking but Jamie was already planning his next campaign. He would gather a petition via his website, calling upon parents to encourage their friends to sign and spread the word until he had 271,677 signatures to hand to Tony Blair. As a result, the British Government promised a cash injection of £280 million over three years into the school meal industry, £60 million of which would come from National Lottery money, with the cost per child rising from 37p to 50p in primary schools and 60p in secondary schools.

The press was predictably cynical. 'A revolution in nutrition? Hardly,' wrote the *Daily Mail*. 'There will be no new money. It probably won't add up to £280m anyway. And much of it won't be spent on better food. We are left with the old, old story: another New Labour exercise that leaves a nasty taste.' But the *Daily Mirror* was determined not to let the opportunity for change pass by: 'Now there is a chance to reverse not only the standard of meals but the absence of somewhere to cook them. Gordon Brown has pledged £9.4bn to revamp school buildings. Ms Kelly must insist that a share of that goes to reinstate kitchens. No school should be without one. They are as important as a gym... The days of inadequate, unhealthy school meals must be ended.'

By 2006 the Government's £280 million had been boosted by £15 million from the Department for Education and Schools for the new School Food Trust, set up to support parents, local authorities and schools in improving school food. Ruth Kelly promised that real results would be seen by the end of the year. 'We will follow the recommendations of the independent School Meals Review Panel, adopting tougher nutritional standards and making it harder for pupils to opt out of healthy food,' she said. 'And we will ensure the removal of chocolate, sugary fizzy drinks and crisps from school vending machines. This will happen in all schools by September 2006; with tougher, nutrient based standards being phased in by 2008 in primary schools and 2009 in secondary schools. And make no mistake, we expect these dates to be the deadline for the last school to meet the standards, not the target for the majority.'

Food consultant Diane McRea said that whether or not we see this happen will be proof of Kelly's political will. 'If we're serious about change, it has to be institutional. Teachers, who have been teaching cookery as part of Design Technology, will have to be trained properly as part of their original training. For schools to have proper kitchens it means putting proper money into it.' 'We will make the provision of new or upgraded school kitchen facilities a priority in our Building Schools for the Future Programme,' said Kelly, 'so that fresh produce can be prepared and served in schools. And we plan to offer a new vocational qualification for school caterers so that they gain their rightful place as valued, highly-trained, members of the school team.'

McRae is cynical about whether or not Kelly will come up with the goods. 'If it doesn't come from the politicians, it has to come from the governors,' she said. 'Health and safety regulations have prevented anyone from taking initiatives in the past. You need to have proper kitchen facilities with places for children to be able to wash their hands. What Jamie Oliver has done is great, but you can see the challenges that he's up against. Greenwich had an unusual number of cooks working in that kitchen, but they didn't have the proper skills between them. There has to be a lot of commitment to follow it through.'

It sounds as if Ruth Kelly is on top of the issue, although only time will tell. 'If we want to cut childhood obesity, we need our pupils to have the skills and knowledge they need to make healthy choices throughout their lives,' she wrote in response to an interview for this book. 'We are working with the Department of Health, investing £5.7 million every year to promote healthy lifestyles to pupils. And through programmes like Growing Schools, we're getting 13,000 more schools to use "outdoor classrooms", learning about health, sustainable development and food. In partnership with the DCMS [Department for Culture, Media and Sport], we are improving school sport – investing over £1.5 billion, so all schools offer pupils at least two hours of quality PE [Physical Education] every week and getting more of them involved in local sports clubs. And with London's successful bid to host the 2012 Olympics, we have a great opportunity to engage pupils even more with the benefits and excitement that sport can bring to their lives.

'We are now in a really strong position to achieve a real transformation in school meals. We are providing the investment, we're engaging parents; we're helping staff to obtain the skills they need. And all within a framework which encourages children to make healthy choices throughout their lives. We have a long way to go, but together we can really make a difference to this important aspect of children's lives.'

By 2005 'Jamie Oliver' was the byword for food campaigning. Radio phone-ins and newspaper essays debated fat taxes and food advertising, cultural laziness and the increase in obesity, but all conclusions came back to the Jamie Oliver effect. Shaming the Government, storming into the school kitchens, embarrassing parents into realising just how they were killing their kids with a diet of junk food and attitude based on sloth, Jamie was our culinary crusader. He somehow managed to have breakfast with Tony Blair and then-shadow leader, Michael Howard, without anyone accusing him of signing on either dotted line. However, when the *Daily Mail* ran a spoof article saying that Jamie was in talks with the Conservative party on 1 April 2005, no one was too surprised. 'Politically I'd have him down as a Tory,' said Rupert Ivey. 'He's that whole Essex boy done good, that Thatcherite aspirational type politics. But the way he does things makes him seem like he's a complete socialist. I don't think he really understands politics, which is excellent. He's only interested in doing good.'

But by October the same year, the Government's programme for improving school food had still only been given half the money it had been promised. Tough new standards that had been recommended by Ruth Kelly's review panel were said to cost around £486m to implement, leaving a gap of £266m. Suzi Leather, who chaired the panel, told a press conference: 'There is clearly a gap between what accountants have told us about the cost and what the government has publicly committed.' The review said that all school meals would have to meet the 14 'nutrient-based' standards on fat, sugar, protein and fibre, and would be cooked on site from fresh seasonal produce procured locally. Dinner ladies and cooks would be given training and qualifications, as well as overtime and extra staff. And in a measure to correct the generation gap of the last 25 years, practical cookery lessons and food education initiatives such as farm visits would be introduced into schools.

Kevin McKay, chair of the Caterers Association, LACA, was not surprised. 'The vision is about developing skills in children, but if you start listening to the Government on this, they'd be the first to admit that the current parents have lost the plot so we have to concentrate on the next generation. That won't just encourage healthier lifestyles but will make them more responsible parents in the future. But it does mean that we have this gap at the moment and we need to work out how to deal with it. We can't rely on the parents.'

All this means thinking time, something Kevin McKay says television hasn't got. 'There hasn't been any change as such yet,' he said. 'Individual authorities are working on their plans and the authority needs to take stock of and work it out for themselves. The DFES [Department for Education and Skills] says that where schools are on their own, they have to think about what their issues are.' McKay said that where schools take their own budgets on, the evidence is that they don't deliver, although Orrey's example was a shining one. 'It's admirable for those schools that do work and can be supported by parents, but what about the huge chunk of schools in rural areas which have to supply free school meals?' he asked. 'You're talking then about £2.50 a meal, which means that the whole thing is reliant on cost subsidisation through large-scale contracts.'

Mention 'large scale' in the food business and you will usually find cuts in standards and bulking agents like monosodium glutamate are not far behind. McKay described how this happened in British schools. 'The large scale private sector was demanding food at a lower cost, so manufacturers went away and examined their processes, and added MSG [monosodium glutamate] and all these other things that bulk up food at no significant increased cost. But the vast majority of suppliers are desperate to find the goal posts. They say, "If you want real food, we'll do that for you and this is the cost for you." The answer is in giving them enough food and clear guidelines.'

Lizzie Vann is rather more straightforward. 'You try to increase your revenue, so you try to cater for as many people as possible as cheaply as possible. The way that you do that is to de-skill your labour force so you end up as we saw on *Jamie's School Dinners* with people opening up cardboard boxes and stuffing them in the oven. That's just not cooking. But it's very cheap and you can pay your operators far less than it would cost to make beef burgers from scratch. That would take a skilled operator far more time to do.'

She points out that those costs have been taken away from feeding more children simply to make more money for the catering company. 'And at the same time, we've never really valued the food that our children are given at school,' she added. 'We do at home – parents will spend as much as they can to feed their children well within their understanding of what that means. But the idea that when a child is out in the world they're fed something cheap and nasty because someone's trying to make a profit out of them is fairly horrifying to a parent. It's a clear exploitation and we haven't been aware of it. I would argue that although the school meal providers recognise that it's a special responsibility to be feeding children, they're operating as companies aiming to make a profit.'

McKay, who now has to deal with the fall-out of this exposé, believes the portrayal of the school meals service was 'largely inaccurate' on *Jamie's School Dinners* although he agreed that it did make exceptionally good TV. He accuses Fresh One of being simplistic and over-generalising the issue, but he does give them some credit. 'Hands up, I did say that there is no such thing as bad food, it's just a bad diet,' he confessed. 'But since *School Dinners*, I would now say that there is such a thing as bad food. And clearly that needs to come out of schools.'

He was glad of the press coverage, though, and if it increased his workload now, he welcomes the challenge. 'It's got everyone talking, including the media and politicians, but it's not representative of the service that is provided.' It's not only that the story varies from authority to authority, but, says McKay, that we're talking business. 'At the moment, you've got a business driven by stakeholders, and all the interested parties have their high moral ground. But the answer still needs to be delivered in a commercial type business. Our competition is not the shops in the High Street but the packed lunches brought from home. Evidence shows that the majority of packed lunches contain fizzy drinks and are less healthy.'

When dinner ladies themselves began to stage their own protest against *School Dinners* after the programme was aired, Jamie leapt into action again with a website campaign to remind us all to give them a little love. But it was too little too late for many of them. 'People were proud of what they were doing,' said Kevin McKay, 'and the last thing they wanted to see was children in tears when they had spent the whole morning producing food for them. I'm sure that the last people he would deliberately hurt would be the school caterers.'

Hazel Green of LACA said there was no doubt that Jamie could not have done that job without the help of Nora Sands. 'She was fantastic – but they all are, right across the country. For most dinner ladies, it's more than a job,' she said, forgetting the dinner ladies in Greenwich who said quite the opposite. 'They are totally committed to feeding children, especially when for some it's the only meal of the day. Despite Jamie knowing what happened and him saying "Support your dinner ladies", it was devastating for many of them.'

She explained that the culture shock of being taken over by big business was responsible for some of the resignation on the part of the dinner ladies about the kind of food they were agreeing to cook and serve up for young bodies. 'Part of the job of working in a school is that you're part of the community,' she said. 'They might have been a parent or grandparent, and when someone comes along and says that they're no longer employed by the school but by the contractor who doesn't speak to them in the same way, they're no longer part of the school and they stop caring quite so much.' She added that teachers have stopped eating school meals with the children, 'because they want to have their non-contact time away from the kids, so where does anyone really get that drive to say that these things really matter in our schools?'

LACA is working on this issue with the Food for Life project through the Soil Association to teach the midday supervisors who have replaced the teachers over lunchtime some of the people skills that Nora Sands and Jamie displayed in the series. 'They'll talk the kids through foods, saying, "Try this", and explaining what it is,' said Hazel. 'But they've got to get all those kids through lunch in 35 minutes. They can make or break a service if they shout at them or don't encourage them, so we've got a lot of work to do with schools to integrate them carefully.'

CHAPTER 31

BACK TO BASICS

Jeanette Orrey is in charge of promoting the Soil Association's message. 'Jeanette's model works,' said Lizzie Vann. 'She ran her own kitchen at St Peter's School, but she had relatively educated parents to deal with. But she also had local pensioners coming in, and she provided the post office with food and so as a local business it worked. You can't do that around the country; there just aren't enough of those people around. You have to do it the way that Jamie did – on a large-scale model. You have to work with parents who aren't as able to support it. If Kevin McKay chooses to take on that model, then that's great and if he doesn't, then we'll see the school meal service deteriorate. There will be so few children eating them that it will collapse in on itself. You'll get the system that exists in America and many places around the world where there just is no school meal service and that's such a shame. And if that happens, we've let down children. We can't let that happen.'

Craig Sams believes Orrey's legacy is in showing what was possible. 'She showed us that the Government can in-source, that they don't have to comply with a one-size-fits-all policy. Jeanette went to her school and suggested that they go to local farmers. She made it work. Jamie did it within a TV format – and you can't do it in a softly, softly way. Camera crews can't sit around while you consult the kids on one menu, so he blasted them and of course some of the message got lost. But what it did was create an awareness that something can be done. Parental pressure is there now on the school to do something about school meals. It develops more outlets for our suppliers so that they all become more economically viable and they grow a greater variety of crops. In Rome 100% of school food is now organic.'

Another of the new initiatives is to teach the cooks to cook. McKay is again defensive. 'Prior to 1989, most authorities had training kitchens,' said the man who closed the last one in Nottinghamshire four years ago. 'The building was physically falling down and it would have cost £¼ million to re-establish it elsewhere,' he explained. 'The training is now done on the job, but we need to remember that the vast majority of cooks can cook. If you look at Kidbrooke Grove, Nora Sands could hardly use a knife to open a bag of peas and she was sent off to Fifteen for training. But there are a vast number of cooks who are still in the system, who have a high level of skills, who wouldn't need that. The issue is about the recruitment and the retention.'

Now new training kitchens have been built, and Jamie Oliver was there to open the first – Ashlyns Organic Farm in Essex – run by the original dinner lady, Jeanette Orrey. Situated on an organic farm and part of the Department for Environment, Food and Rural Affairs (DEFRA) 'Feeding our Future' campaign, Ashlyns has an opportunity to make an even bigger difference to the way Britain thinks about food. Ashlyns was given a grant to establish the training kitchen at the farm, which already supplies a number of schools with fresh organic food, and to set up the kind of network of suppliers that Jamie's mentor Alice Waters has done in California. By encouraging a new generation of dinner ladies to work with organic ingredients, not as luxury products but as the healthiest options on the menu, the future is brighter for the organic and slow food movements. Jeanette Orrey said, 'The Training Kitchen at Ashlyns is hopefully the first of many such projects. It's run on the Soil Association Food for Life project lines – encouraging schools to source unprocessed, local and organic food. School kitchens have suffered from years of neglect and need reinvestment, but many school catering staff are already highly skilled. The idea is to inspire them and provide ideas to take away.'

Lizzie Vann says the issue is about a very British condition. 'I know that there are lots of good schools with lots of dedicated kitchen managers, and they are doing their best but within a very constrained subject. But there is also an issue that Food for Life and Jamie have tackled, which is in the gap in understanding and sympathy between the education staff – the administrators and the head – and the kitchen staff. It's almost like they're two tribes. They don't work together so there is no curriculum support for healthy eating and the kitchens don't support any curricular activity because it's two different worlds. It's like the British approach to class; there's the academic and there's labour, and never the twain shall meet. But we're all servicing children; we're all trying to get the kids at school happy, healthy and educated, and hopefully what we've done over the last few years has made us realise that those two groups of people should work together.'

It will take the revolutionary spirit of parents, teachers and councillors to make *Jamie's School Dinners* a real and sustainable success. The Feed Me Better campaign on www.jamieoliver.com has already created a network of people who want to make a difference in their own schools, with tips and ideas posted onto the site. The starter pack featured on Jamie's website with its stickers and games has been replaced now with regularly updated menus and links to the School Food Trust and Nora's top tips.

Ruth Kelly pointed out that 'many schools are already showing that it's possible to provide healthy, tasty meals for their pupils at a reasonable price'. She gave as an example Ashington Community High School in Northumberland where the cost of school dinners has been halved by ditching expensive convenience food for locally grown produce. 'This has proved popular with children and parents, with 80% of pupils now opting for school dinners,' she said. 'Parents support the school by paying for meal vouchers by cheque, so they can be sure that their children aren't spending their dinner money on sweets instead. Or the specialist sports college, Barking Abbey, which has banned fizzy drinks and crisps, and is educating pupils by creating an organic fruit and vegetable allotment on the school site.'

Robin Gourlay from East Ayrshire Council went one better and created *Hungry for Success*, a campaign for healthy eating and healthy living which brought together an Alice Waters style network of local producers supplying the county's schools. £1.5 million was dedicated to the project over the next three years, with a simple shift of emphasis in the catering industry from a commercial service to a best value service allowing budgets to be reworked to draw from education and social coffers. Gourlay and his team took the inevitable battering from parents who objected to the junk being completely withdrawn from school menus across the county, but with the procurement shift creating new jobs and keeping spending local, the campaign was soon beyond reproach. The initial pilot in Hurlford Primary was extended to another ten schools as a central distribution agency made sure that Food for Life's nutritional guidelines were surpassed with the caterers using 50% organic, 100% unprocessed and 70% local produce. 'If it wasn't organic, it was ethically produced,' said Gourlay.

But Gourlay was lucky; his council supported the campaign and was able to provide the money and the infrastructure to make it work. Head teacher Alan Coode of Gorringe Park School in Mitcham was not so fortunate. He told the Soil Association Conference in January 2006 what he had to do for his own school. Coode resorted to posting digital photographs of the school dinners on the school's website when complaints to the local council, which had taken control of its catering, fell on deaf ears. When the press picked up the pictures showing unrecognisable substances being passed off as a nutritious main meal of the day, the headline on the front page of the *Daily Mirror* in May 2005 was 'Not Fit For a Dog'.

The council and the catering company Coode jokingly calls

'Rentokil' – although he reckons that Rentokil should sue – immediately responded, and Gorringe Park became one of only four schools at the time to pilot Jamie Oliver's menu. Although the children loved it, with numbers rising from 70 to 180 out of the 450 children at his primary school opting for hot lunch, he is cynical, especially as the dinners are gradually reverting to the junk of the old days. 'It's all about money,' he told the conference. He still takes his digital camera into the dining hall and posts the photographs onto the school website, but recognises that real control is out of his hands.

Despite these stories, Lizzie Vann says she is optimistic for the future. 'I think it's been enormously heartening in the last year. The Food for Life campaign led into the Jamie Oliver programme that was the best possible thing to happen. It became a national campaign and led to that enormous petition, and it moved the whole nutrition of children out of the campaigning arena into the mainstream. Parents are saying "I'm going to do something about this; I'm going to give my child a lunchbox, or support the school, become a governor or become a dinner lady again." All of that great stuff happened. You can't put the genie back in the bottle. If LACA still have their dinosaurs, there's a gap opening up between them and their public, and unless they get back in touch with their public, they'll become moribund.'

As to whether or not Jamie himself will continue to bang the drum for organic produce, Craig Sams is realistic. 'He believes in it but he's also a mass-market popular figure,' said Sams. He remembered Jamie's speech to the Soil Association in January 2004. 'The Sainsbury's team were sitting there on the front row, nodding approvingly, but when you're talking about putting food into your mouth, you're really only talking about organic. Jamie didn't say occasionally or usually; he meant always. Organic food is 3–4% of the amount of food we eat in this country so there's a long way to go. Jamie's at the cusp and doesn't want to alienate people by getting too worthy and serious. People would switch off and none of us want that.'

How he continues with the work is by encouraging the public to buy the best, which, according to Sams, 'naturally leads the intelligent consumer to buy from the butcher, which eventually leads to an increased interest in the method of production and onto the issue of organics'. Food for Life undoubtedly planted the seeds for the TV programmes campaigning for better animal welfare three years on.

Under the Food for Life targets, better ingredients included organic ingredients, something that is still a hot potato on the news agenda. The Soil Association was determined to persuade the British Government that if public bodies were allowed to purchase organic food, the public benefits it would deliver would include high animal welfare standards, increased local employment and an improved environment. Craig Sams explained why the Government woke up to organic farming. 'The Soil Association lobbied the Government hard on this and pointed out that everyone in Europe is getting conversion grants. They looked at the impact on the total cost of farming – £100 million is spent on getting pesticides out of water to comply with water purity standards. And it's not just the money; rural economies suffer terribly from centralised mass production and smaller towns become ghost towns. People have to go further to see a doctor. And there's the global warming argument; a quarter to a third of our global warming is due to agriculture. The impact is enormous on society.'

He pointed out that since 1850 a quarter of global warming has been due to the expansion of agriculture, with tractors speeding up the process enormously. 'Vast amounts of carbon go into the atmosphere just because of tractors,' he said. 'If the whole world went organic, a third of the greenhouse gases reduction necessary to achieve climate stability could come from farming. This is gradually sinking in now – not just in Government, but in the public, too.'

'The Food Standards Agency (FSA) is a big stumbling block,' said Joy Carey of the Soil Association. 'Official bodies take their lead from the FSA, which insists that there is no evidence that organic food is beneficial – and, at the same time, seem reluctant to conduct research that could provide evidence. We do, though, draw attention to the fact that organic food is produced without the use of pesticides for which there is plenty of evidence about harmful health impacts.'

Antony Worrall Thompson watched *Jamie's School Dinners* with admiration, but is more sceptical about the level of his success in real terms. 'I tend to feel that Government just want him to go away. They're waiting for it all to die down and then everyone will realise that nothing has really been done about it. Mr Blair will nick £250 million off someone else's budget to put it into meals but there's no point in throwing money at it.'

When Michael Howard rang Antony Worrall Thompson to ask him for his views, he said the then-leader of the Conservative Party nearly fell off his chair when he heard his answer. 'I said, "I'm sorry to say this, but you've got to find a way of doing free school meals."' He told Howard that within 10 years obesity related diseases would be costing the NHS at least five times smoking costs. 'I said, "You look at the cost of the health of the nation and we probably could afford to do free school meals. And we should also tax over-processed foods – what I would call unnecessary foods. That started Mr Howard thinking. And then a couple of months later, the British Heart Foundation came up with exactly the same thing.'

Worrall Thompson also told him not to give kids any choice. 'Sitting down with a teacher at the end of the table saying, "You *will* eat that food" is the only way to get children to eat properly as well as develop the right kind of communication skills.' His book *Real Family Food* is based on the same idea. 'We like campaigns,' he said. 'Jamie's got a young family and I've got a young family, and we want them to have a healthy meal system.' Worrall Thompson has made films about the issue of school meals in London schools with primarily West Indian student populations. 'They've got fantastic food – a great buffet – piri piri chicken and lots of vegetables and salads, and yoghurts and fruit and... chips. And almost to the last one they had chicken and chips. And all that food went in the bin.'

He admits that he's been trying to do what Jamie did 'for ages'. He believes it's now up to parents to take control of children and feed them properly. 'We've got a captive audience and we can put a message across. Jamie's school campaign slightly backfired; so many people were put off with the Turkey Twizzlers that they've taken their kids out of the system and given them packed lunches, which are often just as bad.' Lizzie Vann was quick to disagree. 'I think it's such a knee-jerk reaction to say that the number of children taking school meals has gone down because of low morale among parents and low morale among dinner ladies – just rubbish. I think it's just cheap. Parents are giving their children packed lunches because the food isn't good enough in school. Before they were coming back and asking for packed lunch because they didn't eat the food and they were hungry all afternoon, and now it's being debated in public. Parents won't use their children as guinea pigs and will wait until the food is good enough to put their kids back into the system.'

Hazel Green of the caterer's association LACA said that despite celebrities like Antony Worrall Thompson banging the drum for change, it was only Jamie who actually changed the media agenda. 'I've had more calls from the *FT* in the last year about school meals, and they never went there. Once upon a time it was a switch off.' But if LACA were trying to make the press sit up and take notice of what had been happening in school meals over the last 10 years, Jamie's pressure campaign brought its axe firmly down on the association's head. Did LACA need to be told? 'Clearly we did,' said chairman Kevin McKay. 'We obviously needed a spotlight on what was happening. People were writing to their authorities about the dustbins and the roads, but they weren't writing about school dinners. We could see what was happening from the inside perspective, but the campaigning had started with obesity issues and the healthy living blueprint, all of which were Government initiatives. A lot of authorities were working on that.'

Jamie's School Dinners changed something in our society. It was profoundly empowering, and showed us that it wasn't just the mavericks such as Bob Geldof who could change the world. 'It's about a problem identified and someone who is passionate enough about it to pull you on board and resolve it,' said the editor of *Radio Times*, Gill Hudson. 'It's simple, but it cuts through so much clutter, both on TV and in life. It's about saying, "What I can do?" and finding that the answer is actually, quite a lot. I think it was deeply inspiring.'

CHAPTER 32

SLOW FOOD

Jamie Oliver has exploded an interest in food that transcends age, class and culture and was unseen in Britain before he burst upon our screens eight years ago. As I walked around another annual Good Food Show, I noticed that almost every conversation I overheard was about him. From the old dears sipping cups of tea and cooing, 'Ooh, I wish he was my son; I'd be so proud!' to the screaming nurses who had come to watch him sign books and cook on stage with Gennaro Contaldo, to the middle-aged, middle-class wine buyer on the phone to his wife, 'I'm just going to watch Jamie Oliver, darling, and then I'll head home', everyone was there for Jamie. 'Did you see what happened when Jamie came to Jimmy's stall?' Gennaro asked me. 'He was mobbed.'

Gillian Carter is editor of *Good Food* magazine, which jointly hosts the show with Haymarket Exhibitions. 'Jamie's presence creates a huge buzz at the shows, particularly among the younger visitors,' she said. 'He has reached pop star status with kids, who would mob him given the chance. After the enormous success of *School Dinners*, Jamie did demonstrations specifically for school-children, and these were enthusiastically received and of course, packed out. Jamie's appeal to school-age kids and young adults is all about apparent accessibility, "ordinariness" – the whole "mate" thing. He connects with a young audience immediately, and tailors his show to them.'

The Good Food Show feeds the need for celebrity watchers to get their fix and although trade is good on the stalls, it's the celebrity chefs that most people are here for. 'A hundred thousand people will come from around the country to The Good Food shows, particularly in the Midlands,' said Antony Worrall Thompson. 'Londoners tend to be a bit snobby about food shows. They are the hard core of TV food viewers; they're the *Ready Steady Cook* viewers rather than the dinner party set.' 'Of course a lot of that interest is in the chefs they see on TV,' agreed Gillian Carter, 'or it is certainly bolstered by these appearances. The media coverage of food has increased, which in turns leads to a greater interest in the subject. I don't know how, in an age where media is so dominant, you can clearly separate one from the other. I realise that not everyone is interested in an analysis of food, its cultural importance or the scientific side, but Good Food Show visitors are interested in its variety, and what they see as a fascinating and increasing availability. The link between food and health is also of huge interest and concern. How that squares with the rise in snacking and in obesity levels only goes to show how complex our relationship with food really is.'

The argument proposed by food campaigners from Lizzie Vann and the Soil Association to Alice Waters and Jamie himself is that once you begin to look beyond the packaging, you start to think outside the box. Good Food Show fans may come to see Jamie Oliver cook, but on the way to the auditorium, they will pass stall upon stall offering biltong, flavoured olive oils and venison burgers at Henrietta Green's Food Lovers Fair, whose stalls are part of the show. With producers eager to talk about their products and offering a taste of their lava bread, pâtés or sausages, you can smell the passion at these food shows, and it would take a very single-minded Jamie fan to walk straight past.

Yet Antony Worrall Thompson is keen to put the Jamie Oliver effect into perspective. 'I think we've got a hard core of three million or so who really enjoy food and cooking. There are a lot of women who think "Thank God for chilled foods. I don't have to cook any more and I'm going to hang my apron up because I don't have to do it any more.'" He says it's very rare for anyone to get an audience of more than three million on TV. 'Although,' he pointed out, '*Ready Steady Cook* does in the afternoons.' Sally Clarke is dismissive of the TV chef culture: 'I'm very anti TV chefs altogether,' she said. 'I think Jamie and Rick Stein have been fantastic in what they've done. Stein does it with intelligence and sympathy for the product. It's not done as a laugh and a joke; it's done from the soul. But the ones that leap and do a song and dance – it's about them. I think something like *Ready Steady Cook* is asinine. It doesn't show any sympathy for the food.'

Food historian Colin Spencer believes that the British have been slowly coming to their food senses over the past 50 years since Elizabeth David first reminded us of the flavours and aromas of our ancient ancestry. In his book *British Food; An Extraordinary 1,000 Years of History* he writes, 'Reading Mrs David was like rediscovering a part of oneself that had been so utterly lost we were unaware of its existence.' He reminds us that it was the spices our ancestors were using in the medieval period that we were being served up in the Chinese food brought to Britain by Chinese immigrants in the Sixties. 'Sweet and sour meat dishes were also a favourite medieval dish, so again here was a spectrum of flavours that not so long before had been part of our own cuisine.'

Craig Sams of the Soil Association goes further to suggest that the smells and flavours of our favourite Chinese, Indian and now Italian foods are imprinted on our DNA, giving us a sense of who we are and where we come from. 'We know that junk is imprinted on our DNA, too,' he warned. 'Every time you drink a coffee or take ecstasy, or eat beef, it changes you and becomes part of your heredity.'

Top chef Heston Blumenthal has made memory food his unique selling point, conjuring flavours and smells out of ingredients of another time and presenting them in ways designed to tickle more than your taste buds. 'Although my mother was a very good cook,' he told Matthew Fort in the *Guardian*, 'my childhood memories were not woven with gastronomic experiences. I didn't spend hours beside her, stoning cherries or peeling potatoes. Food nostalgia for my generation was quite heavily influenced by synthetic flavours such as strawberry Angel Delight.'

To have the confidence to sear tuna steaks with crushed coriander seeds, chilli and lime juice à la Jamie Oliver is something even the most unadventurous of home cooks will do now. But back in the Seventies even the most optimistic British foodies would never have guessed that it would be the molecular gastronomy of Heston Blumenthal that would have a self-taught British chef awarded the title of Best Chef in the World by *Restaurant* magazine in 2005. He even beat the previous year's winner, The French Laundry, which is part of Fifteen's employment network into second place. Blumenthal remains unfazed: 'Molecular gastronomy is about making a cup of tea,' he explained. 'Just put tea leaves with boiling water and watch the chemical reaction.'

Monica Brown of Lotus PR, which represents Blumenthal's restaurant, the Fat Duck in Bray, told me how Heston plays with his food. 'Take the bacon and egg ice cream,' she said. 'Basically they bring you a plate with toast soldiers, mushrooms and a jar of marmalade … well, not exactly; the toast is caramelised brioche, the mushrooms are wonderfully rich caramelised morels and the marmalade is a sharp green tea jelly. Then they come to the table with a box of eggs and a frying pan, and put it on a little stand that resembles a small stove. It's fantastic theatre. They crack the eggs into the pan; however, the eggs have been emptied and sterilised, and instead they have injected ice cream custard inside them. They pour liquid nitrogen into the pan and stir it with a whisk. The eye sees scrambled eggs being made but they serve you an egg ice cream, which has a subtle bacon infusion running through it, but it looks like scrambled egg. Altogether it is one of the most amazing desserts you will ever eat.'

She said that the most bizarre thing was that two days later when describing the dish, she described it as being hot. 'My mind still couldn't figure out that it was cold because of what my eyes had registered. Even on the day itself the chefs were laughing at me as I called the green tea jelly "lime marmalade" at least five times. At the time we were eating the dish, three people from other tables were so fascinated they actually stood up to see what was going on. That's what the Fat Duck is all about, having fun, new experiences and just total and utter enjoyment.'

Jamie Oliver and Heston Blumenthal have proved that British chefs can lead the world with the simplest of ideas. Despite what looks like tricky dishes, Blumenthal, like Oliver, strips food back to the basics. 'He has that childlike inquisitiveness,' said Monica Brown. 'When he meets the biggest scientists in the world, he's very open. He'll ask "Why does that bubble, and why does that smell?" He asks the most basic questions of these guys and he doesn't care.' She says that he and Jamie have much the same attitude to food. 'Heston is a big Jamie fan. They're geezers, just blokes. He's very down to earth. He's fascinated in what anyone is doing to change things, and when he and Jamie get together, they gas about everything that the other is doing. They both love asking questions.'

Heston is impressed with Jamie's passion, his energy and determination to improve our love and understanding of food. 'His enthusiasm is contagious and he has influenced people enough to demand better, to source better ingredients and not be scared of handling different produce or trying different tastes and flavours,' he said. 'Food is about fun and enjoyment, not something to be scared of; it's something to be explored.'

Finally Britain has a food movement to be proud of. Even our future king lends his farms to Fifteen's education scheme, and is an unsung hero in the organic movement. But Prince Charles has had a rough ride. Unlike Jamie Oliver, this not so shiny knight had been riding his charger against the tide of public opinion for the past 30 years. But, as Alice Thompson in the *Telegraph* noticed, we are beginning to look again at our national institutions as we move out of Cool Britannia and realise we have had another kilted, jaw-strained, balding Jamie Oliver under our noses. 'Suddenly everyone is talking about Britishness,' she wrote, 'but Prince Charles has been promoting it for years. With David Blunkett, he encouraged the rise of citizenship ceremonies. Tony Blair reignited the debate about "respect", and the emphasis in government is shifting from ASBOs to youth engagement in a bid to counteract "yob culture"; Prince Charles, through his Prince's Trust, has spent decades trying to help disadvantaged children break the mould. The Prince was obsessed by the environment long before every heatwave led to a discussion about global warming. He was railing against bad food in schools years before Jamie Oliver sucked his first Turkey Twizzler.'

By 2004 the Prince was launching a campaign called 'Mutton Renaissance' at The Ritz, with mutton redefined as a revival of the 'classic British dish'. Charles warned that the British rural landscape could become 'rank and ungrazed' if family farmers were not protected. After years of disasters affecting British farming, he said he hoped his efforts could help restore the fortunes of sheep farmers. His interest as patron of the Academy of Culinary Arts – which backed the campaign with the National Sheep Association – extended further than the fields of sheep he himself kept at Highgrove. It was a nod to Jamie and the role of the TV chef when he added, 'In a world where fast food seems to be the order of the day, this may be a message that takes time to percolate beyond the restaurants. But I know from the huge numbers of people who watch the cooking programmes on television that there are some who truly care about how they prepare and cook their food and so, for them, there is a whole new culinary treat in store.'

'There is a total disconnection between the people and the politicians on local food,' said Campaigns Director for the Soil Association, Robin Maynard. 'The public wants local, seasonal food, and understands why. The government still hasn't a clue.'

Perhaps as we read the contents of our junk food, looked at our contact with farms, countryside and local shops, and sent our kids off to school without a clue about what they were eating, we became humbled by our dismissive twenty-first century cynicism. Perhaps something in us longed for good old-fashioned apple pie and real custard, lamb casserole and real sausages baked in red wine and served with onion gravy, and eaten with our parents around a dinner table. Perhaps Jamie Oliver with his Essex lad's meat and potatoes approach and Prince Charles with his aristocratic respect for country ways are what we needed after 20 years of packaged fast food and American junk food values. Certainly, slow food is selling like hot cakes at the increasing number of farmers' markets around the country, even though we're still a long way from the example set by New Yorkers. 'Farmers come to town at lunchtime in New York every day,' said Lizzie Vann. 'You can walk down certain streets and everyone would be out there buying supper. A friend of mine told me that the big banks are installing fridges in their offices so that you can keep your produce cool.'

But with the increase in food shows drawing a celebrity-loving punter towards Henrietta Green's Food Lover's Fairs, perhaps the demand is not too far off. The Patchwork Traditional Food Company has been making pâtés since 1982, with nine of their 39 pâtés made for Prince Charles's Duchy Originals range. Patchwork is one of the hundreds of companies, like Jimmy Doherty's Essex Pig Company, which now sell products at 62 shows including The BBC Good Food Shows and 30 farmers' markets around Britain each year.

'Patchwork Pete' Hansford sells his Duchy Original Devilled Organic Chicken Liver Pâté with Madeira at The Good Food Show in London's Earls Court as if it were a pound of apples at Soho's Berwick Street market, and his customers can't get enough. 'I stand here and I hear people say that this pâté reminds them of the pâté their grandmother or their mother used to make,' he said. 'In 10 years' time we probably won't hear that again, because no one's making pâté now. We're reliant on the supermarkets. I've been preaching to two generations of super-market shoppers who find it easier to go to the supermarket.'

He credits the enormous interest to the freshness of the product: 'Everything we do is by hand. We pan fry everything, reduce everything down, add the ingredients and then we blast freeze them. We do that to seal in the just-cooked taste and we don't use any additives or preservatives. By blast freezing we kill bacteria for about 12 days, so when people defrost, they get a 12-day shelf life without any of those nasty e numbers.'

And to the success of the TV chefs whose live appearances have the punters lining up outside Birmingham's NEC and London's Earls Court exhibition halls, desperate for a glimpse of their heroes. 'They educate people,' he said and, unprompted, he attributed the increase in interest in slow food in particular to Jamie, as his customers, tasting the difference between his Cock Pheasant and Blackberry Pâté with Bramble Wine and his Duck Liver Pâté with Apricot & Apricot Brandy, murmured their agreement. 'It's like when Jamie Oliver first hit the scene, Jamie was teaching people to cook in a different way. He was teaching kids to cook. He was taking raw ingredients and teaching us what to do with them and that's awesome.'

Hansford described Jamie Oliver as teaching a new generation 'to be flirty with food, to use their imagination, to get stuck in. I can't wait for the next generation of kids to come – we'll see them at shows like this in 11 or 12 years' time. The BBC ships in 70 coach loads of kids to fill the theatres. They're enthusiastic and they love Jamie, and so they love food.'

CHAPTER 33

HEART AND SOUL

By 2005, with *Jamie's School Dinners* appearing on TV in Singapore, Hong Kong, Thailand, Canada, Australia, New Zealand, Germany, Norway, Slovenia, Denmark, Finland and the Netherlands, and a special on American television with Jamie transforming the diet of a typical family, the accolades and offers were rolling in. He was even voted sexiest man of the year, along with Brad Pitt.

Jamie Oliver had become a brand. His columns in *Delicious* magazine, *The Sunday Telegraph* and *The News of the World* in the UK joined Jamie Oliver columns and recipes all over the world, from Australia, South Africa and Holland to Sweden, Greece and Estonia.

His books have been translated into 23 languages and have sold more than 12.2 million copies. *Jamie's Italy* broke all barriers by becoming the first non-fiction book to break the 100,000 copies barrier, and easily topped the bestseller lists for Christmas 2005, while *Jamie at Home* shifted 38,000 copies in its first three days on the shelves in 2007. In just five years, the Naked Chef had morphed into one of the most influential political figures in the world, and when he joined the hall of celebrity waxwork models in Madame Tussauds, he was placed next to the then Prime Minister, Tony Blair and US President George Bush. Apparently visitors could touch his tummy as his midriff moved.

According to a poll, he was our middle-class hero at the

beginning of 2006, beating the then new Tory leader, David Cameron, and lead singer of Coldplay and anti-poverty campaigner, Chris Martin in the Class of 2006 on account of his 'irresistible' combination of 'cheek and unthreatening-ness.'

But there was more to Jamie Oliver than met the eye; with the help of his management company, Sweet as Candy, the Jamie brand was also working hard behind the scenes, with property, media and food company interests employing more than 200 employees; 'They're all fucking talented, cool people,' he told the *Independent*. 'And if I meet anyone who's fucking good I'll employ them too.'

With the help of the 'talented, cool' folk at his kitchenware company, Fresh Retail Ventures, he designed a range of quality tableware and serveware for Royal Worcester and launched a range of cookware with Tefal, using his drumming skills to promote them in a Stomp-style ad that was shown across North America and the UK. An own brand range of gifts are sold internationally, and Jamie even found time to 'invent' a new kitchen product called 'Flavour Shaker' which 'bashes, bruises and mixes all the ingredients together' in place of a pestle and mortar.

The business is now one of the fastest-growing parts of the Jamie Oliver empire, with sales of more than £7 million. By autumn 2007, Fresh Retail Ventures was making three appointments for its new headquarters in Manchester to extend its range into the fresh and chilled sector. His Italian food range of artichokes, anchovies, capers, pesto, pasta sauces and infused olive oils, as well as the cookware and tableware, would also undergo a re-launch.

By 2005, Sweet as Candy declared a trading profit of £7.2 million, although according to newspaper reports, its 2007 pre-tax profits fell to £5.7 million, leaving Jamie and Jools on a salary of just £900,000, £1.1 million down on their 2005 pay cheque. Jamie's spokesman explained that the drop was because Jamie had piled his cash into good causes, with £2.5 million in royalties going to charity restaurant group, Fifteen.

He is richer than even Jools could ever dream, worth an alleged £40 million in 2007, his income doubling between 2003 and 2004 and notching up to 15th place in Britain's richest under the age of 30 in 2005. His friends insist that the money is a by-product of what he does. 'I think he feels privileged to be able to do what he's doing, and that what he's doing does make a difference' said Rupert Ivey. 'He gives away most of his money anyway' said Gennaro. Jon Rolfe, one of Jamie's mates, was one of the beneficiaries after Jamie spotted his passion for bread making and allowed him to use the back of the kitchen at London's Fifteen, before Jamie Oliver Holdings set him up in his own artisan bakery, The Flour Station, near Battersea.

Fifteen allowed him to set up more of his mates and protégés in places they deserved to be. Tobie Puttock went home to Australia. Stephanie Alexander is the country's grande dame of good food and although a 'big fan' of Jamie's – and Tobie's, was worried about how the restaurant would fare without Jamie in person. 'His shows are fantastic and it did look like you could have a go,' she told me as Jamie prepared to open Fifteen in Melbourne. But she wondered if he would have his work cut out. 'No-one knows how it will do here,' she said, 'but it will get a lot of publicity and everyone will be very intrigued at the idea. It will probably do very well. It is in the basement of the Windsor Hotel, which is a very venerable institution. It's right in the centre of the city and very well regarded. It has a lot of things going for it. But it also faces huge competition.'

And the snobbery of the Melbourne food crowd. With its Italian heart, its inner city food market to rival New Covent Garden and its Food Festival that outdoes anything we've seen yet in the UK, Melbourne has grown up on good food, and it didn't like being told. 'So eager is Fifteen to brand the Parma ham in the "fantastic salad of peach" that it refers to it as "Marchetti prosciutto." Marchetti is a wholesale small goods delivery company, not a producer of hams!' snorted *The Age*, Australia's heavyweight foodie newspaper.

But Tobie was Jamie's high profile lieutenant as manager of the restaurant and was clearly cut from the same cloth. Even if the restaurant itself was initially dismissed by the gastrocracy, Puttock himself soon melted enough hearts with his tell-it-like-it-is charm. He even got his own TV series out of it; he and sommelier and fellow surfie, Matt Skinner, used their experience in *Jamie's Kitchen* to head off around the world in search of the secrets of the best European cuisine in *Tobie & Matt* for the Lifestyle Food Channel. Meanwhile, the best of the rest, around half the trainees from each year, were successfully placed in professional kitchens, including those of Australia's celebrity chefs, Shannon Bennett and Neil Perry.

By early 2008 though, the Fifteen project was proving that all that glitters is not always gold. The star-studded openings, the worldwide TV profile, the Cinderella-style make-over of disaffected youth had faded to a rather more prosaic reality. Not that it was the bank balance, which had for so long taken its own starring role in the TV series, that had lost its lustre; on the contrary, five years on, Fifteen is turning over £4 million a year. No, in true Jamie style, it was the Fifteen group itself which commissioned a report, *Fifteen: life in the present tense,* concluding that only half of their trainees were emerging as graduates by 2007. 'We did let some of those people down at the time of start up and for some time after that,' it admitted.

Chairman, Liam Black, the son of an Irish bricklayer who had already turned another charity into a multi-million pound social enterprise, wrote in the report just before leaving the company in 2008, 'This is not a typical annual report or PR document, it is a warts-and-all look into the guts of Fifteen, celebrating what's great about this place but acknowledging too when and how we have missed the mark.' Accepting that things were far from perfect, that learning from mistakes is, according to Jamie, the only way to steer a ship through previously uncharted waters; 'We haven't always got it right, but without taking risks we won't make progress,' he said unapologetically.

Dwayne Joseph was one of the lucky ones and graduated in 2006, but says that having Fifteen on your CV is 'a double edged sword.' His first job was not quite the fairy tale he had expected; 'They didn't like it that they'd started as pot washers and we come in up here,' he said. He described Fifteen's training as 'sugar coated.' 'It was a real shock going into the industry,' he said. 'The workload's terrible and they don't care about you. If you don't do it, you're out. You should teach the apprentices how to deal with anger and disapproval.' Had he read Marco Pierre White's accounts of what goes on in the average restaurant kitchen back in 1990 when Jamie was learning his trade, he might have saved himself some of the bruises.

Setting up Fifteen and battling in the school playground with the might of junk culture in *School Dinners*, had been a hard slog and, as Jamie prepared to face the press for *Jamie's Great Italian Escape*, the series that would give him the downtime he so craved, he seemed beaten. He had seen the underbelly of the great British public and it wasn't pretty. The chef whose USP was about telling it as it is, had recognised that our modern food revolution wasn't quite as tasty as it seemed.

At first, it left him floored. He told the press circus as he promoted *Jamie's Great Italian Escape* that he had no ambitions left. 'I haven't got any,' he promised. 'Honestly, I really mean that. I do know Channel 4 want a meeting to see what's next.'

After months of attempting to slice through the fat of British junk culture and watching in horror as Northern European and North American audiences recognised themselves and lapped up his message, Jamie needed to get away. He needed to know that there was somewhere that the last 50 years hadn't microwaved and served up as a ready meal, where people still grew their own herbs and tomatoes on balconies and kept chickens in the back yard.

Cruising down Italy's Amalfi coast in his ancient camper van, he found it and it took his breath away. He had finally set off on the Overseas Experience his Ozzie pals had been telling him about for the past 10 years. But did he even know how to take a break? 'Italy is me time. I want to be fired up,' he told the press. 'Will anyone be filming there?' asked Caroline Stacey. 'Yeah, of course,' he answered as if she was mad.

Warren Beatty said of Madonna, his lover at the time, that life didn't exist for her if the cameras weren't rolling, and hung up his hat in despair. But Jools is made of tougher stuff, and while the tabloids tutted and talked of divorce as he chose the lens over her for his me-time companion, she held out for the moment when the penny would finally drop. It wouldn't be long.

His London dad knew the trip would be good for him on more levels than one. 'I wanted him to go to Italy' said Gennaro whose phone was hot throughout the series as Jamie rang for help. 'I wanted him to understand the Italian way of cooking. He went quickly on a sourcing trip when he was at college but I wanted him to go through the streets. He went to Minori – my village on the Amalfi coast, in the very last programme, and he said that he had come home.'

It was more than the language that Gennaro had taught Jamie over the past 10 years; it was the philosophy which drove Jamie's campaigns. 'It's very traditional,' he explained. 'They do elaborate on the original cuisines, but they use the original ingredients and don't change very much. We like what we have in our own country, so we don't use lemongrass or coriander. I don't even know what to do with it.'

It was as if he was paying homage to the great mentors of his career to date. The local stories and regional recipes he amassed as he drove around Italy in his camper van must have brought memories of the River Café flooding back. Ruth Rogers told me the kind of story that she would have told Jamie during his time there. 'I was baking a whole pig in a wood oven in a little town in Montepulciano and I went into the butcher. I'd ordered this pig and he said to me "how are you going to cook it?" I thought "aha, I'm the chef, so don't think you can intimidate me." So I said "I'm going to get some fennel seeds and sea salt," and he said "but that's what they do in Sienna." Do you know how far away we were from Sienna? Forty-five miles.'

Jamie took us back to basics in Italy, summing up everything that he had shown us from *The Naked Chef* to *School Dinners* and drinking up more than the Italian sunshine. His common touch, it seemed, was universal. But if he sent the shares of Italian rustic holidays into the stratosphere, it seems that little Italy in the heart of the Black Mountains, was less enchanted. Franco Tarruschio, formerly of Abergavenny's Walnut Tree, comes from the Marche area where Jamie sensationally killed a lamb for the cameras. 'My father-in-law said that in 42 years of going to the Marche region, he'd never seen anything so barbaric' said Ann, Franco's wife. 'They are very strict in Italy,' said Franco 'and they would have to take a lamb to the slaughter house. They are not allowed to kill their own lambs – just like in this country. The hygiene standards are so high in Italy that they take farmers from here to the Marche region to show them how advanced they are there.'

As Jamie travelled around Italy, competing with the village nonnas in the local pasta show and stuffing herbs in a way that had never been seen in 1,000 years of night markets, he seemed more thoughtful than we had ever seen. He looked melancholy. *School Dinners* had taken it out of him, he confessed, but on his thirtieth birthday, on a hilltop overlooking the stunning Amalfi coast and the village where Gennaro's father still lived, he said to Andy the gasman that he felt that he had run out of steam. What was he going to do with the next 30 years, he asked his mates. They snorted dismissively, reminding him of his beautiful wife and children, his fantastic job and his vast wealth, and passed him another beer. 'Melancholy?' a friend laughed. 'He was probably just pissed off with working. He's just knackered. He'll go off and lick his wounds then he'll come back. He just works too hard.'

He thinks that it's the performer in Jamie that drives him on. 'There's got to be a lot of addiction in that. He gripes about it a lot and I say, "well mate, give it up." What drives him might ultimately destroy him.'

Gennaro, a deeply religious man, thinks that it was the spirit of

Italy that had got to him. 'He took communion,' he reminded me, referring to the scene in which Jamie went to a monastery. 'It's an important thing to do, even if he doesn't go to Church.' But it was a scene that appalled the Taruschios, both Catholics. 'He blathered on about not having a religion which is fine,' said Ann, 'but then the next minute he had his big tongue hanging out to receive the host.' She said that the Italian Embassy received a barrage of complaints, although the press office declined to comment. 'He was asked to say Grace and he said 'For what we're about to eat, may the Lord be duly thankful.'

But Gennaro, who spends more time with Jamie than most, finds him a silent believer. 'He doesn't show it to anyone else. But you can see it in all that he's doing with the young trainees. If you don't care for anyone, you wouldn't do it.' He says that Jamie has 'God in his heart. It's like a magnet,' he said. 'It draws people to him.'

Gennaro was amazed to find a compilation of pictures of saints on the inside cover of *Jamie's Italy*, the book that accompanied the series. 'I was going bananas,' he said. 'I looked at it again and again.' He showed me the saints on the wall of the office of his restaurant, Passione, and asked me to compare them with those in the book. 'That's Padre Pia from where I come from,' he said animatedly, pointing each one out to me. 'There's San Josef, San Rosalia, San Michael Archangel. Santa Barbara, Our Lady of Saragosa...' He pointed to a picture of Padre Pia. 'I even called one of my daughters Pia. I met him when he was alive, and then I open up this book and, hold on a minute, that's him. And look at these,' he pointed to another photo in the montage. 'This is in Palermo. Our Lady of Pompeii where I come from. What amazes me is how many there are in the book. Looking through the book, you can see all the things that we've talked about for years.'

Gill Hudson, editor of *Radio Times*, noticed that BBC audience research showed that viewers value a good soul. 'If you strip out the soaps and continuing dramas like *Casualty*' she told me, 'the programmes that people are really locked into are things like

Jamie's School Dinners, *Spring Watch with Bill Oddie*, *Cold Blood*, *The Choir*, *Tribe* and *Masterchef*. I remember a reader's comment was quoted, and I really latched onto it. She said that what she really liked about these programmes is that you know that the presenters are the same off screen as they are on. She used the word 'authentic.' I was immensely cheered by that because it means that people absolutely know the difference between something that is pure entertainment and a bit of a show, and something that is absolutely genuine. And not only that it's absolutely genuine, but there's a point and a purpose. It means that you really can tell when something comes from the heart.'

She believes that he is more than just a good soul, that he 'represents the power of the individual, even in a global age when everything is dominated by mega corporations. He shows that an individual can have an effect. I think that's genuinely thrilling.' Jamie showed us the power of TV democracy. 'He bypassed all those Government committees, review boards and Green Papers' said Hudson. 'In the space of eight weeks, he galvanised the entire nation and made Government change its policy. That is phenomenal. It means that if you really want to make a change, you can bypass the things that put people off politics. It politicises people again.'

If it is the big political issues that seem such a monster, Jamie brought it down to a single issue. 'Single issue politics is very powerful,' said Hudson. 'Forget the party politics; it's about "is this right or not?" It doesn't matter which party you belong to, he cut right through all of that entrenched politicism and just got on with it. That is hugely powerful.'

CHAPTER 34

TURNING UP THE HEAT

Jamie's surfie mates told him that there's a reason why people go travelling. Time out to collect your thoughts, to meet people whose life is probably simpler and more balanced than your own, to recognise that the world doesn't stop just because you did, and to realise just what you miss when you leave it behind, all this can be life changing.

Looking out over the Mediterranean that summer, even if the cameras followed his every move, Jamie realised that his life was at home with his family, that although he had work to do, it would no longer be at the expense of his wife and kids. He knew that his purpose, his drive, wasn't going to change, that he was hell bent on changing British food culture, and that very probably he was one of the only people who could. But, as the theme tune of his next series, *Jamie at Home* would croon, he could take time to make himself feel good, to do whatever he wanted, 'cos he could now.

Buying a Grade II-listed Jacobean mansion in Essex, with easy access to his parents, where the kids could help him grow his runner beans and courgettes in a paparazzi-proof walled garden was a start. The swimming pool and boating lake would help when the allure of rotting manure wore off, and the 20 minute drive to Stansted meant that his international career was easier to manage.

But with the smell of the Amalfi coast still haunting him and the words of one of his early mentors and new celebrity mates, Alice Waters, ringing in his head, a germ of an idea, a new challenge was beginning to take root. For Jamie, Alice Waters was more than just one of the best chefs in the world; her love of fresh produce had not only inspired protégées like Sally Clarke to bring the idea of a local and seasonal menu to London in the mid 80's, but had exploded a new way of thinking about food into the American consciousness. It all had to do with food from the land.

It was about slow food for a less hurried, more thoughtful way of life. It challenged the very roots of who we are and pulled together the connection between growing, cooking and eating with friends and family. It was the key to self respect as well as respect for the environment and everyone involved in the food chain – including the animals themselves. It could radically shift our obesity levels as well as our behaviour, in and out of the classroom. In short, it could change the world.

Alice and Jamie shared a dream across the pond. Alice's admiration for his *School Dinners* series and his for her Edible School Yard project had sparked a fire that is still now only burning its way through the kindling. Outside of the deadline-driven media world, their plan to tackle the world's obsession with junk is slowly roasting, teasing the nostrils of some of the most influential people on the planet.

Alice's Edible School Yard is based in Martin Luther King Junior Middle School in her home town of Berkeley, California, with a one-acre organic garden and a kitchen classroom providing what she calls 'edible education.' Launched in 1994, the project treats childhood obesity, nutrition-related illness, the quality of school lunches, and children's ability to learn as related issues.

Alice's experience with a similar project in local prisons proved that good food really does make a difference to behaviour, and she wants to ensure that it starts at the very beginning. She believes that when children grow their own food and it becomes part of their curriculum, this connection with nature nourishes far more than the body. 'We can teach a set of values when we bring an edible education in to school,' she told me. 'We think somehow that education is about a different thing, but it's not – it's about building awareness. It's about relating to everyone else who is sharing this planet and remembering that Nature is our mother. We forget about that.'

She says that it's not just about training school cooks and paying people properly. 'If food became part of the curriculum, people would think differently about it. A new generation would grow up looking after the country in a different way. We're talking about food as a core curriculum in school where students would get grades and it would be part of academia. Every child needs to be involved and food should become an academic subject so that kids learn to participate. Gardens should become labs. The eco-gastro scene should be something that they should study. It opens up people's minds.'

By the time Jamie was mapping out his own edible backyard and inviting the cameras in for his series, *Jamie at Home*, he and Alice had already begun to brainstorm. 'We had such a great time in New York,' she said, referring to a conference on nutrition and childhood obesity organised by the Rudd Institute at Yale in 2005. 'We represent two pieces of a puzzle that fit perfectly together – I'm involved in education around food and he can talk about his personal experience. I can put educational pieces together.' Their aim may be the same; feed school children well and they will concentrate better, achieve more and respect themselves as well as each other, but the impact on a society with as much power as the United States really could change the world. Without it, the growing influence of junk culture could be devastating. 'We're trying to persuade people that you either pay up front or you pay on the way out,' said Alice.

She says that they are looking for the right location, just as Jamie did with *School Dinners* in the UK before they can get a prime time series on TV. 'It has to be somewhere that's already wounded, somewhere like New Orleans,' said Alice. 'There are schools there that are so segregated and he could show what goes on inside there and how to change it.' She thinks that Jamie Oliver is uniquely gifted to take on the job. 'He has that rare quality; his compassion shows through however angry he is. It's never destructive. He's always someone who cares. And Americans really value that – everyone values that. It touches everyone.' I told her that she made him sound like Martin Luther King. 'Yes,' she said, 'I'm thinking of people like him who have that rare combination of radical politics and compassion.'

It says a great deal about the effect that Jamie Oliver has had on the food industry that someone as established and well respected as Alice Waters thinks that she needs him to help her make a difference. 'We can say something together,' she said. 'He's very strong and persuasive.' Alice has friends in high places, and Hillary Clinton is already on her side. 'We can raise lots of money for the project because I have lots of influence here, but when we have a voice in Washington, we can really move on,' she told me. 'Hillary Clinton is someone who really gets this. She's bringing local food into schools already. I have many friends who are influencing her policies. Jamie is unpretentious so he can get to these leaders. I'm just hoping that I can help him situate it. It's all about the time and the place.' They are also talking to Oprah, far away the most influential person in the United States at the moment, and with Jamie's recent appearance on her TV show, *The Big Give,* there's little chance that he would have missed the opportunity to talk about this with her. 'We have lots of access to her but we have to make a strategy,' said Alice.

She showed the Prince of Wales her educational vision when he visited the United States in 2005. 'He's a very important part of this too,' she said. 'He is so exciting. We convinced him to come to see what the slow food movement is about, and I talked to him and encouraged him to see the Edible School Yard in Berkeley. He was very impressed.'

Slowly, the wider influence of the Edible School Yard is reaching around the world, even into schools in Ghana, India and Shanghai. France is also trying to nip the insidious effect of fast food in the bud; Les Defis Ruraux is part of a regional council initiative to boost procurement of local produce in Normandy schools while encouraging its next generation of gourmet kids to keep it real as junk-fuelled obesity becomes a major issue in France.

In Britain, the Soil Association's Food for Life Partnership already has a network of 200 schools committed to transforming their food culture. The original inspiration for *School Dinners* now provides an action framework and award scheme to help schools and their communities serve freshly prepared, well sourced food in their own kitchens. Students are taken to the farms where their food was produced and are encouraged to cook and grow food for themselves in their own school gardens. By 2011, FFL hopes to have 3,600 schools enrolled on the Food for Life Partnership Mark working towards Bronze, Silver and Gold Mark awards. While thousands of schools are still strangled by the hold of their centrally sourcing national caterers, it is, at least, a start.

Alice Waters is pleased. But she is realistic about the future of America. 'It's going to take the governor of California and the mayors of the cities to dedicate the money to make this happen more widely. It can't happen with private philanthropy but what we can do is build the model.'

Even with Alice Water's network of influence, America is a tricky challenge. Without a national press and no real national TV, it is hard to mount a campaign which can not only reach into the sitting rooms of 50 states, but change the habits of the most multi-cultural – and obese – society in the world. Bariatric surgery, with its gastric bypasses and bands is the latest trend to create the perfect body without dealing with the issue of what Americans eat and is on the increase, with personalities like Carnie Wilson, Roseanne Barr and Sharon Osborne living proof of what can happen with some nip and tuck. The one in 50 people dying and many more suing their surgeons has little impact on the numbers queuing up for the op, and when America discovers a weight loss miracle, it's only a matter of time before it crosses the pond.

By 2008, the subject of obesity was racing up the news agenda across the world as health budgets became increasingly weighed down by the impact of junk culture. But the debate about what we eat had broadened at an extraordinary rate to encompass the way we treat our planet, and 'climate change' had become a term that tripped off the tongue. As more people began to think twice about dumping plastic bags in landfill sites already overflowing with the junk generation's nappies, we began to look again at the packaging of our processed food. When Marks and Spencer, that bastion of British High Street value-for-money, announced that its Plan A would zero balance its carbon footprint, we actually knew what it was talking about. Even if it was still a tiny minority who were buying M&S organic fair-trade knickers, the tabloids were bursting with eco-news and green tips. Climate change, and its lesser known but potentially far more sinister partner in crime, peak oil, were prising open the public's consciousness and showing us the gunk of our oil age mentality.

While we were gagging at the sight, Jamie stepped up to the podium. Still stinging from the memory of the mothers who had passed burgers through the school gates, buzzing from his meetings with Alice Waters and remembering the scent of fresh basil from the balconies of Naples, Jamie was getting ready to turn up the heat under our complacent shopping habits. After his latest book, *Jamie at Home*, had galloped up the bestseller lists for Christmas 2007, telling us how to grow our own veggies and garnish our locally sourced lamb with home-grown mint, it was time to leave his wellies in Essex, dress up in his fineries and tackle the great British taste for take-away and cheap-as-chips chicken.

Channel 4's *Big Food Fight* in January 2008 lined up the three heavyweights of British cuisine, Gordon Ramsay, Hugh Fearnley-Whittingstall and Jamie Oliver to step up the debate about our food production and consumption. It was the beginning of the denouement in an extraordinary drama of a British food revolution before an uncertain finale.

Jamie rewound the past 30 years, charting our demise as our food became shrink-wrapped and our waists expanded, putting the contradictions of who we had become on a plate for us to pick at. A mood of reflection seemed to fall over the New Year's obses-sion with diets and resolutions. From the conspicuous consumerism of the Eighties to the dinner parties of the Nineties and Noughties, we had allowed supermarkets to deliver our posh nosh in a packet while our kitchen shelves bulged with unused TV chefs' cook books. We had become a nation of Good Food Show goers whose treat is a Tesco's finest after a busy day at work, Jamie fans who tuck into a tub of KFC while watching his latest series. We had become animal lovers who snack on abused chickens while boasting about the price. 'I buy one and get one free for the dog,' an old dear confided proudly to Hugh Fearnley-Whittingstall in *Hugh's Chicken Run* as part of the season.

Jamie was calling 'Time.' Presenting *Fowl Dinners*, a one off programme for the *Big Food Fight* series, in funereal black tie, he was joined by a host of producers, supermarket buyers, food stan-dard experts and about 150 chickens. His audience which had come expecting a gala dinner, perhaps taking a sneaky peak at a few celebrities on the next table, watched on in horror as he stunned chickens to death before cutting their throats, gassed chicks live and fed members of the audience deep-fried quenelles of mechanically reclaimed meat.

Like the chickens, his audience was stunned, yet the horrors of battery farming are hardly news. Jamie seemed to be a hypnotist who had clicked his fingers and woken us up from another reality. Reaching for the ready meal or the Southern-fried instead of popping into the grocer or butcher on the way home and chatting about a recipe seemed to have performed a collective lobotomy, allowing us to lose any connection with what our bodies really need. His fans were gutted, not just to miss out on the gala dinner, but that they were propping up an industry in which cramped chickens peck at each other as their only stimulation.

Force-feeding an audience, dressed to the nines, the truth about intensive farming was a TV first and hit a bullseye, clearing super-market shelves of free-range and organic chickens overnight and keeping it that way, for a while anyway. By the following month, free-range eggs had captured 53% of the total egg market. Kevin Coles of the British Egg Information Service said 'The only reason can be Jamie Oliver. There's no other explanation for why sales have increased by a third since January.'

Sainsbury's, who declined its invitation to the feast, responded by mailshotting millions of customers pledging to adopt the RSPCA's Freedom Food standard. With more space to grow at slower rates and a more natural environment, Jamie said he had seen the future for chicken farming in this country. It would cost slightly more, and we would eat less; no bad thing according to the climate change and peak oil experts who say that methane produced by animals and the oil used in meat farming is an explosive combination, as climate change and peak oil begin to force us to rethink the way we live.

Tony Wardle of Viva!, the vegetarian campaign group, is quite straightforward about the future: 'You need 17kg of fodder for 1kg of meat product. Animals demand 70% of our land for feed. There is simply no more land available.' In terms of climate chaos, he says we can look no further than animal production as the main offender. 'It's not just about emissions from animals,' he told a Transition Town Lewes debate, 'it's also about the tramping of the soil by animal hooves which releases vital carbon reserves.'

But Tesco wasn't listening. Represented on the show by another empty chair at the table, it later claimed little impact on chicken sales. A spokesperson said: 'Sales of Tesco standard chickens have not been affected by the programmes. This week, national sales of standard whole birds are running around 7% above daily average. Total chicken sales are approximately 10% up on the monthly average, which is great news for British farmers.'

In what could only be seen as a hostile gesture, they even slashed the price of whole chickens from £3.30 to £1.99 in a special 'bargain basement' offer just weeks after *The Big Food Fight*, making its birds the cheapest on the market.

Dr Lesley Lambert, director of research at Compassion in World Farming, was appalled. 'Why doesn't Tesco drop their prices on their higher welfare products and make this affordable to people on all budgets?' she asked. 'While Sainsbury's has committed to massive improvements in animal welfare, Tesco is showing its ethical credentials with this race to the bottom. Scientific research shows that many of these birds are lame and likely to be in pain and live their lives in their own faeces. Consumers have shown they will vote with their wallets on the basis of animal welfare.'

But Tesco's media director, Jonathan Church, chose to ignore the criticism. 'We have been working hard for a while to increase the amount of higher welfare chicken we sell and the recent debate over chickens in the media has helped raise awareness of choice to customers.'

Tesco had badly underestimated Jamie's place in public opinion. A poll of farmers by the National Farmers' Union concluded that 72% of voters supported him and Jamie was vindicated: 'I hope that in a couple of weeks one or two of the supermarkets will say publicly that sales of free-range or RSPCA Freedom Food birds and free-range or barn eggs have gone up while sales of cheap, intensively farmed birds and eggs have gone down,' he said. Chloe Alexander, an RSPCA campaigner, backed him up. 'The programmes have really helped focus attention on to chickens reared for meat. If shoppers can pay a little extra for a chicken which bears the Freedom Food logo, they are buying a bird which has had a better life.'

While Tesco was in denial, independent butcher, Tony Meredith of Natural Farms took the impact full on. After 20 years of selling organic and free-range chickens to nice, middle class types who care about animal welfare, *Fowl Dinners* whipped the rug from under him by selling his chickens to those who hadn't cared two hoots about hen-pecking before Jamie had had a word. 'The Jamie programmes on chickens led to an explosion in demand,' he told me. He says that the supermarkets were the big winners. 'Butchers are at the bottom of the pecking order. Supermarkets gobbled up the suppliers when Jamie's programmes came out. The price was pushed up because the supermarkets have the power to put pressure on the bigger farms to give them their supply. They might be selling half their supply to them anyway, so the supermarkets can turn around and say "we need more." They lean on them.'

For butchers like Meredith, there were simply no organic or free-range chickens available for weeks afterwards. 'It was no bad thing in the end,' he said. 'We found that people would ask us for chickens but when we didn't have any to give them, we could show them other products that they might not have thought about.'

Three months later, he says that it has begun to calm down. 'It hasn't gone back to the way it was – you can't put the genie back in the bottle,' he said. 'Maybe I was naive about the Jamie effect. I wasn't prepared. I just didn't see it coming. Now is the time to capitalise on the interest in good food. It's an issue for people now. It wasn't, but now it really is and that's because of Jamie Oliver.'

But Jamie hadn't finished; when he followed the series with *Eat to Save Your Life*, with the Frankenstein look-a-like anatomist, Dr Gunther von Hagens, performing an autopsy on a 25-stone man who had literally eaten himself to death, it was an iconic moment in TV food history, revealing just what Jamie meant when he accused our junk culture of being full of crap. It was the moment when three million Brits realised that they had lost their way.

Alice Waters said that this is exactly what she is trying to achieve in America. 'This is the way that change can happen. It happens through shock. Then we get a delicious revolution. Jamie's doing therapy and it's a beautiful thing. He's young and magnetic and attractive and he's speaking to a generation which is ready to listen.'

She and Jamie joined American TV chef, Rachel Ray, and a team of American scientists and medics at a debate about obesity as part of the 2008 South Beach Food and Wine Festival in Miami. 'I think obesity is a symptom of an unhappy and wrong thinking culture,' she told me 'and that was one of the things that the doctors were talking about in Miami. It should be talked about in a very different way, other than just a health issue. It's not an easy fix. We need to begin in kindergarten. We need every child in school to be eating something that's beautiful and they need to be engaged in the process of the growing and the cooking. This is what's deeply nourishing and it's what most children don't get. They don't eat with the family. One in two kids in America come from divorced families. Nobody's eating at home. That's why we need a whole education policy in school, physically and spiritually.'

Dr Arthur Agatston, founder of the best-selling South Beach Diet, hosted the event and has pushed the debate deeper into the political agenda as the presidential nominees square up for a place in the White House later this year. 'I've spoken to Hillary Clinton about it and although she's not going to promise me anything, it's her thing,' he told me. 'We're trying to change nutrition in this country in school. We've got a pretty good platform with the South Beach Diet but you run into all sorts of bureaucratic issues, all sort of obstacles.'

Alice Waters is excited about the possibility of a 'kitchen cabinet' she and Mrs Clinton have discussed. 'If she gets into office, I'd love to have Jamie as part of a panel so that he could advise in some way around issues of food in the White House,' she told me. 'I think he would be one of my first choices. He's really an unusual voice. He's a global person. He speaks this other kind of language of truth and care and love and it shines forth. I really believe that it makes a change. He can intimidate and shock and shame people into doing the right thing but I think he can also really inspire people. I think it's probably a once in a lifetime opportunity to radically change the way that America thinks about food.'

Dr Agatston went out for a beer with Jamie the night before the Miami symposium and came home inspired but sober. 'Hearing his stories of how much he overcame was really helpful,' he said. 'He didn't have much help from the medical or the scientific community. He was really on his own and I learnt a lot from what he went through.' Jamie told him how he wanted to use his experience to get to the heart of junk culture. 'Now he wants to do it in this country,' he told me. 'We would love to have his help in doing it together. What I learnt from the symposium is that you just can't go in as an academic, a scientist and change what kids are eating. There's just too much protocol and public relations and diplomacy, and in this country you really need a coalition that runs from the celebrity chefs to the scientists. The title of our luncheon was the Stars Meet the Scientists. It was incredible how mixed it was and how everyone got along. And Jamie was right in the thick of it.'

Alice Waters, who presented Jamie with an award that night, watched in awe as her friend dealt with the media scrum. 'I got to know him in Miami in a way I hadn't before,' she said. 'We were in the throes of such a scene of excess, such wretched excess. It was so over the top but he had to carry on with this entourage of photographers following him. I'm repelled by that and I step away, but he's in the eye of the hurricane. He knows that he can't have one without the other.'

She says his ability to ride the storm is what is amazing. 'He manages the celebrity and he overrides the rest,' she said. 'He can make a connection in what to most people are impossible circumstances.' What makes it possible, she believes, is his integrity. 'He follows his heart. He has the touchstones that really stabilise him in what he's trying to do. His kids and his wife do that for him. His friends do too.'

She says that one of his most endearing qualities is that he says what he thinks and feels. 'Maybe it's because he has endearing childlike ways. He has, in common with some Nobel Prize-winning scientists I've met, the kind of wide-eyed enthusiasm that demands the adjectives "boyish" and "contagious".' The fact that he is able to use his celebrity to expose the immorality of school food, and the next moment to celebrate its opposite: simple, wholesome food, she finds extraordinary. 'He is a very special person on this planet.'

CHAPTER 35

GROWING UP

What does it take to really have an impact on our food culture, to *really* make a difference? Is Jamie Oliver just a clever cook or a real revolutionary whose drive was mistaken by most people for a lust for celebrity and a lot of cash? Perhaps he didn't even know the answer himself until fairly recently; maybe it was simply that magical combination of time and place, the limelight that shone down on him and television that picked him up and catapulted him into a firmament where possibilities are infinite. Once there, maybe the view simply disturbed him enough to want to do something about it, and so he did. Perhaps.

Jamie always says that it was his childhood experience of watching the effect of a bit of smoked salmon, a squeeze of lemon and a twist of black pepper on his gypsy mates back in Clavering that made him want to replicate it for the rest of his life. He always wanted to change people's minds about food, but rather than ram it down their throats, he wanted them to understand where it came from. For him, it came from the producers he met with his dad, the convivial pub where the punters knew his parents and each other by name, and the kitchen where he learnt to chop vegetables in cartoon-style speed, where he learnt young that the crack was to be had.

His desire for a restaurant of his own came from the romantic dreams of two young love birds on a Cretan beach in 1992, along with the home in the country and the couple of kids. He probably had no idea that by the age of 33, he wouldn't just have a restau-

254 \ GROWING UP

rant, but *a brand* of restaurants with 'London, Amsterdam, Cornwall, Melbourne' stamped across it. A team of graduate chefs would already be bleeding his influence and his values into restaurant kitchens across the world, demanding local, seasonal produce, and growers across Britain would be getting seriously excited at the news of a chain of family friendly restaurants, inexpensive versions of the Trattoria at Fifteen London, opening first in Oxford and Brighton where cheap eats would mean regular orders.

Jamie grew up as food grew up; from chicken in the basket to poultry politics, he surfed the wave of gastro-punk through a catering college that taught cockney kids to cook in French and spewed them out into a food industry lapping up the desserts of Thatcher's conspicuous consumerism. As Jamie joined the rack of TV chefs (and their books) in our kitchens and taught us to stay in and stir up a little something, served with a chilled supermarket Chardonnay, the market for fresh produce exploded into town centres.

But as the TV chefs carved up this new market, offering something for everyone; Nigella for the greedy, Delia for the cheats, Gordon for those who want to impress and Jamie for the blokes, it wasn't enough for him. He began to feel stuffed to the gills with fame and fortune and still felt empty.

Hanging out again at Fifteen with another gang of kids who had lost their appetite for life, but for whom a bit of salmon, a squeeze of lemon and a twist of black pepper could raise more than a smile, reminded him that not everyone was invited to the feast. The aching gap between haves and have nots is usually the place where revolutions start, and Jamie chose a kitchen to fan the flames of his.

Seeing first-hand the connection between kids raised on junk in *School Dinners* and kids at Fifteen allowing life to dump on them, divided him from his TV pals. Taking himself off to grow his own vegetables was as symbolic a gesture as Nigella showing us how greed can be good as she settled into her Saatchi lifestyle and Delia warming up a book she wrote in 1971. Jamie was watering something much more sustainable than a career as *The Naked Chef*.

By 2008, he had dissected our foodie habits, and asked us some tough questions about what being interested in food really meant. He appeared at the food festivals and shows alongside the gourmet pâtés and novelty dried meats, but he was also contributing to conferences on obesity and holding secret meetings with some of the most influential people on the planet about the future of food.

Suddenly, watching Delia open a pack of rehydrated risotto and adding porcini mushrooms in a Marsala reduction, or Gordon and Marco competing in a spat of swear-words over their latest TV victim's badly scrambled egg seemed fatuous. We continued to potter around the food programmes now that we had a taste for them, but when Jamie was on telly, we watched in our millions, catapulting the ratings to the top spot. We didn't just watch either; we rowed about the issues with our friends, we ran out of the house to buy organic and free-range chickens and their eggs, we signed petitions. We even signed up for allotments.

From Colchester to Edinburgh, local papers were reporting a run on allotments, with waiting lists of up to six years in Scotland and residents in some London boroughs facing a 10-year wait. Geoff Stokes, of the National Society of Allotment and Leisure Gardeners, wants councils to allocate more land. 'Allotment gardening went into the doldrums in the 1950s–70s. But the 70s saw a revival with the Good Life factor when everyone thought it was a wonderful idea,' he told the press after *Jamie at Home* followed the *Big Food Fight* in January 2008. 'But they didn't realise it is hard work and it dropped off again. Then there was this growing concern with obesity and diet and Jamie was the first to speak out.'

Of course, it wasn't just Jamie. As the national news agenda tied together obesity and junk food, it warned of a future in which oil reserves will run dry and food security will be compromised as the cost of production and animal feed soars, the population rises and land is increasingly dedicated to the growth of bio-fuels in a bid to save our oil age lifestyle. Jamie and Hugh had scratched the surface and left us feeling itchy. William Sitwell, editor of *Waitrose Food Illustrated*, made it worse before it got better with a campaign called 'Pigs Are Worth It,' highlighting the demise of the great

British pig, again backed by celebrities like Gordon Ramsay and Jamie's childhood mate and pig farmer, Jimmy Doherty. This wasn't so much about the conditions of the farming, but of the farmer. 'The average British pig farmer loses £26 on every pig he sells' Sitwell wrote in *The Daily Mail*. 'This appalling state of affairs has come about because feed prices have rocketed while pork prices have fallen. Following last year's foot-and-mouth outbreak, export markets have weakened and not enough of us are supporting our pig farmers by buying their products.'

A global crisis was affecting the lives of the people we live with and we hadn't even noticed. It was all part of the junk culture that was at the root of the climate and peak oil crisis. Leaving lights on, over-heating homes, driving unnecessarily large cars with one passenger when five could be easily squeezed in, were symptoms of our self-centred malaise, and Mother Nature was about to self combust in a terrifying strop.

This was serious stuff and the survivors were already sowing their seeds. A growing number of Transition Towns in the UK – including The Archers' Radio 4 home of Ambridge – are already harnessing local interest in preparing for life without oil. Eating food from our own land and surrounding farms is the answer to our over-reliance on oil, according to Rob Hopkins, founder of Transition Towns and author of *The Transition Handbook*. 'Ultimately, as availability of fossil fuels begins to contract so will our ability to move goods around, and inevitably we will need to start building the infrastructure for local provision,' he writes. 'It is not something we have a choice over – it is an emerging reality; a "when" not an "if".'

Bill Collison of Bill's Produce Store in Brighton, winner of the Observer Food Monthly Readers' Awards' Best of the Rest Breakfasts in 2008, will no doubt be the first door Jamie knocks on when he arrives in Brighton. He has been counting the food miles long before Lewes, home to his original (and better) produce store, became a Transition Town in 2007. 'We're going to have to source more locally,' he said. 'We won't have a choice. We haven't got enough infrastructure to grow as much as is needed, so there's a window there for people who want to grow themselves. It's a valuable thing now to have something that's grown locally with a bit of mud still on it.'

Tim Lang, Professor of Food Policy at City University's Centre for Food Policy in London and one of Jamie's consultants on *School Dinners*, thinks that the surge of interest in small-holdings and allotments is to be welcomed, but also carries the danger of tokenism. 'Land is expensive and ownership is dominated by relatively few landowners. For small-holdings to make a difference to food supply would require a revolution in access to land. For example, Britain now produces just 5% of its fruit' he reminded me. 'You'd need a lot of new fruit growers to alter that figure. You could come to my house and say "how amazing. Tim Lang grows rhubarb, redcurrants, pears, apples." But do I live off it over the year? Of course not. Like everyone in urbanised Britain I am dependent on others.'

An expert in food security, he thinks that we've got to be realistic, tough even, as the oil economy begins to wobble. 'There is a remarkably high awareness of "real" food among the more affluent; in fact it's become a class indicator. But if money is tight, food supply chains focus on "value for money" rather than "values for money".'

He is sober about how effective the campaigns have been. He describes his life's work as 'winning some of the debates while not changing the realities' and he sees the challenge as stark: 'has all the talk of real food so far made a difference to reducing the climate change impact of Britain's food system?' he asks me. 'Not enough. Has it made a difference to the rebirth of British agriculture? A few pockets here and there – there are a few organic growers, but the rest of growing has been seemingly in freefall.'

Change, he believes, will only really happen when meat production is radically reduced. 'We currently fetishise cheap meat and grow huge amounts of grain to feed animals, thereby distorting meat prices, let alone contributing to astronomical commodity prices. Supermarkets are pandering to the pursuit of cheapness without thinking about sustainability issues enough,' he says. 'Morrisons makes much of committing to British beef, but sustainability – not a Union Jack – is what we have to look for. The supermarkets are the gate-keepers of the modern food economy. Until they unleash their power to deliver sustainability and health, the current idiocies of the meat trade look set to continue.'

Lang says that he hasn't talked to Jamie specifically about this subject, but it wouldn't surprise him if he did know about these issues. He will be pleased to hear then about Jamie's next adventure, in which he will appoint himself the unofficial minister of food as he heads back to the school in Rotherham, where local mothers launched a junk food 'meals on wheels service' after students were banned from going out at lunchtimes to the local takeaway.

In a new series inspired by the Ministry of Food's wartime common sense approach to food and health to be aired in Autumn 2008, Jamie will attempt to get to the nub of British food culture. 'We spend over £2 billion a year on ready meals, and that's not even counting junk food and takeaways,' Jamie said. 'Millions of people up and down the country are really busy, they're on tight budgets, and no-one has bothered to teach them how to cook. It's no wonder that the last thing they want to do at the end of the day is cook a meal from scratch.'

With the book to accompany the series going into more detail than his usual style of recipe, Jamie is hoping to change a future in which, for the first time, children are expected to die younger than their parents. 'Rotherham is a typical British town,' he said; 'this isn't about me wagging my finger at people, here or anywhere else, it's about finding out what problems people are facing with time, budget and cooking know-how. Then we can see what help and support they need. Yes, people should take responsibility for their own health, but they need help and the tools to fix it.'

He wants to establish a 'blueprint' that he can replicate across the whole country. 'It may feel like a Mission Impossible, but it's too important for us to give up. I hope that once people see how quick, cheap and easy – as well as rewarding – it can be to prepare good food at home, the ready meals and takeaways will be straight in the bin!'

As the news came out about Jamie's new series, the blogs were bursting with outrage – on both sides of the argument. Incensed-of-Ilkely, aka Ilkblogbabe, was advising him to butt out of her business, while London based journalists, keen to keep credible, were frantically Googling what 'up North' looked like these days. Martin Wainwright of *The Guardian* pointed out that there's nothing wrong with a bit of cod and chips on a Friday night. He had already beetled up to Rotherham to discover that the burgers 'n' bars story was really a bid to keep the school's local food economy buoyant rather than a one-in-the-eye for Jamie. 'One of the main reasons kids left the [school] was to patronise the row of local food outlets, especially Monkwood Fisheries,' he wrote on his foodblog. 'The notion that Keith Allwood's cod could be described as "junk" had the fryer incandescent and with good reason. The sandwich joint in the same parade was selling almost as much tuna filling as cheeseburgers, even if it was called Chubby's.'

Hrhpod (who I can only presume is an organic farmer living in Highgrove) blogged back. 'I'm sorry but I think this is a bit of PC nonsense. There bloody well is a problem. Lots of people eat shit. They spend their money on designer tat and eat crap from Iceland and Farmfoods. How do I know? I see the Iceland and Farmfoods carrier bags dangling from the designer buggies. We are screwed up with food in this country. I know people who express astonish-ment at the fact that my kids eat fruit and veg and ANYTHING that addresses this is to be welcomed. The problem isn't class based so much as aspiration and education based. We don't teach kids to cook and let them be bombarded by adverts for junk food. I've seen the "generous" range of clothes in the BHS kids dept for the obese under 10s so can we stop being woolly liberals worried that we're being patronising? Accept that it's not simply a class issue – it's an educational one but that if it crosses heavily with class issues, well that doesn't mean we shouldn't address the problem. Until people realise that spending 40 quid on a play station game but 89p on the sausages for your tea is fucked up, there's no bloody hope.'

Hrhpod is probably being signed up by Fresh One Productions as I write.

Meanwhile, local farmers will probably be queuing up at Effingham Street on the last Wednesday of each month to join the stalls selling speciality meats and odd-shaped vegetables in time for filming this summer. Ostrich is apparently one of the favourites among Rotherham's more discerning punters.

It seems that Jamie has covered all the corners, but barely begun to pocket the balls. Yet the game has attracted more players than any one individual has ever inspired in the history of food. Elizabeth David would have been proud.

Restaurants across the country are queuing up to talk to people like Tony Meredith of Natural Farms, not just to get a better class of meat but also to get some tips. 'There's even a national chain of inns asking us how they can get hold of meat from the same farm so that they can be sure of its source,' he told me. 'We tell them that they can't, but we advise them how to use less meat from a reliable source in more dishes. It's a great start.'

Meredith supplies Jamie's Brighton neighbours and fellow award winners, Due South and The Real Eating Company as well as Canteen, the London local/seasonal produce restaurants, one of which scooped the Observer Food Monthly Award for best restaurant in 2007. He has watched the story of food unfold over 20 years in the business. 'In the early 80's, it was only individuals who were interested in where their meat came from,' he told me. 'Restaurants were the last to care. They all seemed to work on the basis that once you'd put some sauce on the meat, you couldn't tell where it came from. When I first saw where meat came from, I was horrified. I had been in the police force before becoming a butcher and I saw worse things on those farms than I ever saw as a policeman! There were animals there that were so cramped they couldn't breathe.'

Meredith started to look for meat from farms that treated the animals with respect. 'I began to really enjoy what I was doing. It seemed the respectable thing to do. It was about sourcing with integrity.' These days, his turnover is exploding as the message spreads out to restaurant goers who care about their meat.

The soil is almost as important, and *Jamie at Home* has begun to teach people how to grow again, if only a patch of rosemary in the back garden. Guy Watson of Riverford Organics supplies vegetable boxes through an artery of local suppliers and has mixed feelings. Echoing the words of Alice Waters, he told me 'The more you grow – even if it's just a few perennial herbs on the windowsill, the more you get a connection with the seasons. You realise that things grow faster in the summer, that frost kills things in the winter, that you simply can't have some things at certain times of the year.'

But, like Tim Lang, he says that most vegetable box customers have missed the point. 'All the stuff that I promote about local and seasonal is just so depressing,' he confessed. 'It's all that people talk about but I can tell you from my sales figures that the reality is the opposite. The market for organic peppers (which come from Spain) is £12.7 million a year and the market for all the British cabbages added together is £6.1 million.' Riverford has gathered a huge amount of data over the last two years in an attempt to carbon label every product it sells. But Watson is not happy. 'I have to say, I'm now wondering what the hell I'm going to do with it. People in the business are telling me not to tell my customers all this stuff about carbon footprints. They say it's way too complicated and will put people off.'

Although he calls himself a 'huge Jamie fan' and thinks that he prepares 'fantastic food and makes me want to go and cook,' he puts much of the whims of his customers down to Jamie's influence. 'He's growing chillis, courgettes and tomatoes in his garden and serving them up in Italian style, but they are Mediterranean vegetables. Chillis are in season in the UK at the end of September for about five minutes unless you're using heated glass.' He laughs

262 \ GROWING UP

and admits he's exaggerating. 'OK,' he says, 'but you've got no more than two months of picking time.'

He refers to himself as Mr Doom and Gloom. Despite his eco credentials, he has recently had to buy a farm 200 miles away in Northern France where he can grow what his customers want. 'We have to compromise to retain our customers,' he told me. '80% of what we sell is UK grown and we're constantly pushing our customers in that direction. But our veg boxes are declining and that is our core market. What can I grow that is acceptable to them and acceptable by environmental standards? The French Farm is in a different climatic zone so we will be able to produce green beans in June when people expect them and grow tomatoes for longer. Apart from a tiny minority, that's what people want to buy.'

Amanda Powley and Philip Taylor of Brighton's vegetarian success story, Terre à Terre, will be Jamie's closest restaurateur neighbours. As we tucked into the Terre à Tapas platter of mace cappuccino with porcini, pumpkin and fat garlic confit, balsamic smudge fudge with Slipcote sheep's cheese and fried idli with black onion seeds, Powley said she understands Guy Watson's position. 'Yes, chefs like Jamie have created a taste for Mediterranean vegetables, but all power to it. It's baby steps towards enabling change. You have to be able to reach as many people as possible and to be able to sustain that. When you're as small as us, you have to be commercial and that means giving people what they want on some level without compromising too much. But when the season moves on, so do we.'

She and Philip have also watched the story of food unfold chapter by chapter since setting up their award-winning vegetarian restaurant 16 years ago. From a plucky little town with a big character, Brighton has become a city with a healthy appetite, with more mentions in this year's Observer Food Monthly Readers' Awards than its residents would ever have believed back in 1992. These days, you can't move for locally sourced food outlets, yet when Terre a Terre first opened its doors, its customers were more interested in the wow factor than reading about the provenance.

'People would say we're not really interested in who makes it,' and we'd say, 'well of course you are; you're just about to put it in your mouth and swallow it!' said Powley.

Like Tony Meredith, Amanda Powley was originally inspired to set up her business after witnessing at first hand the horrors of the intensive food industry. 'My life lit up in France where I was living with my parents until I was 16. My culinary fireworks went off as I was following my parents through the markets. They taught me how to cook and how to live.' When she came back to England in the late Seventies, cooking seemed to be the obvious job for her. 'It was a time when things were changing. People were experimenting with their Cordon Bleu recipes but factory farming was the norm. I was horrified. A lot of that extreme, intensive farming was an eye opener.'

Teaming up with business partner, Philip Taylor, she wanted to show people that there was a meat-free choice that was just as interesting, just as creative. 'I can't say I won't eat meat,' she admitted. 'When I used to cook it, I loved the process. I love all the stories behind it, but if there isn't a happy story and a happy ending, I don't want any part of it. Whatever bit of the industry you're in, you have a unique responsibility over the part of the planet that you've got any control over. We're not banner waving. We're not political. We're a very small restaurant trying to do something really quite serious in a jolly way.'

Sixteen years on, Paul McCartney is among Terre a Terre's regulars, and it has just scooped top prize in the Observer Food Monthly's first Best Vegetarian Restaurant category after years of coming runner up in the magazine's Best Restaurant category. She told me that she's looking forward to Jamie coming to town. 'There's so much that's positive that's happening in the food industry now. I think we're on the crest of a wave and the rest of the ride is going to be even more fun.' She admires what Jamie has done to educate people about food, particularly in schools. 'If you can get the message out to school children about the entire food chain,' she said, 'I think the future will be more about produce that's less messed around, hopefully more home-grown stuff and more compassionate farming. If we can accomplish an nth of that, we'll be looking after ourselves and our planet.'

While Jamie gets Rotherham digging for its dinner, the food revolution that has spanned his life is almost coming full circle. As oil prices rise, we'll have to travel less for our food, and our food will have to travel less to get to us. We'll grow our own herbs, maybe even a few potatoes and perhaps keep a small coop of chickens – if only for the eggs. We'll eat less meat, but at least we'll know where it came from and if the chefs and food experts who have mentored Jamie Oliver on his way to the top are right, a new generation will emerge from the oil age with mud on their hands and a smile on their lips.

But if the days of cheap chicken and ready meals are coming to an end, it doesn't mean that the party is over. Jamie's pukka tukka of pasta and fresh vegetables, a little dairy, the occasional excellent meat and a glass of red is the famously healthy 2,000-year-old Mediterranean Diet, the legacy of the Roman Ministers of Fun whose nights in were legendary. As Jamie appoints himself Minister of Food for the 21st century, we know the crack; we've been to his house, we've been to the beach with him, we've even stayed up late with him while he's baked bread at Fifteen. We know it'll be a laugh.

And when Rotherham has been conquered too (and we know it will) could we set a real example in the Western world in dumping the junk? Can we really show America how to chuck a few home-grown herbs into a freshly made tomato sauce, spooned over a bit of pasta that takes less time to cook than a pre-packed chicken korma and rice? And if Jamie does manage to feed America a new diet of conscious cooking, perhaps he will close the chapter on the oil age of excess and begin a new book about a cooler, cleverer culture that eats to save its life.

BIBLIOGRAPHY & FURTHER INFORMATION

Blumenthal, Heston *Family Food*, Penguin 2005.

Contaldo, Gennaro *Passione: The Cookbook*, Headline Book Publishing Ltd 2003.

David, Elizabeth *Elizabeth David Classics: Mediterranean Food, French Country Cooking* and *Summer Cooking*, Grub Street 1999.

Doherty, Jimmy *On the Farm*, Ebury Press 2004.

Fearnley-Whittingstall, Hugh *The River Cottage Family Cookbook*, Hodder & Stoughton Ltd 2003.

Gray, Rose & Rogers, Ruth *The River Café Cook Book*, Ebury Press 1995.

——*River Café Two Easy*, Ebury Press 2005.

Grigson, Jane *English Food*, Ebury Press 1992.

Hildred, Stafford & Ewbank, Tim *Jamie Oliver: The Biography*, Blake Publishing 2001.

Humble, Nicola *Culinary Pleasures: Cookbooks and the Transformation of British Food*, Faber & Faber 2005.

Luard, Elizabeth *A Taste of the Country*, Ebury Press 1993.

Oliver, Jamie *The Naked Chef*, Michael Joseph Ltd 1999.

——*The Return of the Naked Chef*, Michael Joseph Ltd 2000.

——*Happy Days with the Naked Chef*, Michael Joseph Ltd 2001.

——*Jamie's Kitchen*, Michael Joseph Ltd 2002.

——*Jamie's Dinners*, Michael Joseph Ltd 2004.

——*Jamie's Italy*, Michael Joseph Ltd 2005.

Oliver, Jools *Minus Nine to One: The Diary of an Honest Mum*, Michael Joseph 2005.

Orrey, Jeanette *The Dinner Lady*, Bantam Press 2005.

Sands, Nora *Nora's Dinners*, Collins 2006.

Spencer, Colin *British Food: An Extraordinary Thousand Years of History*, Grub Street 2004.

Walker, Caroline & Cannon, Geoffrey *What's Wrong with the British Diet and How to Put it Right*, Ebury Press 1985.

White, Marco Pierre & Carlos Clarke, Bob *White Heat*, Pyramid Books 1990.

Worrall Thompson, Anthony *Real Family Food*, Mitchell Beazley 2005.

Websites

www.feedmebetter.com

www.fifteenfoundation.org.uk

www.foodforlifeuk.org

www.soilassociation.org

INDEX

(JO denotes Jamie Oliver.)